Toward Human Flourishing

Character, Practical Wisdom, and Professional Formation

Endowed by
TOM WATSON BROWN
and
THE WATSON-BROWN FOUNDATION, INC.

Toward Human Flourishing

Character, Practical Wisdom, and Professional Formation

Edited by

Mark L. Jones, Paul A. Lewis, and Kelly E. Reffitt

Mercer University Press
Macon, Georgia

MUP/ P462

© 2013 Mercer University Press
1400 Coleman Avenue
Macon, Georgia 31207
All rights reserved

First Edition

Books published by Mercer University Press are printed on acid-free paper that meets the requirements of American National Standard for Information Sciences—Permanence of Paper for Printed Library Materials.

Mercer University Press is a member of Green Press Initiative (greenpressinitiative.org), a nonprofit organization working to help publishers and printers increase their use of recycled paper and decrease their use of fiber derived from endangered forests. This book is printed on recycled paper.

"The Guilt They Carry" is reprinted by permission from Nancy Sherman, *The Untold War: Inside the Hearts, Minds, and Souls of our Soldiers* (New York: W.W. Norton & Company, Inc., 2010).

ISBN   978-0-88146-436-8
Cataloging-in-Publication Data is available from the Library of Congress

Contents

Acknowledgements	vii
Foreword,	
Daisy Herst Floyd	v
Introduction,	
Mark Jones, Paul Lewis, and *Kelly Reffitt*	1
Part I: Character Development and Moral Formation	15
1: Contemporary Character Education in Context,	
Paul Lewis	17
2: Wisdom as Mature Moral Functioning: Insights from Developmental Psychology and Neurobiology,	
Darcia Narvaez	24
3: Developing the Ethical Thinker and Responsible Moral Agent,	
Thomas Lickona	41
4: The Guilt They Carry,	
Nancy Sherman	68
5: Uncovering the Hidden Values about Values Assessment: Assessing Student Dispositions in Teacher Education,	
Susan Malone, Emilie Paille, and *Kelly Reffitt*	92
Part II: Professional Character and Professional Formation	99
6: Professionalism and Vocation Across the Professions,	
William Sullivan	101
7: Forming Professionals and the Quest for Common Ground in the University, *William May*	115
8: "God at Work": A Reflection on Vocation,	
John Dunaway	134
9: Answering the Call to Service: Vocation and Professional Identity,	
Timothy Floyd	139
10: Reform and Formation: Revisiting the Role of Liberal Education,	
Peter Brown	143
11: Confronting the Three Apprenticeships,	
Jack Sammons	150

Part III: Practical Wisdom in Practical Context	165
12: The War on Wisdom and How to Fight It,	
Barry Schwartz and Kenneth Sharpe	167
13: Practical Wisdom and Vocation in Professional Formation: A Schematic Account,	
Mark Jones	193
14: Being Pragmatic about Practical Wisdom,	
David Ritchie	199
15: Guidelines for Observing Practical Wisdom at Work,	
Jack Sammons	207
Conclusion,	
Mark Jones, Paul Lewis, and Kelly Reffitt	213
Appendix A: Building Bridges and Discovering Commonality: The Story of Mercer University's Professionalism and Vocation Across the Professions Project,	
Mark Jones	217
Appendix B: Moral Development Across Disciplines, Schools, and Life Span: The Phronesis Project,	
Paul Lewis	227
Appendix C: Focus Questions on Professionalism and Vocation in the Professions,	
Mark Jones	233
Appendix D: Case-Study Exercise,	
Alice Baker, Peter Brown, Tom Glennon, Anne Hathaway, Mark Jones, and Stephen Wills	237
Contributors	273
Index	281

Acknowledgments[*]

After trying to put together a project such as this, one is tempted to identify with the unknown editor of Ecclesiastes who observes, "of the making of many books there is no end." Such a dour pronouncement does not, however, adequately capture the joy of such a task. The chance to interact with one another and the people who have contributed to this volume has truly enriched our lives both as scholars and as persons, thereby reminding us that, here and there, now and then, we are part of a true learning community.

In the production of this volume, we must acknowledge the work of Mr. Jonathan Simpson, research assistant for Mark Jones, who graciously and efficiently performed many essential tasks in helping us prepare the manuscript, including finalizing and undertaking preparatory editing of the raw transcripts from two of the Professionalism and Vocation Across the Professions events. This work built on that of Kelley Pierce and Sabina Hussaini, two of Mark Jones' earlier research assistants, who performed invaluable yeoman service by producing the raw transcripts themselves from video recordings of those events. Christina Nosari, a Mercer Law student, and Yonna Shaw, coordinator of Law Review Publishing, compiled the index. Marc Jolley, director of Mercer University Press, has dealt with our myriad anxieties (and questions) with good humor and has encouraged us throughout.

As noted later, the contents of this volume grow out of two previous projects, The Professionalism and Vocation Across the Professions Project and the Phronesis Project, into which the former merged. We therefore acknowledge the people behind the scenes for both of those, whose wise counsel, advice, good humor, and administrative skill made those projects possible.

From the Professionalism and Vocation Across the Professions, we recognize those who helped plan and execute these events: Dayne Aldridge, Jeremy Baham, Alice Baker, Peter Brown, Sabrina Byrne, Jacque Culpepper, John Dunaway, Daisy Floyd, Timothy Floyd, Robert Frasier, Thomas Glennon, Carolyn Goff, Robert Hash, Anne Hathaway, Lori Johnson, Karen Lacey, Patrick Longan, David MacIntyre, Whitney McMath, Doug Pearson, Wil Platt, David

---

[*] Because our activities extend over several years, we should note that some of those mentioned in these Acknowledgements have now retired or moved on from Mercer University to positions elsewhere.

Ritchie, Jack Sammons, Julie Hixson Wallace, and Stephen Wills.[1] Without the assistance of numerous other colleagues, the planning would have been in vain. Although not everyone can be mentioned here, Karen Batts, Debra Boney, Peter Otto, Sandy Studdard, Ina Vaughns, and Susan Wilson assumed major responsibilities in implementing our plans.

For the Phronesis Project, we are especially grateful for the wise counsel and assistance of our collaborating faculty: Jeremy Baham, Thomas Glennon, David Gushee, Anne Hathaway, Julie Jones, Mary Alice Morgan, Doug Pearson, C. Jay Pendleton, Tanya Sharon, and Scott Walker. Again, planning would have been in vain without the able, patient, and gracious help of Nancy Stubbs, whose primary role is Administrative Secretary for the Roberts Department of Christianity, but who found time to handle arrangements for us and help us negotiate the labyrinth of University Accounting. Jessica Gamblin, our student assistant in 2009-2010, did much of the necessary but unglamorous work of assembling conference materials for us and undertaking other miscellaneous tasks for us.

Among those who have been involved in the planning and implementation of the various events that have given rise to so much of the material contained in this volume, we gratefully acknowledge the defining contributions of several people who have been key to these ventures and to whom we owe a special debt of gratitude. The Professionalism and Vocation Across the Professions Project would not have been born if not for the commitment and support of Daisy Floyd, John Dunaway, Peter Brown, Suthern Sims, and Pat Longan. Nor would it have become what it was without the intellectual muscle, advice, and friendship of Peter Brown, Anne Hathaway, and Jack Sammons, our resident expert on Aristotle.[2] The Phronesis Project was made possible by the Academic Initiatives Monetary Fund, an initiative of Mercer President William D. Underwood. Peter Brown also played a critical role as administrator of the AIM Funds via the Provost's Office.

---

[1] As explained in Appendix A, the Planning Committee has changed in composition over the years. The names listed are of those who have served on the Committee at one time or another. Some have remained on the Committee throughout. Members of the Planning Committee have also played critical roles at various Project events—as presenters, as discussion leaders or facilitators, and as discussion observers.

[2] Mark Jones owes an additional personal debt of gratitude to his friend and colleague Jack Sammons. No one has done more to show him what Aristotle's perfect friendship means in practice.

Last, but by no means least, we would like to thank all those who participated in the various Project events, whether as Team members representing their college, school or other educational unit, or in other capacities, as well as the Deans who nominated the Team members. It is their commitment and enthusiastic support that gives our projects their point and purpose. We are especially grateful to the more than a dozen full time practitioners from outside Mercer who so generously shared their time and professional expertise to help make the events a much more enriching and rewarding experience for all of us. And among this group, Maggie Glennon and Jennifer Clements deserve special mention for their extraordinary contribution to our Practical Wisdom Workshops.

Mark Jones
Paul Lewis
Kelly Reffitt

Foreword

Character, Practical Wisdom, and Professional Formation Across the Disciplines

Daisy Hurst Floyd

This publication is a product of the dreams of several dedicated and insightful faculty members at Mercer University, as well as their passion, commitment, and tenacity. It grew from institutional actors who believe that notions of vocation and calling are central to our work as teachers and scholars, who see in their students a desire to develop in ways that allow them to use their talents and gifts to engage with a complex world, and who believe that we have an obligation to those students to be better at helping them realize their desire. This work proves that real change can occur from faculty's asking important questions about their goals and practices: What is it that I want my students to know? What is it that I want my students to be able to do? What kind of people do I want my students to be? And, ultimately: What do I have to do differently as a teacher and practitioner to enable my students to know and do and be these things?

This publication began with a belief that the best way to accomplish these goals was to do two things that universities often fail to do:

1. Encourage conversation and learning among people of different fields and disciplines and among those who teach students at all levels of development, from freshmen to final-year graduate and professional students; and
2. Bring practitioners into the conversation with those of us who spend full-time in the academy, recognizing that preparing our students for the world involves a collaboration among practitioners, faculty, and students.

We spend too much time in the academy focused on what separates us—disciplinary perspectives, the differences between undergraduate and graduate education, and the needs of professional schools versus non-professional schools. In addition, we are most comfortable engaging only with others within the academy, so that our deliberations are too often disconnected from practice.

Instead of focusing on what separates us, however, the writings in this volume – and the projects that gave rise to them – focus on what we have in common, both within the academy and with those who are doing the work for which we are preparing our students. We may use different labels to capture what we seek to do: character development, ethical or professional formation, or teaching towards practical wisdom. The questions we ask may stem from our singular professional or educational context. Whatever we call it and whatever our setting, however, this shared responsibility is at the core of helping our students take their learning into the rest of their lives. Our questions, and the answers they generate, are more alike than they are different. When given the rare opportunity to focus on what we have in common rather than on our differences, unifying questions and answers emerge, and the experience helps us all to be better at what we do.

What other project could give rise to comparisons between the training of teachers of elementary school students and the training of soldiers for the atrocities of war? Between the obligations a reference librarian owes his clients and the duties of clergy to parishioners? For me, the project opened new doors into my understanding of lawyers' decision-making and of ways to better prepare my students for the demands of practice.

As you will see from these pages, shared questions, pursued through both conversation and thoughtful reflection, gave rise to a multi-year journey of exploration focused on understanding how best to educate our students for lives of productive engagement. The dreams of the few ultimately gave rise to involvement by several hundred Mercer University faculty and students from across all eleven of the university's colleges and schools, as well as practitioners from diverse fields. Those project participants were led and inspired by the expert voices of our keynote presenters in a deliberative process skillfully crafted by the projects' lead faculty.

The result is a diverse collection of rich content. It provides both substantive understanding and helpful pedagogy that can be replicated in a variety of settings. Some of the authors explore what constitutes character, professionalism, and practical wisdom. Others explore notions of pedagogy that build upon substantive understanding and raise questions of mission, method, and assessment.

This volume also provides the means for a similar generative experience by others. The appendices set out a format and materials that can be used by those in other institutions who wish to foster cross-disciplinary conversation among those who don't ordinarily have the opportunity to learn from, and to teach, each other. It provides a template for exploring questions across disciplinary fields and across the boundaries that often separate faculty, students, and practitioners.

The meaningful conversations detailed here occurred because of hours of thoughtful and skilled planning about how to bring together the right combination of actors in a setting that empowered all voices (not an easy task when combining students, faculty, administrators, practitioners, and outside experts) and structured the experience around questions specific enough to generate meaningful conversation but general enough to allow for spontaneous ideas and unexpected insights. The organizers dealt with the usual obstacles of tight schedules and tight budgets. But their challenges were exacerbated by the logistical difficulties of achieving a conversation across a complex university (which is located on multiple campuses and operates on multiple academic calendars) and across the lines that separate students, faculty, and practitioners. Had the questions not been as important as they are—and the experience not been as revelatory and rewarding as it was for the participants—the dream may have succumbed along the way to the practical difficulties.

Indeed, it may be that the various projects that led to this volume are an example of the subject of Part III—practical wisdom. As the campus-wide conversation grew, we experienced the moving back and forth between concept and practice, between idea and action, which allows practical wisdom to develop. What grew from individual exploration of the individual educator's mission became an institutional exploration of the mission of the university undertaken by the various project participants and invited scholars: how do we create an environment that fosters discussions of vocation, that cultivates professionalism, and that allows practical wisdom to flourish? It was a rich conversation that has yielded valuable lessons and, as is the case with the best conversations, stimulated powerful questions for the future. In seeking to change our students' lives, we changed our own, changed both the way in which we understand our professional roles and obligations and also the ways in which we engage with the world, including each other. We hope that by providing the details of how this was accomplished at Mercer University, others will learn from our experience, be encouraged to undertake something similar, and experience similar rewards.

Introduction

Mark Jones, Paul Lewis, and Kelly Reffitt

This volume grows out of a series of initiatives undertaken by two interdisciplinary projects involving over 150 faculty and a significant number of students from across Mercer University's eleven colleges and schools in 2005–2010. More specifically, certain contributions grow out of the Professionalism and Vocation Across the Professions Project that held three symposia featuring nationally renowned scholars in 2005, 2006, and 2008:

- A symposium on "Professionalism and Vocation Across the Professions" held in November 2005 with William M. Sullivan as keynote speaker;
- A second symposium on "Cultivating Professionalism and Vocation Across the Professions: Challenges for Higher Education" held in November 2006 with William F. May as keynote speaker;
- A third symposium on "Practical Wisdom: The Character of the Professions" held in October 2008 with Barry Schwartz and Kenneth Sharpe as keynote speakers and including a case-study workshop. The project held a second case-study workshop in November 2009 designed to replicate the experience of the October 2008 Practical Wisdom Symposium for a new group of participants.

The various other contributions in this volume were generated by a conference on "Character Across the Disciplines" that was held in April 2010 with educator Tom Lickona, psychologist Darcia Narvaez, and philosopher Nancy Sherman as keynote speakers. This event was sponsored by the Phronesis Project for the Exploration of Character, Practical Wisdom, and Professional Formation. This center was formed in early 2009 with funding support from Mercer University's Academic Initiatives Monetary (AIM) Fund and combines the work of the Professionalism and Vocation Project, coordinated by Mark Jones, with the work of Paul Lewis in the area of moral development and Kelly Reffitt in the area of character education. We decided to merge our interests and efforts in the Phronesis Project because we became convinced of the need to develop integrated understandings of character development, practical wisdom, and professional formation. While moral education of some sort is "in" these days, such efforts are often theoretically fragmented and pedagogically uneven. It seemed to make good sense, therefore, that colleagues interested in the development of character, moral capacity, and practical wisdom at any stage of the educational continuum should collaborate in a broader endeavor that promises to maximize the prospects for mutual enrichment and synergistic effect. The present publication, of course, is one of the first published fruits of this extended collaboration.

In spring 2010 we were joined by two other co-lead faculty, Daisy Floyd, former Dean of the Law School, and Tanya Sharon, a developmental psychologist. In addition, several other colleagues have been providing indispensable advice and guidance as collaborating faculty.

The Phronesis Project is guided by several important principles:

- Character development is best understood in an Aristotelian sense as the acquisition of an ensemble of deeply ingrained knowledge, skills, and dispositions (the "habits of the heart") by which a person makes good decisions that issue in actions enabling one to flourish as an authentic human being in community with others.
- The "master virtue" of practical wisdom (*phronesis*) lies at the heart of good character by conducting this ensemble in particular situations so that the agent "does the right thing in the right way at the right time."
- Notions of good character and practical wisdom are relevant for decision-making and action in many different contexts, among them the personal, the political, and the professional (where the development of "professional character" is associated with the concept of professional formation).
- Qualities of character can be learned by intentional, guided imitation so that one's reasoning, passions, and actions more closely resemble those of moral experts.
- The development of good character and practical wisdom is intimately linked to, and shaped by, a sense of life's meaning and purpose and hence necessitates raising existential questions that are central to the quest to discover that meaning and purpose: Who am I? What kind of person should I become? What are my core beliefs, values, and commitments? What are my goal and purpose in life? What kind of life should I live?

Introduction

- The development of good character, practical wisdom, and sense of identity occurs over the course of a whole lifetime as it is lived in life's various contexts, including the educational process, whether K–12, undergraduate, postgraduate, professional, or continuing education.

The Phronesis Project is discussed further in appendix B to this volume as described below.

* * *

The basic organization of this book is straightforward. Part I explores character development and moral formation in general, and the cultivation of character and moral capacity throughout the educational spectrum. Moving from the general to the particular, part II then explores the particular topic of professional formation and the development of professional character, and part III explores the particular topic of practical wisdom. Those readers especially interested in pre-professional education may want to read part I and then continue with part III before reading part II for additional perspective. And those readers especially interested in professional education may want to begin with part II and continue with part III before reading part I for additional perspective. It should be noted that several of the contributions represent edited, and in some cases expanded and/or updated, versions of the author's presentation at the original event and that other contributions have been specifically prepared for the purposes of publication in this volume.

In introducing the contents of this volume, we can do no better than to quote from Tom Lickona's paper in part I:

> Character matters—in every sphere of society. It matters in families, the cradle of learning and the first school of virtue. It matters in schools, which must teach students to get along with people different from themselves, work hard to develop their minds and talents, and become good citizens of their communities. It matters in colleges and universities, which have the responsibility of developing critical ethical thinkers and the capacity for ethical leadership. It matters in the workplace, where the quality of craftsmanship affects other people's lives, and in the boardroom, where the absence of a moral compass can wreak widespread social havoc. It matters in the worlds of sports, entertainment, and the media, which shape the often toxic popular culture in which we are all

immersed. And it matters in the halls of political power, where decisions impact not only our own country's welfare but, in many cases, the state of our increasingly interconnected world. At the end of the day, the most important measure of a society is not its economic wealth, its technological genius, or its military might; it is the character of its people.[1]

The contributions in part I, exploring character development and moral formation in general, address a range of important questions such as: What are the elements of good character? Why is good character important? How is the development of good character related to moral formation? How are character development and moral formation related to human flourishing? How are they related to the cultivation of practical wisdom? How can the development of good character and moral capacity be promoted? How may their development be impeded? How can such impediments be appropriately addressed?

We begin part I with Paul Lewis's paper "Contemporary Character Education in Context." As the title suggests, this is intended to help the reader situate the remaining contributions in part I in a broader historical context by identifying some of the most important reasons for the decline of character education in the twentieth century and surveying some of the alternative schools of moral education that sought to fill the resulting vacuum. These include cognitive developmentalism, values clarification, citizenship education, and a revitalized character education movement. In addition, the author provides a broader intellectual context by identifying several scholars engaged in relevant psychological research and proposing a framework for synthesizing their perspectives that focuses on the expert integration of skills in the areas of Knowing, Desiring, and Doing. He also reflects on the need for further work aimed at providing a comprehensive and integrative account of character development and moral formation.

Three of the four remaining contributions, by Darcia Narvaez, Thomas Lickona, and Nancy Sherman, are the authors' keynote papers from the Phronesis Project Conference on "Character Across the Disciplines" in April 2010. The fourth is authored by three colleagues from Mercer University's Tift College of Education. The first keynote paper is by psychologist Darcia Narvaez, one of the psychologists whose work is addressed in Paul Lewis's paper discussed above. In this paper entitled "Wisdom as Mature Moral

---

[1] See p. 41.

Introduction

Functioning: Insights for Developmental Psychology and Neurobiology," the author equates mature moral functioning with practical wisdom and suggests that it requires expertise in the areas of "ethical sensitivity (noticing and interpreting events), ethical judgment (reasoning and deciding on moral action), ethical focus (prioritizing moral action), and ethical action (having the wherewithal to complete the moral action)." She explains how moral character and moral functioning are significantly influenced by three basic ethical orientations (the Ethic of Security, the Ethic of Engagement, and the Ethic of Imagination) that are themselves rooted in neurobiological capacities and unconscious emotional systems that are both shaped by experience. These orientations, she suggests, predispose one to perceive, act, and react in particular ways, with the caveat that these orientations can be promoted and activated by particular types of situations. She further describes an empirically driven model of integrative ethical education that proposes five ways and numerous concomitant practices for educators to foster moral wisdom in their students by helping them cultivate a "mindful morality" rooted in engagement and communal imagination and develop the skills necessary for moral expertise.

Drawing upon his work in the Smart & Good Schools project, Thomas Lickona identifies two interdependent components of character in his keynote paper entitled "Developing the Ethical Thinker and Responsible Moral Agent." He distinguishes between moral character and performance character, suggesting that "[i]n a flourishing life ethics and excellence go hand in hand." He further resolves these two components into eight interdependent strengths of character that include lifelong learner and critical thinker, diligent and capable performer, socially and emotionally skilled person, ethical thinker, responsible moral agent, self-disciplined person who pursues a healthy lifestyle, contributing community member and democratic citizen, and spiritual person engaged in crafting a life of noble purpose. In a discussion that resonates with and complements the discussion in Narvaez's paper, the author focuses on two of these strengths with special relevance for the secondary and postsecondary years (ethical thinker and responsible moral agent). In doing so, he examines several practices for character development that educators can use to help students develop four interdependent components of integrated ethical thinking (moral discernment, conscience, moral identity, and moral competence) and the attributes necessary for respectful and responsible moral agency enabling them to translate ethical thinking into ethical action.

We find some interesting points of convergence in these two papers, as Narvaez explicitly, and Lickona implicitly, suggest that their theoretical frameworks for understanding moral expertise can be regarded in effect as addressing the subject of practical wisdom. We will undertake a more advertent and sustained treatment of this subject in part III below where we will explore the significance, contours, and operation of this "master virtue" in the fittingly practical context of the professions. Moreover, both acknowledge that the "ethical learning community" to which one belongs plays an important role in character development and moral formation, and both recognize the formative value of studying moral exemplars.

These latter points are vividly illustrated by Nancy Sherman's poignant stories of members of the U.S. military suffering different forms of battlefield guilt (accident guilt, luck guilt as a form of survivor guilt, and the guilt of collateral damage) in her keynote contribution, "The Guilt They Carry," which is reprinted from her book *The Untold War: Inside the Hearts, Minds, and Souls of Our Soldiers* (2010). The reader will certainly be struck by the author's depiction of a "brotherhood" that "involves 'mothering' activity at its core—including caregiving, profound emotional love, and a willingness to die as if for your own child"—and will be moved and inspired by the stories of moral exemplars operating in extreme circumstances who strive to reclaim a sense of moral agency and moral autonomy, and thereby to reaffirm their humanity, as they struggle with the emotion of guilt arising from acts or omissions for which they hold themselves responsible even though they are neither legally nor morally culpable. Furthermore, the author's different-tiation of the various types of battlefield guilt can be seen as demonstrating a critical feature of practical wisdom in its discernment of the particulars that call forth varied responses to different contexts.

Susan Malone, Emile Paille, and Kelly Reffitt provide a further striking illustration of the important role played by the learning community in character development and moral formation, and the experience of moral struggle within that community, in their paper "Uncovering the Hidden Values about Values Assessment: Assessing Student Dispositions in Teacher Education." There, they chronicle the process by which Mercer University's Tift College of Education developed an assessment of dispositions of professional teacher candidates. As the learning community responsible for the character development and moral formation of their students, Tift College faculty realized that they needed to identify relevant dispositions and implement measures to assess their development. In this respect, the

Introduction

training of good teachers by Tift College is similar to the training of the good soldiers who are the subjects of the stories told by Nancy Sherman. In the case of Tift College, however, the narrative of struggle is not the struggle of the individual within the learning community, but the struggle of the community itself as it discovers and confronts its own disagreements and seeks practically wise ways to overcome those disagreements in an effort to develop an assessment process that is "fair, equitable, and meaningful."

Nancy Sherman's highly personal narratives from the "profession of arms" and Tift College's institutional narrative from the profession of teaching form an appropriate bridge to part II, which explores the particular topic of professional formation and the development of professional character through several contributions generated by the Professionalism and Vocation Across the Professions Project. We consider that the moral ideal of professionalism is at the heart of professional character and professional formation. Thus, we are concerned with a range of different questions in part II, such as: What is professionalism? Why is it important? How is it related to a sense of professional calling or vocation? How is it promoted? Is it under threat? If so, why is it under threat? And what is the appropriate response to such threat? Moreover, we are concerned with such questions across the entire range of professions—both the traditional, centuries-old "learned professions," such as law, medicine, and the ministry, as well as those occupations, such as engineering, accountancy, nursing, pharmacy, and teaching, that have joined the ranks of the professions much more recently.

These are, of course, the sorts of questions we identified in part I with regard to character development and moral formation in general. Now, however, we raise them in the particular context of the professions and with a particular focus on the ideal of professionalism. Moreover, we are concerned with the answers that have been given in this particular context and with that particular focus. That said, we consider that the contributions in part I are clearly relevant in the present context, too. We offer the contributions in part I, therefore, with this purpose in mind as well. This reflects our conviction that we need to pursue an integrative approach to issues of character development and moral formation throughout the entire educational continuum. By the same token, insights gained in the particular context of professional formation may also be relevant for our understanding of character development and moral formation in general.

The historical development and current state of the ideal of professionalism and related sense of professional vocation are, of course, inextricably intertwined with the historical development and current state of the professions themselves, of professional education, and of the larger society of which the professions are an integral part. Although the precise details and relative emphasis vary across the different professions, observers have discerned a broad trajectory from an ideal of professionalism in which technical expertise is combined with a commitment to public service and public purposes, towards an ideal of professionalism in which the element of commitment to public service and public purposes has become seriously attenuated relative to the element of technical expertise.[2] William Sullivan, for example, uses the terms "civic professionalism" and "technical professionalism" to describe the two poles of this trajectory, the outcome of which is a sense that the professions are currently in a state of some crisis.[3]

In a very real sense, Mercer University's Professionalism and Vocation Across the Professions Project can be seen as responding to this sense of crisis. Moreover, we have been told by the distinguished scholars who addressed us at our various symposia that it is rare, perhaps even unique, to involve so many participants from across an entire university. Because we believe that readers may be interested in our story for these two reasons, and also because it will provide context for what follows in part II and part III, readers may first wish to read Mark Jones's narrative of the project in appendix A, discussed further below, before reading the remaining contributions.

Part II begins with William Sullivan's keynote paper from the project's inaugural event, the 2005 symposium on "Professionalism and Vocation Across the Professions," bearing the same title as the symposium, followed by William May's keynote paper from the 2006 symposium on "Cultivating Professionalism and Vocation Across the Professions: Challenges for Higher Education," entitled "Forming Professionals and the Quest for Common Ground in the University." These two contributions introduce influential notions and conceptual frameworks originated by their authors. The first conceptual framework is William Sullivan's "three apprenticeships of

---

[2] For an illuminating account of the relevant history, see William M. Sullivan, *Work and Integrity: The Crisis and Promise of Professionalism in America*, 2nd ed. (San Francisco: Jossey-Bass, 2005).

[3] Ibid.

Introduction

professional education": the academic apprenticeship focused on cognitive or intellectual knowledge, the practical apprenticeship focused on skill or practice, and the socio-ethical apprenticeship focused on identity and purpose, central to which is his notion of "civic professionalism." The second framework is William May's "three marks of the professional" (the intellectual, the moral, and the organizational) and their three correlative virtues (practical wisdom, fidelity, and public spiritedness). These pieces also discuss several other important matters such as the idea of professional calling or vocation, the history of higher education and professional education in the United States, the challenges posed by the institutional and social context in which the professions are practiced, and possible strategies for professional educators to meet these challenges in the process of professional formation.

The other four contributions in part II, authored by participants in the Professionalism and Vocation Across the Professions Project, elaborate upon and/or otherwise respond to themes in the keynote papers. The first two contributions, John Dunaway's reflection entitled "'God at Work:' A Reflection on Vocation" and Timothy Floyd's "Answering the Call to Service: Vocation and Professional Identity," are based upon the authors' joint panel presentation at the 2005 symposium. As the titles suggest, these two contributions elaborate upon the topic of vocation, in particular its religious dimensions, although they both share Frederick Buechner's capacious understanding of vocation as "the place where your gladness meets the world's deep need." The two remaining contributions are by Peter Brown and Jack Sammons. Both authors served as observers of the lunchtime discussions at the 2005 symposium and in other critical roles during the preparation and execution of project events, and they have provided much of the intellectual muscle powering both individual project events as well as the development of the project as a whole. Peter Brown's paper, entitled "Reform and Formation: Revisiting the Role of Liberal Education," is not based upon the reflections he delivered during the summing-up session following the lunchtime discussions at the 2005 symposium but, in part at least, upon his presentation at the second symposium in 2006. Drawing upon the particular experience of Mercer University, he emphasizes and explores how a strategy of "teaching against the grain" in higher education can answer the summons in the two keynote papers for a liberalized professional formation and can help resist those cultural forces that threaten to corrupt our professional practices. Jack

Sammons's paper entitled "Confronting the Three Apprenticeships," which *is* based upon his reflections during the summing-up session at the 2005 symposium, itself goes against the grain of much other thinking. Thus, the author suggests that, before they do anything else, professional educators would do well to recognize the ultimate goal of helping our students become good practitioners, that is to say, practically wise practitioners, who submit to the moral authority of the practice and, with this goal in mind, to discover the hidden potential revealed by shifting our perceptions to see the holistic nature of what we are *already* doing.

A detailed set of focus questions designed to help guide ongoing exploration and research on professionalism and vocation is reproduced in appendix C and addressed further below.

Part III undertakes an advertent and sustained exploration of the particular topic of practical wisdom, a notion that we already have encountered a number of times, in the practical context of the professions. We consider that practical wisdom is a central unifying theme and focus for character development and the development of moral capacity throughout the educational continuum as well as in the cultivation of professionalism, and indeed that attaining practical wisdom can be regarded as a culminating achievement in life. This explains why we have separated out the materials undertaking the advertent and sustained exploration of this topic, and indeed postponed that exploration until the final part of the book, instead of including these materials in part II, even though they were generated by the third symposium held by the Professionalism and Vocation Across the Professions Project in 2008. In this part we are again concerned with a set of questions similar to those we identified with regard to part I and part II, such as: What is practical wisdom? Why is it important? How is practical wisdom related to rules and to character virtues? How is it related to the ideal of professionalism, and how is the practical wisdom of the good practitioner related to a sense of professional calling or vocation? How is practical wisdom cultivated? Is it under threat? If so, how and why is it under threat? And what is the appropriate response to such threat? And of course, once again, in keeping with our conviction that we need to pursue an integrative approach to issues of character development and moral formation throughout the entire educational continuum, we consider that the contributions in part I and part II are relevant in seeking answers to these questions, just as the insights gained in part III are relevant for our understanding of character development and moral formation in general and the moral ideal of professionalism in particular.

Practical wisdom is commonly defined as the ability to act well in context, to do "the right thing in the right way at the right time." We begin part III with Barry Schwartz and Kenneth Sharpe's keynote paper from the 2008 symposium, entitled "The War on Wisdom and How to Fight It." Emphasizing that practical wisdom involves the combination of ethical intelligence (moral skill) and ethical motivation (moral will), the authors explore why practical wisdom is necessary in professional life, identify six moral abilities of the practically wise person (ability to attend to the particular circumstances, to find the mean, to improvise, to empathize, to aim at the right things, and to draw on experience, take initiative, and learn from mistakes), and show how practical wisdom is threatened by the unwise use of rules and incentives. They also suggest ways in which practical wisdom can be defended in the professions and professional education.

Three additional contributions elaborate upon several of the themes in this keynote paper. In the first piece entitled "Practical Wisdom and Vocation in Professional Formation: A Schematic Account," Mark Jones re-emphasizes that the good practitioner in a professional practice is the practically wise practitioner. A person of practical wisdom (a *phronimos*) acts well in a situation (i.e., engages in good practical reasoning and translates thinking into action) by calling into play relevant attributes from an ensemble of deeply ingrained and seamlessly integrated attributes (theoretical knowledge, practical skills, and qualities of character) in a manner that is appropriately responsive to context. It is this ability that constitutes the "master virtue" of practical wisdom, enabling the *phronimos* to conduct the entire ensemble appropriately. He also seeks to show how becoming a practically wise practitioner is related to a sense of professional vocation.

The remaining contributions, authored by two participants in the Professionalism and Vocation Across the Professions Project, complement each other in exploring further both the substance and the procedure of practically wise decision-making. In a paper with a more procedural focus entitled "Being Pragmatic about Practical Wisdom," David Ritchie draws upon John Dewey's pragmatic epistemology to analyze five "distinct steps" of "inquiry" in the pragmatic reasoning characteristic of the competent practitioner who makes practical and wise decisions (i.e., "(1) a felt difficulty; (2) its location and definition; (3) suggestion of [a] possible solution; (4) development by reasoning of the bearings of the suggestion; and (5) further observation and experiment leading to its acceptance or rejection...," quoting Dewey). With a focus more on substance, Jack Sammons's "Guidelines for Observing Practical Wisdom at Work" analyzes five components of practically wise deliberation (the deliberation involves means and ends, is driven by the actual particularities of context, relies heavily upon internalized past experiences, is sufficiently aware of itself to consider and correct for its limitations, and considers the character and not just the consequences of the action to be taken). These five components and their multiple subcomponents resonate with and complement Schwartz and Sharpe's account of the moral abilities of the practically wise person and the accounts of moral expertise given by Narvaez and Lickona in part I.[4]

In the conclusion we consider what we have learned through our work in the two projects and the contributions of this volume as well as some important opportunities and challenges for the future.

There are four appendices. Appendix A contains Mark Jones's narrative entitled "Building Bridges and Discovering Commonality: The Story of Mercer University's Professionalism and Vocation Across the Professions Project," which discusses the origins and development of the Professionalism and Vocation Project from 2005 until 2010, including its incorporation into the broader Phronesis Project in 2009, as well as the goals, scope, and focus of the project and our evolving understanding and evolution of project emphasis during the course of its development. For the reasons discussed above, we believe that this history may be of interest to the reader.

In appendix B, Paul Lewis continues the narrative in his "Moral Development Across Disciplines, Schools, and Life-Span: The Phronesis Project." In addition to discussing the genesis of the Phronesis Project, as

---

[4] We should note that David Ritchie illustrates his account by reference to the case-study exercise reproduced in appendix D and his experience as an observer in the 2009 Practical Wisdom Workshop that used that exercise. Moreover, as the title of his piece suggests, Jack Sammons, who also served as an observer at the 2009 workshop as well as at the 2008 workshop for which the exercise was originally developed, wrote his "Guidelines" to assist the observers in the two parallel case study discussion groups at the workshops. Although the substantive discussion of practical wisdom in the "Guidelines" warrants including them as an independent contribution in part III, they also should be regarded as part of the case-study materials and therefore are addressed again below in that context.

well as its goals, objectives, guiding principles, and various activities, both completed and continuing, the narrative situates the Phronesis Project within the historical context of Mercer University's longstanding commitment to transformative education and curricular innovation, concluding that the project should be seen as a natural and authentic expression of the character of Mercer University.

Appendix C reproduces Mark Jones's detailed set of focus questions along a vertical (profession-specific) axis addressing the history, current state, and future of professionalism and vocation in the United States. These questions expand upon the original five questions along the vertical axis that, together with five questions along a horizontal (cross-professional) axis, were formulated to focus our inquiries at the first symposium held by the Professionalism and Vocation Across the Professions Project in 2005. This expanded list of questions along the vertical axis, as well as the original five questions along the horizontal axis, is designed to help guide ongoing exploration and research within the project. Both sets of original questions and the expanded list of questions are discussed further in Mark Jones's narrative in appendix A.

Appendix D reproduces the materials developed for the case-study workshop that was part of the third symposium held by the Professionalism and Vocation Symposium in 2008, and repeated for a new group of participants in 2009. The planning committee for the 2008 symposium decided to draft a difficult hypothetical case study focused on disability law and the challenges in providing adequate educational, medical, and social services for an autistic child for discussion in two parallel interdisciplinary breakout groups at a case-study workshop held the next day following the previous evening's keynote address. Observers attached to each breakout group at the workshop sought to identify those elements of practical wisdom that were being manifested in the discussions. Following the breakout group discussions, the observers reported their observations to the entire group of participants and led a plenary discussion analyzing and evaluating our experience at the workshop. The same case study was used in the repeat of the workshop in 2009. Our particular purpose in holding the case-study workshops was to enable the participants to learn more about the nature of practical wisdom, especially the similarities and differences among the practical wisdoms of our different professions as these were manifested in the group deliberations, as well as to field test a promising interdisciplinary pedagogy. However, such a case-study workshop also could be usefully conducted for participants from the same discipline or professional field.

The appendix includes "Case Study Part I: Whose Decision Is It Really?", drafted by Peter Brown; "Case Study Part II: Best for Whom?", drafted by Tom Glennon, Anne Hathaway, and Stephen Wills; "Case Study Supporting Materials," prepared by Alice Baker; "Guidelines for Observers," prepared by Jack Sammons and already reproduced in part III as "Guidelines for Observing Practical Wisdom at Work," as discussed above; and a "Teaching Note: 'Difference, Disability, and Professional Judgment'," prepared by Peter Brown that, unlike Jack Sammons's generic guidelines, focuses specifically on the facts of our particular case study. Although we decided to use only the guidelines at the workshops, we also include the teaching note for those who would like to use the same case study and who want to give the observers more structured guidance either instead of, or in addition to, the guidelines. Mark Jones's "Introduction to Case Study Exercise" at the beginning of the appendix explains how we structured and conducted the workshops, and how we asked the participants to prepare for them, in case those readers who would like to use such a case-study exercise themselves may find our own experience helpful. Such readers also may be interested to know that, although the participants in the 2008 and 2009 workshops were mostly faculty, the same case study also has been used successfully, both at the undergraduate level and at the graduate professional school level, with various interdisciplinary groups composed exclusively of students.

Part I: Character Development and Moral Formation

1

Contemporary Character Education in Context

Paul Lewis

In *Meno*, Plato asks whether virtue can be taught, and while he hedges his answer there, he later suggests an affirmative answer in *The Republic* as he explores the origins of the just person. What Plato suggests, his pupil Aristotle makes explicit by saying that the only reason to study ethics is to become a good person—in short, to become a person of character.[1] The notion that character development is therefore a legitimate goal of education is thus deeply imbedded in Western civilization and endures in the United States until the twentieth century when it comes under siege. In this essay, I will briefly identify some of the most important reasons for the decline of character education, sketch out some of the alternative schools of moral development that took its place, and conclude by outlining an account of character and its formation that is emerging in contemporary psychology.

Many scholars trace the decline of character education in the United States to the work of Yale psychologists Hugh Hartshorne and Jim May.[2] In

---

[1] Aristotle, *Nicomachean Ethics*, trans. Martin Ostwald (New York: Macmillan Publishing Company, 1986) 1103b.

[2] My summary of this widely shared sense of the history of moral education draws heavily from B. Edward McClellan, *Moral Education in America* (New York: Teachers College Press, 1999); Clark Power, Ann Higgins, and Lawrence Kohlberg, "The Habit of the Common Life: Building Character Through Democratic Community Schools," in *Moral Development and Character Education*, ed. Larry P. Nucci (Berkeley: McCutchan Publishing Corporation, 1989) 125–43; Craig A. Cunningham, "A Certain and Reasoned Art: The Rise and Fall of Character Education in America," in *Character Psychology and Character Education*, ed. Daniel K. Lapsley and F. Clark Power (Notre Dame: University of Notre Dame Press, 2005) 166–200; Thomas Lickona, *Educating for Character* (New York: Bantam Books, 1991) 6–12; James Davison Hunter, *The Death of Character: Moral Education in an Age Without Good or Evil* (New York: Basic Books, 2000) 31–204; and Robert J. Nash, *Answering the Virtuecrats: A Moral Conversation on Character Education* (New York: Teachers College Press, 1997) 6–10. For a treatment that focuses exclusively on the decline and revival of

the 1920s, they studied the behavior of over 10,000 children, only to find that there was little match between moral convictions and behavior. This finding led them to conclude that prior efforts at character development were failures. Additionally, the philosophy of positivism began to take hold in Anglo-American circles, a philosophy that in the arena of morality led to the conclusion that values are intangible and therefore matters of preference rather than fact. Moreover, in the aftermath of World War II, trends toward increasing pluralism and geographic mobility intensified, with the result that whatever common social convictions and arrangements remained were stretched, and at times even sundered, especially when coupled with the sexual, feminist, and civil rights "revolutions" of the time. Another blow to character education at this time was the perceived technological superiority of the Soviet Union that led to an educational emphasis on science and math so that the United States could "overcome the communist menace." In short, by the mid-1960s, what had been a relatively homogenous and stable consensus about the legitimacy and shape of character education had broken down.

Moral education did not go away, however, as four competing schools of thought emerged. The first school of moral education to appear, cognitive developmentalism, emerged in the mid-1950s and has had a long-lasting influence. Rooted in the work of Lawrence Kohlberg and William G. Perry, this school, which worked initially with a college undergraduate population, sought to understand and track the development of moral reasoning over a series of stages that move from what are taken to be less sophisticated to more mature forms of reasoning. Cognitive developmentalism has been criticized on many counts, e.g., for being too wedded to a problematic philosophical understanding of moral agency, for being too male, and/or for defining the moral domain too narrowly.[3] In response to these criticisms, the

---

moral education in higher education, see Elizabeth Kiss and J. Peter Euben, "Debating Moral Education: An Introduction," and Julie A. Reuben, "The Changing Contours of Moral Education in American Colleges and Universities," both in *Debating Moral Education: Rethinking the Role of the Modern University*, ed. Elizabeth Kiss and J. Peter Euben (Durham NC: Duke University Press, 2010) 3–26 and 27–54, respectively.

[3] See Daniel K. Lapsley and Darcia Narvaez, "Moral Psychology at the Crossroads," in *Character Psychology and Character Education*, ed. Daniel K. Lapsley and Clark F. Powers (Notre Dame: University of Notre Dame Press, 2005) 22–23. See also Carol Gilligan, *In a Different Voice* (Cambridge MA: Harvard University Press, 1993).

latest researchers have expanded its horizons by recognizing that other processes than reasoning are at play in moral behavior, such that cognitive developmentalism has remained a vibrant, evolving school, even though it is now, in the minds of some thinkers, searching for a post-Kohlbergian direction.[4]

A second school—and the shortest lived—is that of values clarification, first proposed by Louis E. Raths, Merrill Harmon, and Sydney Simon in 1966 and later modified by others. Stressing both the personally engaging nature of values and a smorgasbord philosophy that encouraged people to choose from a range of possible values, proponents of this school saw the point of moral education as that of helping students to identify or clarify their own values in a supposedly nondirective and value-free way. This movement came under withering criticism for its inability to be morally neutral and was largely abandoned by the mid-1970s.

In the 1990s, a revitalized character education emerged as a third approach to moral development, led most publicly by then Secretary of Education, William Bennett, but also championed by academic educators Thomas Lickona and Larry P. Nucci. This approach to moral education focuses primarily on elementary and secondary-age students (although it resonates with efforts in professional schools to form professional character or identity in their students). While taking various forms, most versions trace their roots back to Aristotle and stress the development of dispositions and habits among students. Critics of this resurgent character education often argue that it is philosophically and pedagogically naïve, dangerously authoritarian, and unsuited to the needs of a pluralistic democracy.[5]

The fourth and most recent school of moral education is that of citizenship education, which focuses mostly on secondary and postsecondary populations. Such education seeks to instill in students a variety of competencies, such as a knowledge base, thinking skills, social

---

[4] One example of the evolving shape of the Kohlbergian paradigm can be found in James Rest's Four Component Model, which emphasizes the interaction between moral sensitivity, moral motivation, and moral character, as well as moral reasoning. James Rest, "Background Theory and Research," in *Moral Development in the Professions*, ed. James R. Rest and Darcia Narvaez (Hillsdale NJ: Lawrence Erlbaum Associates, 1994) 22–25. On the search for direction after Kohlberg, see the September 2008 issue of *The Journal of Moral Education* that was devoted to exploring new directions.

[5] See, for example, Nash, *Answering the Virtuecrats,* 31–52.

skills, and dispositions to act, often through the use of service-learning or other engaged pedagogies. Signs of interest in citizenship education include the growth of an organization that promotes service-learning, Campus Compact, from a few campuses to 1,200 member campuses across the country. Moreover, the publication of the Princeton Review's *Colleges with a Conscience* identifies schools that promote community involvement. Critics of this school of moral education sometimes claim that its engaged pedagogies sacrifice academic rigor and that it is insufficiently critical of the prevailing culture.[6]

At this point, I return to character education today. We have seen that neither is it the only approach to moral education around at present, nor is it without its critics. Nonetheless, another part of the story is that the work of several psychologists seems to be converging on a somewhat unified understanding of the moral person or moral character.[7] James Rest identifies four mutually influential psychological processes that are components of moral behavior. Darcia Narvaez, a former associate of Rest, refines and expands his model (see her contribution elsewhere in this volume). She compares the development of character to the development of expertise at a number of levels that must coordinate in order to achieve moral action. Marvin Berkowitz describes a "moral anatomy" that consists of four skills and characteristics that are part of a fully functioning moral agent. Paul Baltes and Ursula Staudinger, in their treatment of wisdom and its development, talk about developing expertise in bringing factual and

---

[6] For examples of these criticisms and rebuttals, see many of the essays in *Introduction to Service-Learning Toolkit,* 2nd ed. (Providence RI: Campus Compact, 2003).

[7] James Rest with Muriel Bebeau and Joseph Volker, "An Overview of the Psychology of Morality," in *Moral Development: Advances in Research and Theory* (New York: Praeger, 1986) 3–18; Marvin Berkowitz et al., "Educating for Positive Youth Development," in *Handbook of Moral Development*, ed. Melanie Killen and Judith G. Smetana (Mahwah NJ: Lawrence Erblaum Associates, 2006) 689–91; Paul B. Baltes and Ursula M. Staudinger, "Wisdom: A Metaheuristic (Pragmatic) to Orchestrate Mind and Virtue Toward Excellence," *American Psychologist* 55/1 (2000): 12–136; Robert J. Sternberg, "A Balance Theory of Wisdom," *Review of General Pyschology* 2/4 (1998): 347–65. For a more detailed discussion of the work of these psychologists and for my argument that this emerging synthesis echoes Aristotle's ancient account of moral character, see "In Defence of Aristotle on Character: a Synthesis of Recent Psychology, Neuroscience, and the Thought of Michael Polanyi," *Journal of Moral Education* 41, No. 2 (2012): 155-170.

procedural knowledge to bear on conduct. Robert Sternberg, now at Oklahoma State University, describes wisdom as skill in applying tacit knowledge to the task of achieving the common good.

This understanding may provide invaluable input into efforts in character education—indeed, in many ways it already has. From this work, we might propose to define character as the expert integration of skills in three areas. Following Lickona, I call them Knowing, Desiring, and Doing.[8] Such language keeps with the Aristotelian understanding of character as the integration of thinking and desiring for the sake of doing the right thing in the circumstances. Of course, these divisions between knowing, desiring, and doing should not be taken to be hard and fast. Character is a living, organic, systemic entity in which knowing, desiring, and doing interact and overlap in complex ways that are difficult, if not impossible, to tease apart. This treatment attempts to distinguish some of the key features of character, but without dissecting character, for dissection kills the living entity that is being dissected.

The skills involved in the cognitive or knowing dimension of character are many—and the contemporary literature is helpful in identifying these sub-skills. One is perception—that is, the ability to interpret the moral aspects of a circumstance, the ability to perceive ethical salience, or one's ethical sensitivity. A second cognitive skill is that of reasoning, which includes facility at decision-making and judging in ambiguous and/or complex situations. This skill is the one that cognitive developmental theories emphasize and arguably measure through the Defining Issues Test or other instruments. A third cognitive skill is what some call perspective-taking, the ability to examine a situation from a viewpoint other than one's own.[9] A fourth is an understanding of the self, of one's own perspective, convictions, even treating morality as a central part of one's self-identity. These skills of knowing operate at both tacit and explicit levels and deal with matters of both content and process.

---

[8] Lickona, *Educating for Character*, 53–62.

[9] This ability is sometimes referred to as empathy and construed as part of the emotional or desiring dimension of character. The most extensive psychological work on empathy has been done by Martin L. Hoffman. See his *Empathy and Moral Development: Implications for Caring and Justice* (Cambridge and New York: Cambridge University Press, 2000).

The second skill set has to do with desiring. According to these authors, to be of good character, one must desire what is morally good, a term often understood as referring to pro-social attitudes and behaviors. In addition, one must give priority to moral values in decision-making. Another necessary skill of desiring is that of self-regulation, the ability to control or temper one's desires that is sometimes called emotional competence. The final skill set is that of doing, the ability to put the pieces together for the sake of moral action.

In sum, we have seen that character education has a long but contested history in Western education, especially in the United States. Called into question early in the twentieth century, it gives way to other schools of moral education but later experiences a resurgence of interest even as it remains contested. Nevertheless, a new psychological account of character seems to be emerging that shows promise for helping us better understand what character is and how it develops.

At the same time, there is much work to be done, and this emerging view of character would benefit from greater attention to more and varied student populations, most notably college undergraduates since they are largely left out of studies on character education. At the practical level of pedagogy, we know a bit about strategies that promote the development of moral reasoning and civic engagement—at least studies suggest that cognitive development is spurred best by dilemma discussions and service-learning does seem to correlate positively with ongoing civic engagement. We know something about pedagogies that develop expertise. On the whole, however, we do not reflect enough on the theoretical assumptions behind the pedagogical practices and the practical implications of theories of moral development.

What we need, therefore, is a comprehensive account of moral education that undertakes several tasks. This first is to connect and unify the competing emphases on moral reasoning, virtues/character, and citizenship.[10] The second is to integrate information about brain development and the biology of habituation from the neurosciences into our

---

[10] Wolfgang Althof and Marvin W. Berkowitz hint at the need for such coordination in their "Moral Education and Character Education: Their Relationship and Roles in Citizenship Education," *Journal of Moral Education* 35/4 (2006): 503.

accounts.[11] The third is to reflect more critically on the actual needs of a pluralistic democracy so as to better understand the skills needed for effective citizenship.[12] The fourth is to stimulate critical reflection on pedagogies in order to refine older strategies and develop new ones. The final task is to find ways to assess character development that are appropriate to the subject matter, for to paraphrase Aristotle, ethics is not physics and the degree of precision sought must fit the subject matter.[13]

---

[11] Darcia Narvaez is one of those making an effort at this broad integration, as is apparent in her contribution to this book. For an overview of her work, see my "The Emerging Comprehensive Moral Psychology of Darcia Narvaez," in *Tradition and Discovery* 34/4 (2011): 9–17.

[12] The essays collected in part III of *Debating Moral Education* represent a solid beginning at this task.

[13] Aristotle, *Nicomachean Ethics*, 1094b.

2

Wisdom as Mature Moral Functioning:
Insights from Developmental Psychology and Neurobiology

Darcia Narvaez

The goal of this chapter is to examine briefly the nature of mature moral functioning, or wisdom, from the broad view of human development. Although wisdom has been studied for some time, here I try to fill in some gaps in its conceptualization by addressing the development of emotion and expertise (e.g., specific skills and self-monitoring). It is assumed here that under optimal conditions, all (normal) persons are able to develop wisdom.

The Nature of Wisdom

What is wisdom? Perhaps we know it when we see it, but researchers cannot agree on a definition. Some define it as cognitive expertise, others as a personality factor or a matter of ego development.[1] Moreover, researchers typically either collapse moral and practical wisdom or emphasize practical wisdom as a priority. For example, Kramer defines wisdom as "excellent judgment about human affairs."[2] Life-span researchers define wisdom as a form of practical wisdom: "a metaheuristic to orchestrate mind and virtue toward excellence," an "expert knowledge system concerning the fundamental pragmatics of life," or "expertise on the conduct and meaning of life."[3]

Research on wisdom, defined broadly, has made several key findings, based largely on interview data using scenarios for judging and deciding a

---

[1] D. J. Shedlok and S. W. Cornelius, "Psychological Approaches to Wisdom and Its Development," in *Handbook of Adult Development*, ed. J. Demick and C. Andreoletti (New York: Springer, 2003) 153–68.

[2] D. Kramer, "The Ontogeny of Wisdom in Its Variations," in *Handbook of Adult Development*, ed. J. Demick and C. Andreoletti (New York: Springer, 2003) 131–52.

[3] P. Baltes and U. Staudinger, "Wisdom: A Metaheuristic (Pragmatic) to Orchestrate Mind and Virtue Towards Excellence," in *American Psychologist* 55 (2000): 122, 123, 124.

course of action. One is that wisdom is apparent in only 5–10 percent of subjects. It also seems that wisdom does not show a general age trend, although it is found more commonly among older than younger adults.[4] Moreover, wisdom arises in early adulthood and is further refined throughout adulthood with particular experience.[5] In addition, all age groups are better at reasoning wisely when the scenarios are familiar to their age group, suggesting that there is an experiential element.[6] Finally, wisdom is correlated with particular personality characteristics (e.g., openness, creativity) and requires basic levels of intelligence.[7] Again, these findings reflect interview data, a method that taps explicit knowledge.

In contrast, Robert Sternberg, who perhaps has the strongest generalist definition of wisdom, emphasizes non-conscious or implicit knowledge.[8] He describes a balance theory of wisdom, which is mediated by values: "Tacit knowledge underlying practical intelligence is applied to balance intrapersonal, interpersonal, and extrapersonal interests to achieve a balance of the responses to the environmental context of adaptation to, shaping of, and selection of environments in order to achieve a common good."[9] (Again, practical and moral wisdom are collapsed.) In this paper, I adopt an expertise view of wisdom as comprised of both non-conscious intuitions built from experience and deliberate conscious understanding.

The research on wisdom described so far has focused primarily on judgment or decision-making. This work can be enriched by combining it with research in moral psychology that has also emphasized judgment, but has focused on reasoning used to advocate a certain action choice in a moral dilemma. In this tradition, researchers find that people conceptualize moral

---

[4] P. B. Baltes and J. Smith, "The Psychology of Wisdom and Its Ontogenesis," in R. J. Sternberg, ed., *Wisdom: Its Nature, Origins, and Development* (New York: Cambridge University Press, 1990) 87–120.

[5] P. B. Baltes and U. Kunzmann, "Wisdom," *The Psychologist* 16/3 (2003): 131–33.

[6] Kramer, "Ontogeny of Wisdom."

[7] U. Staudinger and M. Pasupathi, "Correlates of Wisdom-Related Performance in Adolescence and Adulthood: Age-Graded Differences in 'Paths' Toward Desirable Development," *Journal of Research on Adolescence* 13/3 (2003): 239–68.

[8] R. Sternberg, "Abilities Are Forms of Developing Expertise," *Educational Researcher* 3 (1998): 22–35.

[9] Ibid.

problems differently, based on age and education.[10] As individuals develop in moral judgment, transformations occur in how they construe their obligations to others. Kohlberg described these changes in complexity as stages of moral reasoning.[11] These transformations also can be viewed as alternative moral schemas about how it is possible to organize cooperation.[12] As moral judgment matures, an individual's concerns expand, and he or she is able to consider the welfare of more and more "others" when conceptualizing ideal forms of cooperation (e.g., at the lowest schema, one is primarily concerned for self, whereas in the most developed schema, one includes concern for those one will never meet). These changes certainly contribute to wisdom.

So far, we have seen that in the attempt to understand wisdom, some psychologists emphasize practical intelligence, whereas others emphasize the integration of virtue and expertise.[13] We also have seen that other research on moral reasoning can tell us more about the processes involved in the development of wisdom. But philosophical reflection also needs to inform our understanding of wisdom.

In the history of philosophy, a distinction has been made between *phronesis*, practical wisdom used to meet one's goals, and moral virtue. Narvaez, Gleason, and Mitchell identify three perspectives on the relationship between practical wisdom, *phronesis*, and moral virtue.[14] One view considers practical wisdom and virtue as essential to, if not separable from, the virtues.[15] Aristotle contended that *phronesis* unites and powers the

---

[10] For example, Lawrence Kohlberg, *The Psychology of Moral Development: Essays on Moral Development*, vol. 2 (San Francisco: Harper & Row, 1984); and J. R. Rest, *Development in Judging Moral Issues* (Minneapolis: University of Minnesota Press, 1979).

[11] Kohlberg, *Psychology of Moral Development*.

[12] James Rest, D. Narvaez, M. J. Bebeau, and S. J. Thoma, *Postconventional Moral Thinking: A Neo-Kohlbergian Approach* (Mahwah NJ: Lawrence Erlbaum Associates, 1999).

[13] For an example of the first type, see R. Sternberg, "Abilities Are Forms of Developing Expertise," in *Educational Researcher* 3 (1998): 22–35. For an example of the second, see Baltes and Staudinger, "Wisdom: A Metaheuristic."

[14] D. Narvaez, T. Gleason, and C. Mitchell, "Moral Virtue and Practical Wisdom: Theme Comprehension in Children, Youth, and Adults," *Journal of Genetic Psychology* 171/4 (2010): 1–26.

[15] Plato, *The Republic*, 2nd ed., rev., trans. D. Lee (London: Penguin Books, 1955/1987).

use of the virtues, making moral virtue impossible without *phronesis*.[16] In this case, the two cannot be separated. The second view divides practical wisdom from morality entirely.[17] In Kant's view, the human being has an empirical side driven by prudential self-interest. Humans also have a rational side, which allows the individual to set aside self-interest and use moral reasoning as a guide to behavior. In this view, *phronesis* is primary and moral virtue comes later with the skills of rationality. A third view, which Narvaez and colleagues call the "developmental view," emphasizes the role of experience in wisdom development.[18] Because experience is founded in sociality, moral virtue develops first, and because life experience occurs over time, *phronesis* develops more slowly. The latter requires domain-specific experience for its success and can take years to develop. On the other hand, the development of moral virtue starts from birth and is necessary for social survival. Narvaez and colleagues' developmental studies supported the third view, showing that moral understanding comes first before practical wisdom, findings that conform with virtue ethics theory.[19]

The Development of Wisdom and Virtue

According to some modern virtue theorists, practical wisdom cannot be found in the young. Although children and adolescents may have developed moral virtue appropriate for their ages, they lack real world experience on how to apply moral virtue well. According to Hursthouse, "Both the virtuous adult and the nice child have good intentions, but the child is much more prone to mess things up because he is ignorant of what he needs to know in order to do what he intends."[20] In other words, practical wisdom involves knowing what ends are good and how to reach them in a beneficial way. Hursthouse implies a developmental story to wisdom development that has been corroborated by research.[21]

---

[16] Aristotle, *Nicomachean Ethics*, trans. W. D. Ross (London: Oxford, 1925/1988).

[17] Immanuel Kant, *Grounding for the Metaphysics of Morals*, trans. James W. Ellington (New York: Hacket, 1785/1993).

[18] D. Narvaez et al., "Moral Virtue and Practical Wisdom," 363–88.

[19] Ibid.

[20] R. Hursthouse, "Virtue Ethics," in *The Stanford Encyclopedia of Philosophy*, vol. 3, ed. E. N. Zalta (Stanford, CA: Stanford University, 2003) http://plato.stanford.edu/archives/fall2003/entries/ethics-virtue/ (Accessed August 8, 2012).

[21] D. Narvaez et al., "Moral Virtue and Practical Wisdom," 1–26.

Nevertheless, moral character is often discussed from the viewpoint of an adult—almost as if you are born with it, or not. Some subscribe to a biological determinism (i.e., "bad seed," "poor genes"), a perspective not rooted in valid empirical evidence.[22] Genes might play a role in character, but there are many other factors that also play a role, making the role of genetics very small (but easiest to measure).[23] Also, something might look genetic, like temperament, but only because other environmental factors have not been examined, such as gestational and perinatal experiences that make deep impressions on the child and the mother-child relationship.

If moral character is not genetic or inborn, how does it develop? We know quite a bit about how relationships with caregivers in early life influence well-being and personality throughout life.[24] Caregivers actually shape the systems and functioning of body and brain, the latter of which is only 25 percent complete at birth. For example, the functioning of the vagus nerve, which is implicated in the proper performance of all major body systems and also linked to capabilities for compassion, is dependent on warm responsive care. Caregivers also help determine how emotion systems develop—which ones become habitual or are easily triggered by outside events. They form implicit understandings of what relationships are for—in warm, responsive settings, relationships are enjoyable, whereas in neglectful and abusive settings, relationships are for manipulation and power. Caregivers instruct the child on how to manage emotions (e.g., as informative or as dangerous) and how to deal with the needs of the self (e.g., kindly or harshly). Factors like these shape moral character from birth.

Although there are other sensitive periods in life, none seem to be as sensitive as the first years of life when irreversible designs are established. Other periods of increased plasticity include early adolescence, therapy, but most important for this paper, emerging adulthood (ages 18–26). During these periods the brain is more malleable than it normally is, allowing for a greater impact of experience. In sum, most critical for moral formation,

---

[22] Although it was rooted in bad science, see R. C. Lewonton, S. Rose, and L. J. Kamin, *Not in Our Genes: Biology, Ideology, and Human Nature* (New York: Pantheon, 1984).

[23] R. C. Richardson, *Evolutionary Psychology as Maladapted Psychology* (Cambridge MA: MIT Press, 2007).

[24] For more information, see D. Narvaez, J. Panksepp, J. Shore, and T. Gleason, eds., *Evolution, Early Experience, and Human Development* (New York: Oxford University Press, 2012).

perhaps in contrast to other areas of expertise, are personal relationships—beginning with the mutual co-regulation established with the caregiver and the lifelong co-construction by parents, friends, mentors, and others. So if you want to be a socially or morally adept person, you should be immersed, like an apprentice, in an environment where good social skills are encouraged and supported by those with more capacities. We look next at the moral propensities that humans carry.

The Beginnings of Moral Character: Triune Ethics

Evolution predisposes human beings to three basic ethical orientations, according to Triune Ethics Theory (TET).[25] These moral orientations are rooted in unconscious emotional systems shaped by experience and predispose one to react to and act on events in particular ways. The three ethical orientations proposed by Triune Ethics Theory are called Security, Engagement, and Imagination.

Table 1. Triune Ethics Moral Orientations

Triune Ethics
Major Types and Sub-Types
Engagement Calm and Communal Imagination
Mindful Morality (The "Moral Zone")
Imagination
Detached Imagination (Intellectualized Morality)
Vicious Imagination (Righteous Morality)
Communal Imagination (Agape Morality)
Engagement
Engagement Distress (Co-Dependent Morality)
Engagement Calm (Harmony Morality)
Security
Wallflower Security (Submissive Morality)
Bunker Security (Challenging Morality)

---

[25] I develop these ideas in greater detail in my "Triune Ethics: The Neurobiological Roots of Our Multiple Moralities," *New Ideas in Psychology* 26 (2008): 95–119; "Triune Ethics Theory and Moral Personality," *Moral Personality, Identity, and Character: An Interdisciplinary Future*, ed. D. Narvaez and D. K. Lapsley (New York: Cambridge University Press, 2010) 136–58; and "Moral Complexity: The Fatal Attraction of Truthiness and the Importance of Mature Moral Functioning," *Perspectives on Psychological Science* 5/2 (2010): 163–86.

The Ethic of Security is based in instincts for self-preservation, often relying on defensive aggression (bunker security) or conditioned submission (wallflower security). The conditioned, primitive ethic (security) perceives choices with filters of threat and safety. When emotions are dysregulated, the security orientation may dominate in situations of threat either as an externalizing, aggressive morality (bunker security), or an internalizing, collapsing morality (wallflower security). The individual has a difficult time dealing with social stress and is caught in a self-centered manner of making moral decisions.

The Ethic of Engagement is oriented to face-to-face emotional affiliation with others in the present moment and is linked to the pro-social emotions of compassion and gratitude. It represents full presence in the moment for intersubjectivity and resonance with the Other. Engagement is a more non-verbal, right-brain-dominant ethic that is able to perceive life holistically, in rich context and with reverence.[26] An exemplar is the devoted mother who is in love with the child but at the same time respects the child's individual dignity.

The Ethic of Imagination is able to abstract from the present moment, which is helpful when pro-social emotions are engaged (communal imagination), but potentially harmful when detached from emotion (detached imagination) or related to morally mandated aggression toward and dominance of others to satisfy ego needs (vicious imagination). When emotions are discouraged or discounted in formative years, the more verbal, more left-brain ethic (imagination) may become dominant in one's personality. One may adopt a more detached approach to relationships and moral functioning, focusing more on abstractions like decontextualized principles or non-human areas of life. Human life itself may be less valued.

Each ethic is dominated by different parts of the brain, influenced by physiological systems that can unconsciously shape perception and action choices. Each ethic can distinctively influence ideological choices, perception, attention, and information processing. When an orientation is used as a driver of moral action, trumping other choices, it becomes an ethical orientation.

---

[26] P. Woodruff, *Reverence: Restoring a Forgotten Virtue* (New York: Oxford University Press, 2002).

In contrast to moral development theories that focus on top-down, deliberative reasoning,[27] Triune Ethics Theory focuses on bottom-up construction of moral propensities shaped by experience. Their availability and interplay are shaped by experience during sensitive periods. One may be dispositionally oriented to an ethic based on early life experience. In several studies, Narvaez, Brooks, and Mattan found that attachment was related to personality factors and both to the ethical orientation one adopts or strives for.[28] Those with poor attachment were more likely to have a security orientation, whereas those with good attachment were more likely to have an engagement or imagination orientation. Moreover, one's ethical orientation was related to moral behavior. For example, those with security identities were less likely to report being honest, having integrity or taking action for the less fortunate, whereas the opposite was found for those with engagement identities. Thus, capacities for moral functioning begin from a young age and are based in emotion development.

Situations can promote one ethic or another. Fearful situations activate the security ethic, whereas nurturing situations are likely to activate the engagement ethic. An active ethic influences sensibilities such as perception, for example, narrowing vision in the case of security and widening it in the case of engagement.[29] However, when an ethic is primed by the circumstance, it occurs in interaction with personality disposition. For example, when agreeable people are provoked, they are less likely to aggress subsequently, unlike those who are less agreeable.[30]

So far we have expanded the notion of wisdom to include emotion development. However, there is more to be accounted for beyond reasoning and emotion. Mature moral functioning requires expertise in the components and subcomponents of ethical sensitivity, judgment, motivation,

---

[27] For example, Kohlberg, *Psychology of Moral Development*.

[28] D. Narvaez and J. Brooks, *A Multidimensional Approach to Moral Identity: Early Life Experience, Prosocial Personality, and Moral Outcomes*. Manuscript submitted for publication, 2012.

[29] T. W. Schmitz, E. DeRosa, and A. K. Anderson, "Opposing Influences of Affective State Valence on Visual Cortical Encoding," *Journal of Neuroscience* 29/22 (2009): 7199–207.

[30] B. P. Meier, M. D. Robinson, and B. M. Wilkowski, "Turning the Other Cheek: Agreeableness and the Regulation of Aggression-Related Primes," *Psychological Science* 17/5 (2006): 136–42.

and action.[31] It is this broader view of moral and practical wisdom that is described here.

Fostering Mature Moral Functioning

Integrative ethical education provides an empirically derived model for fostering mature moral functioning.[32] It proposes five ways to foster moral wisdom: through relationships, climate, skills development through apprenticeship, self-authorship, and community integration and support. I discuss them in three groups here.

Relationships, Climate, and Practices. As mentioned previously, relationships and culture are vital for moral character formation. Establishing secure relationships with students establishes lines of influence and calm interactions that promote more engagement and imagination. TET points out how one's moral orientation or mindset can affect moral behavior. Moral mindsets are fostered by the situational climate and group culture. Others have pointed out how particular attitudes influence moral decisions and behavior, such as how "five dangerous ideas" (superiority, vulnerability, injustice, distrust, helplessness) can lead to aggression between individuals and groups.[33] Fostering a cooperative, rather than competitive, climate in the classroom or group allows for engagement and imagination to flourish as well.

---

[31] D. Narvaez, "Moral Complexity," 163–86. Elsewhere my colleagues and I report on a set of skills that need fostering for moral action capabilities (Narvaez et al., "Integrative Ethical Education," in *Handbook of Moral Development*, ed. Melanie Killen and Judith Smetana (Mahwah NJ: Erlbaum, 2006) 703–33; and D. Narvaez, T. S. Bock, L. Endicott, and J. Lies, "Minnesota's Community Voices and Character Education Project," *Journal of Research in Character Education* 2 (2004): 89–112.

[32] I develop this approach to education in more detail in my "The Neo-Kohlbergian Tradition and Beyond: Schemas, Expertise, and Character," in *Nebraska Symposium on Motivation: Moral Motivation Through the Lifespan*, vol. 51, ed. G. Carlo and C. Pope-Edwards (Lincoln: University of Nebraska Press, 2005) 119–63; as well as my "Integrative Ethical Education" and "How Cognitive and Neurobiological Sciences Inform Values Education for Creatures Like Us," in *Values Education and Lifelong Learning: Philosophy, Policy, and Practices*, ed. D. Aspin and J. Chapman (Dordrecht, The Netherlands: Springer Press International, 2008) 127–59; and my "Triune Ethics: Neurobiological Roots," 95–119.

[33] R. Eidelson and J. Eidelson, "Dangerous Ideas: Five Beliefs that Propel Groups Toward Conflict," *American Psychologist* 58 (2003): 182–92.

Students of all ages can be made aware of how their moral orientations can shift from one ethic to another depending on the situation, the person with whom they are relating, and a host of other factors. Educators can promote a common understanding of the different ethical orientations and how they are rooted in a different brain/body system and emotional sets. Students can learn to attend to the type of emotion and attitude they are promoting in their action choices and how these emotions and attitudes affect their subsequent behavior. (See Table 2.) The instructor is also careful to select activities that foster positive emotions and imaginative response, which are related to mindful morality.

Table 2. Skill and Knowledge Base for Mindful Morality

KNOWLEDGE
  Competing moral mindsets within the self (TET types and subtypes)
  How emotions and habits foster a mindset

DISPOSITIONS
  Fostering of positive emotions
  Non-judgmental of others
  Sympathy for others
  Taking perspective of others

SKILLS FOR MINDFULNESS
  Self-awareness of feelings
  Maintaining presence in the moment
  Self-monitoring of habit development (e.g., controlling social bias)

ETHICAL PROCESS SKILLS (see Table 3)
  Ethical sensitivity
  Ethical judgment
  Ethical focus
  Ethical action

Mindful Morality. Major religions and scholars of morality suggest that human potential lies in compassion and the positive emotions of gratitude, love and forgiveness, behaviors reflecting presence, I-Thou relationships, hospitality, and agape love. Feminist scholars have emphasized similar constructs, pointing to the greater capacities of women to be governed by such orientations at least in Western societies of this era.[34]

Mindful morality uses the whole brain. It involves both a here-and-now orientation, "Engagement Calm" or "Harmony Morality," full emotional presence and responsivity in the moment, and "Communal Imagination," the capacity to maintain a sense of emotional relatedness to the Other (right-brain engagement) while at the same time using the abstraction capabilities of the left brain to solve moral problems. Also necessary is extensive experience in a particular domain for on-the-ground understanding of context. Mindful morality makes moral innovation possible, as represented in the work of Geoffrey Canada, who uses communal imagination to envision and establish the Harlem Children's Zone, an alternative to the piecemeal efforts on behalf of poor children.[35]

Mindfulness has to do with staying emotionally and attentionally present in the moment and can be practiced through meditation and prayer. Mindfulness has all sorts of positive effects, including improved health, well-being, and pro-social behavior.[36] To practice, one must pay attention to the newness of the current experience (rather than drift off absentmindedly). Free play with others is a technique for learning mindful presence. Savoring is a similar idea in which one pays attention to the positive feelings one has in life.[37] This can be facilitated through journaling about positive or negative events and becoming more in tune with one's reactions. For those whose emotions were habitually negated and suppressed in some fashion, change

---

[34] For example, C. Gilligan, *In a Different Voice* (Cambridge: Harvard University Press, 1982); N. Noddings, *Caring: A Feminist Approach to Ethics and Moral Education*, 2nd ed. (Berkeley: University of California Press, 2003).

[35] Paul Tough, *Whatever It Takes: Geoffrey Canada's Quest to Change Harlem and America* (New York: Houghton Mifflin, 2008). Moral exemplars like Canada exhibit at the same time higher affiliation with others (communion and compassion) and higher self-efficacy or agency. (See L. J. Walker and J. Frimer, "Moral Personality Exemplified," in *Personality, Identity, and Character: Explorations in Moral Psychology*, ed. D. Narvaez and D. K. Lapsely [New York: Cambridge University Press, 2009] 232–55.) These capacities are best cultivated from a young age in the methods described above. However, there are ways to foster such virtues in adults and emerging adults, which I outline below.

[36] Ellen Langer, *Mindfulness* (New York: Da Capo Press, 1989).

[37] Fred B. Bryant and Joseph Veroff, *Savoring: A New Model of Positive Experience* (Mahwah NJ: Erlbaum, 2007).

may require a responsive, caring relationship that repairs the systems of trust and attachment to others.[38] In one way or another, for mindful morality, it is important to learn to be socially mindful—to be aware of the relational context and the uniqueness of those with whom one relates. Table 2 shows several skills needed for the practice of mindful morality.

Students can learn to increase positive (and decrease negative) emotions and attitudes towards others. Learning the habits of positive social emotions such as gratitude (keeping a gratitude journal), sympathy (learning to give people the benefit of the doubt), and compassion (taking the perspective of another) lubricate the opportunity for mindful moral action. Working with others of equal status towards a common goal can increase empathy and understanding.[39]

Skills for Moral Action Learned through Apprenticeship

Although the language can sound technical, expertise development is how people become virtuous.[40] Through the course of building perceptual skills (sensibilities), motivational skills (focus), reasoning skills (judgment), and action skills (implementation), individuals move towards expertise. There are many kinds of skills necessary for moral or ethical expertise, including procedural and conditional knowledge that can be employed automatically when needed (doing the right thing at the right time in the right way).

Rest proposed a four-component model to delineate the processes of moral behavior, which Narvaez has used as a guide for developing educational interventions.[41] The four components include capacities for

---

[38] Daniel J. Siegel, *The Developing Mind: How Relationships and the Brain Interact to Shape Who We Are* (New York: Guilford, 1999).

[39] Consider the social contact theory associated with Gordan Allport, *The Nature of Prejudice* (Garden City NJ: Doubleday and Company, 1958).

[40] F. Varela, *Ethical Know-How: Action, Wisdom, and Cognition* (Stanford CA: Stanford University Press, 1999).

[41] For the original model, see J. R. Rest, "Morality," in *Handbook of Child Psychology, Vol. 3: Cognitive Development*, 4th ed., ed. P. Mussen, J. Flavell, and E. Markman (New York: Wiley, 1983) 556–629; and D. Narvaez and J. R. Rest, "The Four Components of Acting Morally," in *Moral Behavior and Moral Development: An Introduction*, ed. W. Kurtines and J. Gewirtz (New York: McGraw-Hill, 1995) 385–400. For my appropriation of it, see my "Neo-

ethical sensitivity (noticing and interpreting events), ethical judgment (reasoning and deciding on moral action), ethical focus (prioritizing moral action), and ethical action (having the wherewithal to complete the moral action). Like other kinds of intelligence, moral intelligence is embodied in action.[42] It is not enough to be ethically sensitive (e.g., to feel empathy or sympathy) or to make a good moral judgment or to be motivated to take a moral action. Ultimately, it is the accomplishment of the action that matters most (which of course relies on these other processes).[43] A great deal of practice is required to make these skills and processes automatically available when needed.

Table 3. Ethical Process Skills

ETHICAL SENSITIVITY
    Involves picking up on the cues related to
        ethical decision-making and behavior;
    Interpreting the situation according to who is involved,
        what actions could be taken, what possible reactions
        and outcomes might ensue.
    Sample Ethical Sensitivity Skills:
        connecting to others, responding to diversity,
        interpreting situations, communicating effectively
    Exemplar: Mother Teresa

ETHICAL JUDGMENT
    Reasoning about the possible actions in the situation
        and judging which action is most ethical.
    Sample Ethical Judgment Skills:
        using context-specific codes of conduct; coping and resiliency;
        understanding consequences; reflecting on the process and outcome
    Exemplar: King Solomon

Kohlbergian Tradition," 119–63; "Integrative Ethical Education," 703–33; and "Minnesota's Community Voices," 89–112.

    [42] Varela, *Ethical Know-How*.

    [43] J. D. Trout, *The Empathy Gap* (New York: Viking/Penguin, 2009).

ETHICAL FOCUS
>Prioritizing the ethical action over other goals and needs
>>(either in the particular situation, or as a habit).
>Sample Ethical Focus Skills:
>>respecting others, cultivating conscience, acting responsibly, helping others,
>>finding meaning in life, valuing traditions and institutions,
>>developing ethical identity and integrity.
>Exemplar: Martin Luther King, Jr.

ETHICAL ACTION
>Involves implementing the ethical action by knowing how to do so and following through despite hardship.
>Sample Ethical Action Skills:
>>resolving conflicts and problems, asserting respectfully,
>>taking initiative as a leader, planning to implement decisions,
>>cultivating courage, persevering.
>Exemplar: Paul of Tarsus

Some suggested skills are listed in Table 3. Skills in ethical sensitivity include connecting to others, using appropriate emotional expression, taking the perspectives of others, and controlling social bias. Skills in ethical judgment include understanding ethical problems, predicting and responding to consequences, choosing good environments, and developing resilient thinking. Skills in ethical focus include valuing community traditions, cultivating conscience, respecting others, and developing ethical integrity. Skills in ethical action include resolving conflicts, taking initiative as a leader, asserting respectfully, planning, and implementing decisions.

It is obvious that only knowing *about* skills is not enough. How does one actually learn them as capacities that become available for deployment at the right moment and in the right way? Capacity or skill development, in education circles, is understood as a matter of expertise development.[44] Children are universal novices and, through education, can develop multiple

---

[44] *How People Learn: Brain, Mind, Experience, and School*, ed. J. D. Bransford, A. L. Brown, and R.R. Cocking (Washington DC: National Academy Press, 1999).

skills towards expertise in every domain, including the skills and capacities for moral action.

What does instruction for expertise look like? Education towards expertise is best fostered by an apprenticeship model. People learn best from immersion in experience accompanied by a mentor who guides perception and offers explanation. An apprenticeship model can provide a step-by-step but holistic experience that fosters growth and change.[45]

What does the novice learn? Expert knowledge includes both deliberative and intuitive systems "knowing that" (semantic knowledge) and "knowing how, when, and how much" (conditional and procedural knowledge).[46] All of these types of knowledge are fostered in mentor-guided immersion. Also, two types of understanding are cultivated in apprenticeship for expertise; good intuitions, and deliberate understanding. Good intuitions are cultivated through immersion and good feedback from the contexts of learning (thus fostering implicit or intuitive understanding). Perceptions and sensibilities are fine-tuned and developed into chronically accessed constructs and actions.[47] Deliberative understanding is developed by the mentor providing theoretical grounding and meta-cognitive guidance. Interpretive frameworks (schemas) are learned and, with practice, applied automatically (thereby fostering semantic or explicit knowledge). Frameworks are applied for information processing, judging options, taking action.

My colleagues and I have applied expertise development to moral formation.[48] We have identified four levels that instructors can use to guide students towards expertise. The first, immersion in examples and opportunities, involves immersing students in the "big picture," showing them exemplars of action. At the second level, attention to facts and skills, instructors help the student make important distinctions within the domain. Different skills are practiced until they become second nature. The third

---

[45] Barbara Rogoff, *Apprenticeship in Thinking: Cognitive Development in Social Context* (New York: Oxford University Press, 1990).

[46] R. M. Hogarth, *Educating Intuition* (Chicago: University of Chicago Press, 2001).

[47] D. K. Lapsley and D. Narvaez, "The Psychological Foundations of Everyday Morality and Moral Expertise," in *Character Psychology and Character Education,* ed. D. K. Lapsley and F. C. Power (Notre Dame IN: University of Notre Dame Press, 2005) 140–65.

[48] See my "Minnesota's Community Voices," 89–112, and "Integrative Ethical Education," 703–33.

level, practice procedures, allows students plenty of practice in the practice of skill sets. At the final level, integrating across contexts, students have opportunities to practice the skill in different contexts. All these are done under the supervision and guidance of the instructor.

Self-Authorship and Community Integration

The typical goal for education, including moral education, is for students to be able to monitor their own performances. Ultimately the teacher wants to be not needed. Indeed, as Aristotle pointed out and modern research confirms, virtuous character takes a lot of immersed *practice* in an environment that provides good, rather than poor, information on performance ("kind" versus "wicked" environments) with a more expert *guide* at your side.[49] Aristotle pointed out the need for mentors in guiding actions and choices until one is able to mentor oneself.[50] In an apprenticeship model, the expert scaffolds the learning experience, stepping away more and more as the apprentice is able to function well enough on his or her own. Yet the apprentice continues to consult with the mentor when things are challenging. It is good to remember that we all need mentor advice from time to time throughout life.

In the same way, all people need a community of support for their learning and behaving. It is only in the West that a person is viewed as an individual who can (and should) stand on his or her own. In the rest of the world, typically, persons are understood only as members of communities— no one lives life alone and to try to do so is madness. The individual is comprised of his or her relationships. How well he or she is doing depends on how well the relationships are doing. A virtuous person is aware of this level of embeddedness, the nesting of the individual person in a network of relationships, an ecological context that includes other life forms as well as human beings. The virtuous person knows what Aristotle pointed out, that a person learns and practices virtue within a community, and that the practicing of virtue leads to individual and community flourishing.

---

[49] Hogarth, *Educating Intuition*.
[50] J. O. Urmson, *Aristotle's Ethics* (Oxford: Blackwell, 1988).

Conclusion

In this chapter, I have integrated research on wisdom with my own work on educating moral exemplars. In doing so, I have suggested that we should treat wisdom as mature moral functioning, something that develops over time. I have identified three different ethical orientations that are grounded in neurobiological structures and shaped by both general experience and skills training. Treating moral development as a form of expertise development, we see that, by apprenticeship, one is able to develop the moral self-authorship that is a sign of mature moral functioning.

Although the detailed work is yet to be done on the day-to-day development of moral expertise, prior scholarship suggests that the college years are particularly good (i.e., a sensitive period) for making students aware of their potential—for good or for ill—and for fostering the habits and attitudes that will accompany them through life.[51] The development of self-awareness, including one's moral propensities and how to foster them, can get a good start in these impressionable years. Although many years of practice are required, college can shape the path towards moral wisdom.

---

[51] For example, see the work of Anne Colby, E. Thomas, E. Beaumont, and J. Stephens, *Educating Citizens: Preparing America's Undergraduates for Lives of Moral and Civic Responsibility* (San Francisco: Jossey-Bass, 2003); and Sharon Daloz Parks, *Big Questions, Worthy Dreams: Mentoring Young Adults in Their Search for Meaning, Purpose, and Faith* (San Francisco: Jossey-Bass, 2000).

3

Developing the Ethical Thinker and Responsible Moral Agent

Thomas Lickona

The psychiatrist Frank Pittman observes, "The stability of our lives depends upon our character. It is character, not passion, that keeps marriages together long enough to do their work of raising children into mature, responsible, productive citizens. In this imperfect world, it is character that enables people to survive, to endure, and to transcend their misfortunes."[1]

Character matters—in every sphere of society. It matters in families, the cradle of learning and the first school of virtue. It matters in schools, which must teach students to get along with people different from themselves, work hard to develop their minds and talents, and become good citizens of their communities. It matters in colleges and universities, which have the responsibility of developing critical ethical thinkers and the capacity for ethical leadership. It matters in the workplace, where the quality of craftsmanship affects other people's lives, and in the boardroom, where the absence of a moral compass can wreak widespread social havoc. It matters in the worlds of sports, entertainment, and the media, which shape the often toxic popular culture in which we are all immersed. And it matters in the halls of political power, where decisions impact not only our own country's welfare but, in many cases, the state of our increasingly interconnected world. At the end of the day, the most important measure of a society is not its economic wealth, its technological genius, or its military might; it is the character of its people.

Because character matters, education rightly conceived has historically had two great goals: helping students become smart and helping them become good. They need character for both. For the past two decades, a recovered sense of character's importance has led to a renewal of character education in American schools. This can be seen in a proliferation of

---

[1] Frank Pittman, "On Character," *Networking* (1992): 63.

grassroots character education initiatives at the K–12 level; a spate of character education books[2] and curricula[3]; federal and state funding of character education; the establishment of national character education organizations such as the Character Education Partnership (www.character.org) and the Character Counts! Coalition (www.charactercounts.org); the creation of college-based centers for character education; the emergence of a *Journal of Research in Character Education*; (www.characterandcitizenship.org); reports on how to prepare future teachers to be character educators[4]; and handbooks describing efforts to foster the growth of ethics and character during the postsecondary years.[5]

Smart & Good Schools

The evolution in our own thinking about character and character education has emerged from our ongoing Smart & Good Schools work.[6] In the first phase of this work, we conducted a two-year study of twenty-four diverse, award-winning high schools in order to (1) develop a theoretical model of a high school that integrates the pursuit of excellence and the pursuit of ethical behavior in all phases of school life, and (2) identify promising practices that would render character education more relevant to the academic and behavioral challenges faced by high schools. The resulting report, *Smart & Good High Schools: Integrating Excellence and Ethics for Success*

---

[2] See, for example, Thomas Lickona, *Educating for Character* (New York: Bantam Books, 1991); William Kilpatrick, *Why Johnny Can't Tell Right from Wrong* (New York: Simon and Schuster, 1992); Madonna Murphy, *Character Education in America's Blue Ribbon Schools* (Lancaster PA: Technomic Publishing Co., 1998); and Kevin Ryan and Karen Bohlin, *Building Character in Schools* (San Francisco: Jossey-Bass, 1999).

[3] For a monograph on character education programs that have research to support their effectiveness, see Marvin Berkowitz and Melinda Bier, *What Works in Character Education* (Washington DC: Character Education Partnership, 2005) http://www.character-andcitizenship.org/research/wwceforpractitioners.pdf (Accessed August 18, 2012).

[4] See Mary M. Williams and Eric Schaps, *Character Education: The Foundation for Teacher Education* (Washington DC: Character Education Partnership, 1999).

[5] See *Colleges That Encourage Character Development* (West Conshohocken PA: Templeton Foundation Press, 1999).

[6] Major grant support for the Smart & Good Schools research and development has been provided by the John Templeton Foundation and the Sanford N. McDonnell Foundation.

in School, Work, and Beyond, set forth our theoretical model and described more than 100 high school character development practices, drawn from our research, showing how to implement the Smart & Good vision.[7] Many of those practices, along with the core theoretical ideas of the model, have since been used or adapted by elementary and middle schools as well as high schools, and are also adaptable, as I hope to show in this chapter, to the college level.[8]

Smart & Good High Schools called for a paradigm shift in character education—from focusing only on developing moral character (being one's best ethical self in relationships) to focusing equally on developing performance character (doing one's best in all areas of endeavor). We argued that these two parts of character are interdependent (see Table 1), both necessary for a life of character. Without moral character, we can easily fall into using unethical means to achieve our performance goals. Without performance character, we will have difficulty developing our human potential and enacting our moral values effectively.

Table 1. 8 Strengths of Character: Assets Needed for a Flourishing Life

1. Lifelong Learner and Critical Thinker
    Strives to acquire the knowledge that characterizes an educated person
    Approaches learning as a lifelong process
    Demonstrates skills of critical analysis
    Takes seriously the perspectives of others
    Seeks expert opinion and credible evidence
    Makes connections and integrates knowledge
    Generates alternative solutions
    Demonstrates willingness to admit error and modify thinking

---

[7] Thomas Lickona and Matthew Davidson, *Smart & Good High Schools* (Cortland NY: Center for the 4th and 5th Rs; Washington DC: Character Education Partnership, 2005). The full report may be downloaded from our website, www.cortland.edu/character.

[8] For examples of teachers and schools that have implemented the Smart & Good model at different developmental levels, see our center's newsletter, *Excellence & Ethics*, at www.cortland.edu/character.

2. Diligent and Capable Performer
    Strives for excellence; gives best effort
    Demonstrates initiative and self-discipline
    Knows standards of quality and creates high-quality products; takes pride in work
    Sets personal goals and assesses progress
    Perseveres in the face of difficulty

3. Socially and Emotionally Skilled Person
    Possesses a healthy self-confidence and a positive attitude
    Demonstrates basic courtesy in social situations
    Develops positive interpersonal relationships that include sensitivity to the feelings of others and the capacity for "confrontation"
    Communicates effectively
    Works well with others
    Resolves conflicts fairly
    Demonstrates emotional intelligence, including self-knowledge and the ability to manage emotions

4. Ethical Thinker
    Possesses moral discernment, including good judgment, moral reasoning, and ethical wisdom
    Has a well-formed conscience, including a sense of obligation to do the right thing
    Has a strong moral identity defined by moral commitments
    Possesses the moral competence, or "know-how," needed to translate discernment, conscience, and identity into effective moral behavior

5. Responsible Moral Agent
    Respects the rights and dignity of all persons
    Understands that respect includes the right of conscience to disagree respectfully with others' beliefs or behaviors
    Possesses a strong sense of personal efficacy and responsibility to do what is right
    Takes responsibility for mistakes

Accepts responsibility for setting a good example and being a positive influence
Develops and exercises capacity for moral leadership

6. Self-Disciplined Person Who Pursues a Healthy Lifestyle
Demonstrates self-control across a wide range of situations
Pursues physical, emotional, and mental health
Makes responsible personal choices that contribute to continuous self-development, a healthy lifestyle, and a positive future

7. Contributing Community Member and Democratic Citizen
Contributes to family, classroom, school, and community
Demonstrates civic virtues and skills needed for participation in democratic processes
Appreciates the nation's democratic heritage and democratic values
Demonstrates awareness of interdependence and a sense of responsibility to humanity

8. Spiritual Person Crafting a Life of Noble Purpose
Considers existential questions ("What is the meaning of life?" "What is happiness?" "What is the purpose of *my* life?")
Seeks a life of noble purpose
Formulates life goals and ways to pursue them
Cultivates an appreciation of transcendent values such as truth, beauty, and goodness
Pursues authentic happiness
Possesses a rich inner life
Pursues deep, meaningful connections—to others, nature, a higher power, and so on

Various studies show the contributions of performance character and moral character to human development and achievement. In their handbook *Character Strengths and Virtues*, Peterson and Seligman[9] identify the cross-

---

[9] Christopher Peterson and Martin Seligman, *Character Strengths and Virtues* (New York: Oxford University Press, 2004).

cultural importance of performance character attributes such as creativity, curiosity, love of learning, and persistence. Longitudinal studies such as *Talented Teenagers*[10] find that gifted adolescents who develop their talents to high levels, compared to those who do not, show high levels of performance character qualities such as goal-setting and wise time management. Colby's and Damon's study, *Some Do Care: Contemporary Lives of Moral Commitment*[11], reveals how strong performance character and strong moral character work synergistically to account for exemplars' achievements in fields as varied as civil rights, education, business, philanthropy, the environment, and religion. Such exemplars do good, and do good *well*. In a flourishing life, ethics and excellence go hand in hand.

Eight Strengths of Character

The *Smart & Good High Schools* report also identified eight strengths of character, developmental outcomes that "unpack" the constructs of moral and performance character. Philosophers have long asked, "What does it mean to be a complete human being?" Educators have long argued that we need to educate "the whole person." The eight strengths of character are the outcomes we think schools at any level should aim for if they are serious about developing the whole person. These eight strengths are: (1) lifelong learner and critical thinker, (2) diligent and capable performer, (3) socially and emotionally skilled person, (4) ethical thinker, (5) responsible moral agent, (6) self-disciplined person who pursues a healthy lifestyle, (7) contributing community member and democratic citizen, and (8) spiritual person engaged in crafting a life of noble purpose. See Table 1 for subcomponents of each of these eight strengths.

We drew these eight strengths of character from our own grounded theory research in schools; cross-cultural research on character[12]; theory and research on intellectual character[13]; classical conceptions of a meaningful life

---

[10] Mihaly Csikszentmihalyi, Kevin Ratunde, and Samuel Whelan, *Talented Teenagers: The Roots of Success and Failure* (New York: Cambridge University Press, 1997).

[11] Anne Colby and William Damon, *Some Do Care: Contemporary Lives of Moral Commitment* (New York: Free Press, 1992).

[12] Peterson and Seligman, *Character Strengths and Virtues*, 33-52.

[13] See Ronald Ritchhart, *Intellectual Character* (San Francisco: Jossey-Bass, 2002); and Robert Sternberg, *Successful Intelligence* (New York: Penguin, 1997).

(for example, Viktor Frankl)[14]; positive psychology[15]; moral psychology[16]; research on social-emotional learning[17]; educational research[18]; research on service learning[19]; and work on the development of purpose[20] and the role of spirituality in education.[21]

Just as moral and performance character are interdependent, the eight strengths of character are conceptualized as interdependent, each needed for the optimal functioning of the others. For example, being a diligent and capable performer (the second strength of character), affects how hard we work at developing all the other strengths of character. Diligent effort and practice are clearly needed to become a socially and emotionally skilled person (the third strength of character); consider the challenges involved in becoming a good listener and learning to work out mutually acceptable solutions to conflicts. Being an ethical thinker (the fourth strength)—bringing our best moral judgment to bear on every situation—guides how we live out the other strengths of character (how, for example, we function as responsible moral agents or democratic citizens). As we grow as spiritual

---

[14] Viktor Frankl, *Man's Search for Meaning* (Boston: Beacon, 1959).

[15] Martin Seligman, *Authentic Happiness* (New York: Free Press, 2002).

[16] See Augusto Blasi, "Moral Functioning: Moral Understanding and Personality," *Moral Development, Self, and Identity*, ed. Daniel K. Lapsley and Darcia Narvaez (Mahwah NJ: Lawrence Erlbaum, 2004) 335–47; Lawrence Kohlberg, "Moral Stages and Moralization," *Moral Development and Behavior*, ed. Thomas Lickona (New York: Holt, Rinehart, and Winston, 1976): 31–53; and Daniel Lapsley, *Moral Psychology* (Boulder CO: Westview Press, 1996).

[17] See, for example, CASEL (Collaborative for Academic, Social, and Emotional Learning), *Safe and Sound: An Educational Learner's Guide to Evidence-Based Social and Emotional Learning Programs* (Chicago: CASEL, 2003); Maurice J. Elias et al., *Promoting Social and Emotional Learning* (Alexandria VA: Association for Supervision and Curriculum Development, 1997); and Daniel Goleman, *Emotional Intelligence* (New York: Bantam, 1995).

[18] Robert Marzano, Debra Pickering, and Jane E. Pollock, *Classroom Instruction That Works* (Alexandria VA: ASCD, 2001).

[19] Shelley H. Billig, "Research on K–12 School-Based Service-Learning: The Evidence Builds," *Phi Delta Kappan* 81/9 (May 2000): 658–64.

[20] William Damon, Jenni Memon, and Kendall C. Bronk, "The Development of Purpose During Adolescence," *Applied Developmental Science* 7/3 (2003): 119–28.

[21] See, for example, Rachael Kessler, *The Soul of Education* (Alexandria VA: ASCD, 2000); and Parker Palmer, "Evoking the Spirit in Public Education," *Educational Leadership* 56/4 (1999): 6–11.

persons with a deepening sense of our life's purpose (the eighth strength of character), that brings greater energy to the development and consistent application of all the other strengths. And so on.

Much of our *Smart & Good High Schools* report was devoted to describing practices for developing these eight strengths of character. Although we think all eight strengths are needed to lead productive, ethical, and fulfilling lives, this chapter focuses on two, *ethical thinker* and *respectful and responsible moral agent*, that we think have special relevance for the secondary and postsecondary years and are often neglected during those important developmental periods.

Evidence of the Need

Many of us who work in a college setting are likely to have had experiences with students who leave us realizing that we need to do more to help them grow in their operative level of moral reasoning and behavior.

In 1968, I was a young psychology professor at another SUNY campus when U.S. Congressman Sam Stratton came to speak in defense of the Vietnam War, which many of us at the time opposed as unjust. Unfortunately, a number of the students who turned out for Stratton's speech, instead of challenging him with questions or rational arguments, tried to shout him down with words that can't be printed here.

In the early 1990s, at my current college, I became faculty advisor to Collegians for Life, a student pro-life group. One semester we met with the student newspaper's business manager to place, and pay, for an "advertising insert titled 'She's a Child, Not a Choice.'" On the day when the newspaper staffers were putting the inserts into the papers, however, the paper's editor examined—for the first time—the inside contents of the insert, which included photos of prenatal development, a testimony by a college girl who regretted her abortion, and medically accurate descriptions of five kinds of abortion procedures. He reportedly became furious, ordered his staff to stop, and pulled the inserts out of the papers that already had them. Later that day, our group approached him to point out that we had made the required arrangements with the business manager and paid the paper's advertising fee (not to mention spending $300 of our group's funds to acquire the inserts); that he didn't have to agree with the insert's contents in order to allow our organization to express its views; and that the airing of different views about controversial issues was, after all, one of the purposes of a student press. But those arguments all fell on deaf ears. His response was, "The women I know would be really p----d off if this went out!"

A final story: About two decades ago, a small group of faculty on our campus, concerned about what seemed to us increasingly common academic dishonesty and increasingly casual student attitudes toward it, designed an anonymous questionnaire on academic attitudes and behavior and had faculty administer it to a representative sample of 300 graduate and undergraduate students. The questionnaire asked, "Do you consider the following behaviors wrong?" and listed seven behaviors (e.g., using crib notes on a test, copying another student's answers, plagiarizing a paper) commonly used to cheat. Students could answer, for each item, "Yes," "No," or "It depends."

Upwards of 90 percent of our students said yes, these behaviors were wrong. But when we listed the same seven behaviors on a different page and asked, "Would you ever do the following if you were sure you wouldn't get caught?", the percentages shifted dramatically. Now about half of the students said yes, they would do these things if they could get away with it. Finally, we asked students to indicate how often, if at all, they themselves had actually cheated during their college careers and, if they admitted to cheating, to explain why they had done so. A typical answer from a self-confessed cheater (this from an elementary education major): "I'm not saying it's right to cheat, but it's a tough world out there, and sometimes you have to cheat in order to survive."

Persons familiar with Lawrence Kohlberg's stages of moral development[22] are likely to recognize immature stages at work in these three examples. The anti-war protesters who shouted obscenities to try to drown out the pro-war speaker, and the students who said on our survey that you need to cheat to survive in a tough world, were displaying what sounds like Kohlberg's stage 2 instrumentalism ("Do whatever works for you"). The student newspaper editor who didn't want to offend his female friends by allowing the anti-abortion insert seems like an example of Kohlberg's stage 3 interpersonal conformity ("What will people think of me?"). Kohlberg, at the completion of his landmark twenty-year longitudinal study of moral stage development (which began with ten- to sixteen-year-olds and followed them

---

[22] Lawrence Kohlberg, "The Claim to Moral Adequacy of a Highest Stage of Moral Development," *The Journal of Philosophy* 70/18 (25 October 1973): 630-646.

into their thirties), reported this sobering finding: Only 14 percent of his adult subjects (eight of fifty-eight) showed any evidence of stage 5 principled thinking, which recognizes the universal obligation to respect the human rights of all persons and the need for a social system that protects those rights.[23] If that's true, it means that most American citizens don't understand the fundamental moral principle underpinning our democracy.

Stories and studies like these are supported by recent research indicating that moral reasoning among college students is becoming more self-centered,[24] at the same time that empathy among college students is decreasing.[25]

Developing the Ethical Thinker

What can we do as educators to address these character challenges? The first challenge in educating for mature ethical thinking is to define and develop it in a way that maximizes the probability that ethical thinking will lead to ethical behavior. If we conceptualize ethical thinking too narrowly—as merely being "book smart" about ethics—then we are likely to end up using narrow, overly intellectualized instructional strategies that merely teach students how to "talk a good game" rather than disposing them to actually lead an ethical life.

Most of us could cite examples—including some from our own behavior—of the difference between knowing the ethical thing to do and actually doing it. Consider one particularly striking instance. Some years ago, the *New York Times* published a story about an author who had his manuscript, "Telling Right from Wrong," accepted by Random House for

---

[23] For a brief summary of Kohlberg's longitudinal study, see Anne Colby and Lawrence Kohlberg, "Invariant Sequence and Internal Consistency in Moral Judgment Stages," *Morality, Moral Behavior, and Moral Development*, ed. William M. Kurtines and Jacob L. Gewirtz (New York: John Wiley and Sons, 1984) 4–51.

[24] Stephen J. Thoma and Muriel J. Bebeau, "Moral Judgment Competency Is Declining Over Time: Evidence from 20 Years of Defining Issues Test Data," paper presented to the American Educational Research Association, New York, NY, March 24-28, 2008.

[25] Sara Konrath, Edward H. O'Brien, and Courtney Hsing, "Changes in Dispositional Empathy in American College Students Over Time: A Meta-Analysis," *Personality and Social Psychology Review* (August 2010): 180-198.

publication. Random House's editor-in-chief was quoted as saying he considered it a "brilliant" treatment of everyday ethics, but he halted publication upon discovering that the author had completely forged several prestigious "endorsements" of his book. Confronted with his fraud, the author defended it as "vigorous gamesmanship."

As educators, would we be satisfied if we developed in our students the kind of ethical thinking exhibited by this deceptive author? Here was a person who understood ethics well enough to write a brilliant book about it but obviously didn't feel any obligation to *act* ethically himself.

The Four Components of Integrated Ethical Thinking

In view of the gap that often exists between knowing what's ethical and acting ethically, we must conceptualize ethical thinking broadly—to include other components of ethical consciousness besides mere moral knowledge or reasoning. We believe there are at least four components of ethical thinking that must work together, in an integrated way, to dispose a person toward ethical behavior. The components of integrated ethical thinking are:

(1) *Moral Discernment.* Being able to discern what is right and wrong, recognize when a situation involves a question of right and wrong, and make well-reasoned decisions about moral matters ranging from simple questions ("Should I return a lost wallet?") to complex ones ("What is the responsibility of the United States to alleviate global problems such as AIDS and poverty?"); and having wisdom about what constitutes good character and an ethical life.

(2) *Conscience.* Awareness of what is right or wrong with respect to our own conduct, intentions, and character, coupled with a sense of obligation to do what is right.

(3) *Moral Identity.* The degree to which our moral character and commitments are central to our sense of self ("I am a person who does the right thing; my moral commitments define who I am").

(4) *Moral Competence.* Having ethical skills (such as knowing how to be helpful in a particular situation) that enable us to translate discernment of what's right, conscience, and moral identity into effective moral action.

In developing ethical thinkers, we should do everything possible to avoid fostering "dis-integrated thinking"—that is, ethical judgment divorced from conscience, moral identity, and the competence to act ethically. Instead, our goal must be to develop ethical thinkers characterized by the integrated functioning of these four components. Finally, whenever possible, we should employ teaching methods that have the potential to develop more than one of these components simultaneously.

Examining Lives of Character

Studying lives of character—men and women who embody courage, love, justice, and other virtues—is one way to help students see what good character looks like ("other-study"), develop a desire to have a good character, and take steps to work on their own character development (self-study).

Studying lives of character can also function as an antidote to moral relativism. According to Christina Hoff Sommers, editor of *Vice & Virtue in Everyday Life*[26] and a former professor of ethics at Clark University, many students come to college "dogmatically committed to a moral relativism that offers them no grounds to think" about cheating, stealing, and other moral issues.[27] We interviewed high school teachers who said they also saw among their students a trend toward greater moral relativism, showing up as an increased reluctance to make moral judgments. A history teacher commented: "Students used to be more willing to say, 'It's not okay for kids to be doing X, Y, or Z,' whether the issue was using drugs, getting drunk, or being violent. Now they seem to be adrift about what's moral. They're willing to say, 'Personally, I don't think that's right'—to talk about what *they* would do—but they are less and less willing to make a moral judgment, to impose any kind of standard."

Why this apparent increase in the reluctance to make moral judgments? Some observers cite the influence of multiculturalism and the idea that we should not criticize the views or values of other groups or cultures. Others cite a cultural emphasis on tolerance that tends to inhibit people from making judgments about right and wrong and holding others accountable to moral standards. Correctly understood, of course, tolerance as an ethical virtue does not require us to approve of other people's beliefs or behaviors;

---

[26] Christina Sommers and Fred Sommers, *Vice & Virtue in Everyday Life: Introductory Readings in Ethics*, 4th Ed. (New York: Harcourt Brace College Publishers, 1997).

[27] Christina Hoff Sommers, quoted in J. Leo, "No Fault Holocaust," *U.S. News and World Report* (July 21, 1997 p.14), rep. in *The American Feminist* (Vol.4 No.4, p.9).

it does require us to respect their freedom of conscience, as long as the exercise of that freedom does not violate other people's rights.

Rather than engaging students in an abstract philosophical debate about relativism—often an unsuccessful strategy—we can involve them in what is ultimately likely to be a more fruitful project: studying virtue ("What does good character look like?") and reflecting on their own character development ("How can I become a better person?"). Sommers found this approach effective with her own college students. She writes:

> An exposure to what Aristotle says about courage, generosity, temperance, and other virtues makes an immediate inroad on dogmatic relativism. ...Once a student becomes engaged with the problem of what kind of person to be, and how to *become* that kind of person, the problems of ethics become concrete and practical. For many a student, morality itself is thereafter looked on as a natural and even inescapable personal undertaking. I have not come across students who have taken a course in the philosophy of virtue saying that they have learned there is no such thing as morality.[28]

The academic curriculum is full of opportunities to examine lives of character. In their book, *Building Character in Schools*, Kevin Ryan and Karen Bohlin argue that:

> The curriculum is a primary source of our shared moral wisdom. Stories, biographies, historical events, and human reflections provide us with a guide to what it means to lead a good life and possess strong moral character. This moral heritage also includes encounters with human failure, tragedy, injustice, and weak and sinister characters. In effect, the curriculum can be used to sharpen our students' capacity to see what it means to lead one's life well or poorly.[29]

In any academic discipline, a teacher can introduce students to men and women of exemplary performance character and moral character and ask: (1) What strengths of character enabled this person to do what he or she did, even in the face of obstacles? (2) What can you observe or infer about this person as an ethical thinker? What evidence do you see of moral discernment, conscience, moral identity, and moral competence? (3) What particular

---

[28] Christina Hoff Sommers, "Teaching the Virtues," *Imprimis* 20/11 (November 1991): pp.5-6.

[29] Ryan and Bohlin, *Building Character in Schools*, 93–94.

character strengths did this person possess that you feel you also have, at least to some degree? What is something you could do to further develop that quality? (4) What is one character strength possessed by this person that you do *not* now have but would like to develop? How could you do that?

Lives of Character in Literature

Literature provides abundant opportunities to focus on ethical thinking and character. The teacher, however, must know how to capitalize on the character-building potential of a novel, short story, or other literary work. Consider, for example, one of the most memorable moments in Mark Twain's classic, *Huckleberry Finn*: The bounty hunters are searching for Jim, the runaway slave and Huck's river raft companion, and ask Huck if he has seen him. Huck decides to lie to protect Jim—even though he knows the law requires the return of a runaway slave and even though he thinks he might go to hell for doing so.

For an example of a teacher who puts the focus on character, Ryan and Bohlin take us into the eleventh-grade English class of Mrs. R. as they reach the point in the novel where Huck lies to save Jim. She asks her students to take twenty minutes to write an in-class reflection:

> What does this decision reveal about Huck—about the kind of person he is becoming? Drawing from our previous discussion of virtues, which virtue is he beginning to show in this scene? Or is he simply acting out of enlightened self-interest? Give evidence from the text to support your response.

At the end of the twenty minutes, Mrs. R. engages the class in a discussion of their papers:

Mrs. R.: What kind of person is Huck becoming?

Deborah: I think Huck is really changing. He stands up for what he believes is right, even if he has to lie.

Steve: Yeah, Huck shows a lot of guts. He's changed a lot from the beginning of the novel.

Mrs. R.: How has he changed?

Steve: I'd say he's gained courage.

Danielle: I don't think so. Huck needs Jim, and he doesn't want him taken away. I think he's acting out of his own self-interest.

Norma: No—for the first time, Huck realizes that Jim is a person, not property. It reminds me of people who hid Jews in their homes during the

Holocaust and then lied to the Nazis. Huck shows respect for Jim—*and courage*.[30]

Lives of Character in Current Events

Current events are an ongoing source of lives of character. Students can be asked to read the newspaper, for example, to find persons who have put their ethical principles into practice. One example: In 2003, the Nobel Prize for Peace was awarded to Shirin Ebadi, the first Muslim woman to be chosen and the first person from Iran to win this award. Her story, used as the basis of a lesson on human rights and courage by the online character education resource Virtue in Action,[31] is a compelling portrait of a principled ethical thinker who acts on her ethical convictions without counting the cost.

In 1978, Shirin Ebadi was a respected judge in Iran striving to fulfill her dream of promoting justice in her society. When radical Islamic clerics came to power in 1979, they banned women judges and stripped her of her title. Many other professional women left Iran to escape the repressive laws, but Shirin Ebadi stayed to protest them. She stated: "Any discrimination based on gender, race, or religion is a challenge to our basic humanity. There is no future for mankind without human rights." She continued to practice law and took on cases representing women and political dissidents who had been imprisoned for speaking out against the government. When people who criticized the government were killed, she pressed for an investigation of their deaths and the prosecution of the killers. Subsequently, she was beaten many times by radical groups and arrested.

Iranian law under this government permits a father to kill his wife, sister, or daughter if he believes she is guilty of infidelity. When a father did take the life of his daughter, Ebadi represented the girl's mother. In an interview, she said, "We asked people who opposed this law to throw white flower petals into the street. In a few minutes, the whole street was white with petals." This action reflected her belief in nonviolent protest. To make the world aware of Iran's human rights abuses, Shirin Ebadi has written a book, *The History and Documentation of Human Rights in Iran*.

Virtue in Action suggests the following questions for student reflection

---

[30] Ryan and Bohlin, *Building Character in Schools*, 30–31.

[31] *Virtue in Action*, October 2003. Http://www.virtueinaction.com (accessed October 12, 2012).

and action: (1) Why do you think Shirin Ebadi stayed in Iran when other professional women were leaving? What did she believe about human rights? (2) Where does courage come from? (3) In working for human rights, what can we do? Choose one idea as a class to implement.

Shirin Ebadi's principled stand for universal human rights offers a model of social activism springing from the highest levels of ethical thinking. There are many such contemporary examples from which young people can draw inspiration.

Moral Discernment

The holistic approach of studying lives of character can be complemented by attention to developing the individual components of integrated ethical thinking. As noted, the first component of integrated ethical thinking is moral discernment. The ethicist Richard Gula observes, "We cannot do right unless we first see correctly."[32] In his book *The Art of Virtue*, Ben Franklin wrote, "The foundation of all virtue and happiness is thinking rightly."[33]

All of us face a common ethical challenge: to use our powers of moral discernment to construct what one school headmaster called a "go-to" ethical framework. He said, "To me, character requires a 'go to' ethical framework. In times of stress, we can call upon that ethical framework and rely upon its guidance. It isn't all that valuable if it doesn't come to our aid in the face of unexpected challenges."[34] A go-to ethical framework is another name for a well-formed conscience. It consists of ethical beliefs or standards that are based on correct discernment of what's right and good—standards we can apply with confidence, and with good outcomes, when making moral decisions.

Understanding the Functioning of Conscience. The dictionary defines conscience as "consciousness of the moral goodness or blameworthiness of one's own conduct, intentions, or character, together with a feeling of obligation to do right or be good."[35] Note that conscience applies our powers

---

[32] Richard Gula, *Ethics in Pastoral Ministry* (New York: Paulist Press, 1996) 38.

[33] George L. Rogers, ed., *Benjamin Franklin's The Art of Virtue: His Formula for Successful Living* (Eden Prairie MN: Acorn Publishing, 1996).

[34] Quoted in Lickona and Davidson, *Smart & Good High Schools,* 138.

[35] *Webster's New Collegiate Dictionary* (1959). Springfield, MA: G.&C. Merriam Co., 1959.

of moral discernment to our own behavior and adds a crucial component: *the feeling of obligation* to do what we have discerned to be right.

With respect to conscience, each of us has two duties: (1) to form our conscience well and (2) to follow our conscience faithfully. Discussions of conscience sometimes emphasize following one's conscience but neglect the prior, crucial task of conscience formation. If we aren't discerning right and wrong correctly, we will form our conscience poorly. Most of us can think of examples of poorly formed conscience.

One survey of middle school students found that two-thirds of boys thought it was "acceptable for a man to force sex on a woman if they have been dating for six months or more." Even more astonishingly, so did 49 percent of the girls.[36] From all indications, suicide bombers who blow up innocent people are following their consciences. Throughout history, badly formed consciences have been the source of much evil. Many things can contribute to poor conscience formation, including ignorance, a low level of moral reasoning, misinformation, prejudicial attitudes, bad teaching, and bad example.

We can begin to help students, even as early as elementary school, form their consciences well by helping them understand what a conscience is and how it operates. A fifth-grade teacher asked his students to write in response to three questions: "What is a conscience? When does your conscience appear? Do you listen to it?" One ten-year-old boy wrote: "A conscience is the part of your mind that has the job of decision-maker. My conscience appears just before an incident occurs. Most of the time I listen to it, but sometimes my conscience sleeps through an incident." Clearly, there's material in this boy's response for classroom discussion: Why does our conscience sometimes "sleep through" an incident? How can we keep it awake and on the job?

Here are other thought-provoking questions teachers can ask about conscience: (1) Does everyone have one? (2) How is a conscience formed? What role do other people play in forming your conscience? What role do you play? (3) What is the difference between a "well-formed" conscience and a "badly formed" one? How can you tell whether you have formed your conscience well or poorly with regard to a particular moral issue—such as

---

[36] Rhode Island Rape Crisis Center, National Symposium on Child Victimization, Anaheim CA, April 1998.

stealing, cheating, sex, drugs, and drinking? (4) Does conscience change over time? If so, why? What contributes to positive conscience development? To changes for the worse? (5) Do we always follow our conscience? If not, why not? What happens to our conscience if we repeatedly ignore it?

In her book *In Good Conscience: Reason and Emotion in Moral Decision-Making*, psychologist Sidney Callahan examines the self-deceptive strategies that even basically good people often use to keep their consciences from working fully. Self-deception, she observes, is often "motivated by the desire not to face demanding truths that are suspected or already halfway known."[37] We sense that something is wrong in our lives, but we turn away because the truth would be painful to face. She notes that psychotherapists must often "spend many hours slowly and gently getting persons to confront what their self-imposed blinders hide from themselves."[38]

Helping Students Learn to Make Good Moral Decisions

In using their ethical framework, young people also need decision-making skills that help them *apply* general principles about right and wrong to particular situations. They need "ethical tests"—questions they can ask themselves when faced with a moral decision. Here are eight such tests we can teach students: (1) The Golden Rule (reversibility) test: Would I want people to do this to me? (2) The fairness test: Is this fair to everybody who might be affected by my actions? (3) The "what-if-everybody-did-this?" test: Would I want everyone to do this (lie, cheat, steal, litter the school, etc.)? Would I want to live in that kind of world? (4) The truth test: Does this action represent the whole truth and nothing but the truth? (5) The religion test: If I have religious beliefs, how do they apply to this action? What would a respected member of my religion advise? Are there any religious texts that I could draw on for guidance? (6) The conscience test: Does this go against my conscience? Will I feel guilty afterwards? (7) The consequences test: Might this action have bad consequences, such as damage to relationships or loss of self-respect, now or in the future? Might I come to regret doing this? (8) The front-page test: How would I feel if my action were reported on the front page of my hometown paper?

---

[37] Sidney Callahan, *In Good Conscience* (San Francisco: Harper, 1991) 155.
[38] Ibid.

Developing Students' Moral Reasoning

Students' ability to make good moral decisions is aided by the above ethical tests, but it is also a function of their developmental stage of moral reasoning. As noted in the earlier discussion of Kohlberg's work, reasoning about right and wrong develops through a series of stages, each of which is better at perspective-taking and has a wider understanding of what it means to treat all persons with the respect and justice they are due as human beings.

At stage 1, which often appears around age five, children think it's right to obey parents and teachers, but their best reason for doing so is, "You'll get punished if you don't." At stage 2, which usually emerges in the primary school years but tends to persist much longer, children's sense of fairness becomes a tit-for-tat morality: what's right is to return favor for favor and blow for blow. At stage 3, which, in a supportive moral environment, can begin to break through in the later elementary years, children think that what's right is to be a nice person, so that others will think well of them and they can think well of themselves. At stage 4, an important developmental goal for the high school years, young persons think that what's right is to fulfill their responsibilities as members or citizens of a larger social system. Young adults who go on to reach stage 5 have the capacity to criticize their social system when it falls short of justice for all.[39] Research shows a positive correlation between maturity of moral reasoning and maturity of moral behavior, such as lower levels of cheating and substance abuse.[40]

Moral dilemma discussions, if led by a facilitator with good Socratic questioning skills, can bring about advance to higher stages of moral reasoning. Dilemma discussions engage students in considering or debating different ways to solve difficult, often complex moral problems. These might be interpersonal dilemmas (for example, "Your best friend, in danger of failing a course, asks to copy your homework, which violates your school's

---

[39] For a more complete description of the stages of moral reasoning and how parents can promote progress through the stages, see Thomas Lickona, *Raising Good Children* (New York: Bantam Books, 1983).

[40] Marvin W. Berkowitz, Nancy G. Guerra, and Larry P. Nucci, "Sociomoral Development and Drug and Alcohol Abuse," in *Handbook of Moral Behavior and Development: Vol. 3. Application,* ed. William M. Kurtines and Jacob L. Gewirtz (Hillsdale NJ: Erlbaum, 1991) 35–54.

honor code. What should you do?"); historical dilemmas (e.g., "Should the United States have dropped the atomic bomb on Japan?"); or one of the many social/political issues that are often hotly contested in the public arena ("Did the U.S. have legal and ethical grounds to justify a pre-emptive war in Iraq?" "Is killing human embryos in stem cell research justified if such research might someday cure serious illnesses?"). In their 2005 report *What Works in Character Education*, Berkowitz and Bier state: "Moral dilemma discussion has been studied for over three decades, and numerous meta-analyses of close to 100 studies have demonstrated its effectiveness in promoting the development of moral reasoning. When students engage in guided peer discussions of moral dilemmas, they show accelerated development in moral reasoning capacities."[41]

Teaching the Value of a Virtue

Moral discernment also includes understanding what good character is—and why the virtues that make up good character are important. With regard to moral character, no virtue is more important than honesty.

Evidence of the widespread erosion of integrity can be found in David Callahan's *The Cheating Culture: Why More Americans Are Doing Wrong to Get Ahead*.[42] An estimated half of résumés now contain lies. Duke University's Center for Academic Integrity, in its survey of more than 18,000 students at sixty-one U.S. high schools, found that 76 percent admitted to cheating. The data show a steady increase in cheating over the past several decades, accompanied by the growing attitude that cheating is the way the world works.[43] One high school boy said, "Politicians cheat, businessmen cheat, athletes cheat—why not students?"

How can faculty, whether high school teachers or college professors, encourage students to value honesty as important in school and life, and be motivated from within to acquire and practice this virtue? If individual teachers work to create a culture of integrity in their classrooms, institutional honor codes are likely to be more successful in creating a school-wide

---

[41] Berkowitz and Bier, *What Works in Character Education*, 10.

[42] David Callahan, *The Cheating Culture: Why More Americans Are Doing Wrong to Get Ahead* (New York: Harcourt, 2004).

[43] Don McCabe, "Cheating: Why Students Do It and How We Can Help Them Stop," *American Educator* (Winter 2001): 38–43.

culture of integrity. Former high school history teacher Hal Urban, in his article "Honesty: Why It's Still the Best Policy,"[44] explains how he tried to develop his students' intrinsic motivation to be honest. He says: "I wanted my students to realize that when we choose to be honest—or dishonest—something happens inside of us. *It affects the kind of person we are becoming.*"

To help them see why this is true, he began by asking them to write thoughtful answers to a series of questions about honesty: (1) A prospective employer or college writes to one of your teachers for a recommendation. The writer says, "We know this student has good grades. What about his/her character?" What would you want the teacher to say about your character? (2) Is "Everybody's doing it" a valid reason to do something dishonest? (3) Is cheating in any of the following circumstances less wrong than cheating in the others: (a) school, (b) business, (c) income taxes, (d) athletic event, (e) job or college application? Explain. (4) How do you gain the trust of another person? How do you destroy it? (5) What are some of the consequences of being dishonest? (6) What are some of the rewards of being honest?

Urban's students then shared their answers in small groups, followed by reporting out and whole-group discussion. Discussion typically identified the following costs of dishonesty: (1) Dishonesty turns us into phonies. (2) Dishonesty always carries a cost, internal if not external. (3) Dishonesty often can't be hidden because our deceptions eventually catch up with us. (4) Dishonesty ruins relationships because it destroys trust. (5) Dishonesty prevents our fulfillment because it undermines our self-respect.

Class discussion also typically identified the following rewards of honesty: (1) Honesty brings peace of mind. (2) Honesty builds our character and reputation. (3) Honesty strengthens our relationships. (4) Honesty is good for our mental health because it frees us from guilt and worry and builds our self-respect. (5) Honesty enables us to be authentic—true to ourselves.

Following discussion, Urban asked his students to write again on the initial questions about honesty, and compare their two sets of responses. He comments: "As a class, we discussed how their answers may have changed and why. This activity helped them see that honesty is a choice, one that

---

[44] Hal Urban, "Honesty: Why It's Still the Best Policy," *The Fourth and Fifth Rs* (Spring 1999): 4, http://www.cortland.edu/character/newsletters/99spring.pdf (Accessed August 18, 2012).

matters. They had a better grasp of why honesty is essential if they want to have self-respect and fulfilling relationships—now and throughout their lives."[45]

Responsible Moral Agency

Although integrated ethical thinking increases the likelihood of ethical behavior, it does not guarantee it. We can discern what is right, feel obligated in conscience to do it, think of ourselves as someone who normally does the right thing, and have the skills needed to act ethically—but still fail to do so. To cross the bridge from ethical thinking to ethical action, we need responsible moral agency.

Responsible moral agency is a combination of confidence, courage, and a strong sense of responsibility for the welfare of others. Studies of persons who rescued Jews from the Holocaust shed light on the role of this kind of moral agency in a life of character. In *The Altruistic Personality*, researchers Samuel and Pearl Oliner reported their research on 406 rescuers who had helped to save Jews in Nazi-occupied Europe.[46] For purposes of comparison, they also interviewed 126 non-rescuers. The Oliners found three kinds of "moral catalysts," sometimes operating in combination, that moved people to rescue.

For the majority of rescuers (52 percent), a *norm-centered motive*—allegiance to the pro-social moral code of their social group—led to their first helping act. For example, the wife of a German minister initially took Jews into her home because her church was engaged in rescue activity.

For more than a third of the rescuers (37 percent), *an empathic orientation*—a response of the heart to people in pain—motivated their first helping act. For some of these individuals, merely knowing that others were suffering was enough to motivate action; for others, a direct encounter with a person in distress led to helping.

For a small minority of rescuers (11 percent), the first helping act was motivated by a *belief in universal ethical principles of justice or caring*. For example, a high school mathematics teacher was deeply involved in saving children—hiding them in various schools. She had not directly witnessed the

---

[45] Ibid.

[46] Samuel P. Oliner and Pearl M. Oliner, *The Altruistic Personality: Rescuers of Jews in Nazi Europe* (New York: Free Press, 1988).

mistreatment of Jews. Asked why she helped them, she responded simply: "All men are born free and equal by right."

These three moral orientations—norm-centered (acting in accord with the values of one's group), empathic (moved by another's distress), and principled (committed to a universal ethic of justice or care)—were three different paths to the virtuous act of rescuing. What they have in common, the Oliners concluded, is the *capacity for extensive relationships*—a feeling of responsibility for the welfare of others, including those outside one's immediate family and community circle. This kind of feeling of responsibility for others' welfare thus appears to be a central component of responsible moral agency.

Facing History and Ourselves

How can the academic curriculum be used to develop responsible moral agency, in particular moral courage and a sense of obligation to intervene in the face of injustice? One curricular example is *Facing History and Ourselves* (www.facinghistory.org), one of thirty-three programs identified as having research validation by the report *What Works in Character Education*.[47]

Used at the middle and high school levels, *Facing History* is an eight-week unit that examines the Nazi Holocaust, the Turkish persecution of the Armenians, and other large-scale violations of human rights. Students view films; engage in class discussions; hear guest speakers, including survivors of the Holocaust, the Armenian persecution, and the Cambodian genocide; examine historical documents; and discuss readings that address issues of power, morality, justice, and caring for others. In studying the Holocaust, students investigate questions such as: How did individuals decide whether to support or oppose the Nazi regime? What were the motivations of those who decided to help the persecuted minorities—and of those who remained silent? How did leaders of foreign nations respond to reports of Nazi persecution of minorities?

A Harvard University evaluation of *Facing History* reported, "Students' moral reasoning scores significantly increased. Program students showed increased relationship maturity, decreased fighting, and reduced racist

---

[47] Berkowitz and Bier, *What Works in Character Education*, 13-16.

attitudes."[48] Students also kept journals during the eight weeks of the *Facing History* unit. Their entries reflected the curriculum's impact on their character. One thirteen-year-old girl wrote: "I'm glad this unit was taught to us, and especially to me. At the beginning, I have to admit I was prejudiced against Jews and was glad they were killed. I know this is awful, especially if that is your religion. Then you and the class discussions proved to me I was wrong. Jewish is just like me and other people."

Teachers testify that years after the *Facing History* course, students come back and say that it changed them as persons. Some students, after examining prejudice in their own lives, wanted to know what they could do to help prevent prejudice and improve society. That led *Facing History* creators to design a curriculum sequel, *Choosing to Participate*[49], that not only examines moral agency in history but challenges students to develop their own moral agency by getting involved. The curriculum examines all the ways that people historically have participated—through human service, politics, social activism, and other voluntary activity—in creating a society that seeks justice and dignity for all its members.

The Impact of Service on Moral Agency

Opportunities for moral action are a crucial catalyst for the development of responsible moral agency. In "The Healing Power of Altruism," Richard Curwin describes an experiment that demonstrates the power of service to provide such action opportunities.[50] Tough adolescents from alternative schools—many who had been involved in gangs—were paired with seniors in geriatric nursing homes and with children in hospitals for physically disabled kids. These teens helped the elderly with their exercises, read stories to and played games with the children, and in general did what they could to be helpful. The results, Curwin reports, were remarkable: "For a majority of the youths in the program, significant

---

[48] Lynn H. Schultz, Dennis J. Barr, and Robert L. Selman, "The Value of a Developmental Approach to Evaluating Character Development Programs: An Outcome Study of Facing History and Ourselves," *Journal of Moral Education* 30 (2001): 3–27.

[49] http://www.facinghistory.org/resources/publications/choosing-participate. "Choosing to Participate" (Brookline, MA: Facing History and Ourselves Foundation, 2009). Download available at (website above). Accessed August 23, 2012.

[50] Richard L. Curwin, "The Healing Power of Altruism," *Educational Leadership* 51/3 (November 1993): 36–39.

changes in attitudes and behaviors have occurred. Having formed close attachments with the people they help, they go out of their way to listen to their problems and offer advice. Not only do these formerly difficult youths become enthusiastic about and reliable in their new roles, but many now say they want to go into a 'helping profession.'"[51]

The lesson here: If we want young people to develop responsibility, we should give them responsibility. Especially with students who are not succeeding in school, having real responsibility for another human being can make an important contribution to the development of responsible moral agency.

Research on Service Learning

Service learning links service activities to academic learning, usually by including a reflection component, by granting academic credit, and sometimes by designing the service experience to be an integral part of a history, science, or other academic course. Billig's review of ten years of research on service learning finds that it strengthens social responsibility and citizenship skills, enhances school climate, increases respect between teachers and students, and improves students' ability to relate to diverse groups.[52] In another research review, the U.S. Department of Education reports that high school students engaging in service learning, compared to those who do not, are: more likely to treat each other kindly and show acceptance of cultural diversity; higher in their self-esteem; more likely to develop bonds with teachers and a variety of other adults; less likely to be absent or tardy; less likely to drop out; less likely to be referred to the office for discipline problems or to experience arrest; more likely to care about doing their best in school; and more likely to perform well on state-mandated tests.[53]

Service learning projects vary in their ability to develop ethical thinkers and responsible moral agents. Thomas Martin and Scott Richardson, in their essay "Making Citizens Out of Students," observe, "Too many service

---

[51] Curwin 36-39.

[52] Shelley Billig, "Service-Learning Impacts on Youth, Schools, and Communities: Research on K–12 School-Based Service-Learning, 1990–1999" (Denver CO: RMC Research Corporation, 2000).

[53] Cited in Lickona and Davidson, *Smart & Good High Schools*, 183.

learning projects often come in the form of short, one-day activities like cleaning up a park. Instead of ending a project when the park is clean, teachers should encourage students to address a public policy or community practice that would keep the park clean for the long term."[54] Students at one middle school, Martin and Richardson say, did just that.

> After cleaning up the park, a sixth-grade class worked with the city council to improve park maintenance. Their efforts ensured that the park would be a clean community resource well into the future. The students also conducted an educational campaign at area schools that resulted in a significant decrease in vandalism and litter at the park. The students walked away from the experience understanding how to interact with their elected officials and shape public policy.[55]

Conclusion

Plato argued that we become good by knowing the good. Aristotle said we get better at being good by doing good. Educating for ethical thinking builds on Plato's insight, educating for responsible moral agency, on Aristotle's.

At the college and university level, as much as possible, we also need to connect the effort to foster these personal strengths of character to the world of work that our students will soon be entering. Some years ago, I attended a day-long Harvard seminar on ethics teaching at the college level; I remember one of the final comments by a seasoned observer of "ethics in the real world":

> Most people will become functionaries in large institutions, subject to the decisions of others rather than making decisions. Do we merely raise their anxieties by talking about ethics and character? We must open their eyes to the opportunities for ethical choices—show them how given institutions, say, have reconciled profit and a concern for human welfare. Let people see examples of opportunities to do good in the world and still work within the organization.

As they live out their lives, the ethical behavior of our students will be the result of both character and culture. Their individual strengths of

---

[54] Thomas Martin and Scott Richardson, "Making Citizens Out of Students," *Education Week* (7 May 2003): 48.
[55] Ibid., 35.

character will interact with social environments that, to varying degrees, are concerned with—or indifferent to—ethics and character.

4

The Guilt They Carry

Nancy Sherman

> What I expected, was
> Thunder, fighting,
> Long struggles with men
> And climbing.
> After continual straining
> I should grow strong;
> Then the rocks would shake
> And I rest long.
>
> What I had not foreseen
> Was the gradual day
> Weakening the will
> Leaking the brightness away,
> The lack of good to touch,
> The fading of body and soul
> Smoke before wind,
> Corrupt, unsubstantial.
> —Stephen Spender, "What I Expected,"
> from *Poems*, (London: Faber & Faber, 1933) 25-26

Living with Guilt

Lt. Cdr. Tom Webber is a Navy chaplain who has talked to thousands of Marines as they prepare for war, deploy, and return home. In 2002 he was with the 1st Marine Division at Camp Pendleton, California as they mobilized for the first wave of the war in Iraq. In 2003 he deployed for eight months advising many soldiers who had never really experienced war:

> Probably the thing that was the most difficult to get the men ready for is to get them to understand life and death. ...The junior troops, the lance corporals, corporals, and even sergeants had never really seen battle. Many of them up until that point had never even fired a weapon at

another human being. So, just about to a man—and I was with an all-male unit—they all wanted to find out "Will God still appreciate me if I have to pull the trigger on another human being?"[1]

These Marines don't use the word "guilt," but that is what they worry about: how will they judge themselves or be judged by a higher being for what they do in war? Their worries are not about war crimes or indiscriminate killing, i.e., killing in malice. They trust that they will not commit such acts and instinctively understand the moral issues at play there. They worry about what they regard, by and large, as *just* killing in war: despite their training, the prospect of *that kind of* killing does not always sit easy. Other military personnel—whether sailors, soldiers, Marines, or airmen—struggle with guilty feelings about past acts for which they are not legally or even morally culpable. Army Major John Prior, who was in charge of an infantry company in Iraq, told me in an interview some three years after his return from Iraq that he struggles with his "own personal guilt" about the accident in which one of his privates was killed by a gun that misfired from a Bradley fighting vehicle. Still others struggle with guilt for what would be transgressions in peacetime circumstances, but are less clearly so in wartime. So an eighty-year-old World War II veteran who was part of the Normandy invasion in 1945 tells a younger neighbor sixty years later that the beachhead was far from glorious.[2] It was awful, he says, remembering vividly what happened. As soon as they landed, they looted the bodies of their own dead. Stripping the dead, even of arms, offended his civilian mentality. Ralph (Rogow) Roger, a friend's father who served with the Canadian army in World War II, wrote home in February 1945 about the plentiful German chickens they had been feasting on: "Naturally we don't steal the chickens. We just happen to be passing by when they fly into our vehicles." As his daughter Robin Roger later commented in poring through his letters, "even in the relatively minor matter of helping themselves to food, my father needed some rationales." But, too, as the war drew to a close, "empathy provoked by direct contact with Germans" made the "guilt

---

[1] From an interview with Lt. Cdr. Tom Webber and author, 21 October 2005.

[2] From conversation with Steven Lagerfeld of the Woodrow Wilson International Center for Scholars, spring 2007.

of triumph so significant that it can't be spoken of."[3] A psychiatrist who has supervised cases at a veterans' administration hospital tells me that one veteran reported that he felt his act of killing the enemy was fine until he approached the body and took out the wallet with its family portraits. The pictures were like those he carried in his own wallet. That empathic moment unleashed profound guilt.[4]

The emotion of guilt, as these examples suggest, is janus-faced. We think of it as typically focused on the past, on the thought of wronging another (or on the future, in contemplating wrongdoing, where the bite of conscience, the "pang" of guilt, acts as a check against it). But as we know well, individuals can feel guilt about actions for which they are not at fault yet for which they nonetheless hold themselves responsible. In some cases they may be *causally* but not *morally* responsible. That is, the injury or death is something they "brought about," but as the result of non-culpable ignorance, as in the case of the Bradley misfiring. In other hard cases, it may be a soldier's finger that pulls the trigger and kills an innocent; though he foresees the risk, he does not intend it. In yet other cases, an individual knowingly and intentionally kills justly in the role of soldier, though if he steps out of role, it feels like a gross transgression of his humanity.

Guilt for these various actions can seem both rational and irrational.[5] Personal agency is implicated, but there may be legitimate excuses or, indeed, justification. But what is typically overlooked in discussions is that even when guilt is irrational, it can be an important sign of a soldier's humanity, and something admirable. Though we might not blame those who lack a feeling of guilt in comparable cases, we still tend to feel moved, morally moved, by those who show it. In the case of a soldier, it is often a testament to a sense of moral accountability in the use of lethal force. It is an expression of personal responsibility often squeezed out by fighting in large, bureaucratic armies.[6]

Of course, that very guilt that can be admirable can easily turn excessive and pathological. So Friedrich Nietzsche warns, standing morality on its head: "bad conscience" can become "torture without end," undoing

---

[3] I am indebted to Robin Roger, a psychoanalytic psychotherapist, for sharing with me portions of her father's correspondence, and her astute analysis of it.

[4] From conversation with Dr. Richard Waugaman (spring 2007).

[5] Where I mean by "rational," here, something like "strictly speaking appropriate."

[6] I thank Peter Railton for help in seeing this point.

any prospects for happiness. Sigmund Freud famously elaborates upon the theme: enduring the recriminations of a harsh super-ego (his term, more or less, for "conscience") is the cost of civilization. The anger of the super-ego, like Seneca's notion of the thirst for revenge, can leave its possessor more tormented than satisfied. And this is a double-bind felt all the more intensely by soldiers, for if recognizing the incredible responsibility they bear is necessary to wage war justly, the weight of this terrible recognition deepens the guilt they may feel when they exercise their wartime duties, justly or not. And whereas wrath is punishment outward, guilt is punishment inward, a self-indictment of having harmed or violated or betrayed another. It is an accusation and conviction against self for actions done.

We tend to worry about war desensitizing warriors, about soldiers getting used to killing and accepting how cheap life can be. This may happen to some. But this was *not* the prevalent theme I heard in my interviews. The soldiers to whom I've talked feel the tremendous weight of their actions and consequences. Sometimes they extend their responsibility and guilt beyond what is reasonably within their dominion: they are far more likely to say, "If only I hadn't," "If only I could have," than "It's not my fault."

Yet for all this, the subject of guilt does not come up easily in talking to soldiers. The topic is rarely discussed openly or systematically. It is the elephant in the room. And it is so, in part, because guilt feelings are often borne with shame. Shame, like guilt, is also directed inward. Its focus, unlike guilt, is not so much on an action that harms *others* as on *personal* defects of character or status, often felt to be exposed before others and a matter of social discredit.[7] But on the battlefield, where the destruction of others is the *modus vivendi*, it is guilt for causing that suffering that is inescapable.

---

[7] In the last century philosophers have talked considerably about shame in an attempt to reinstate it as an important moral feeling in the way it once was in ancient moral philosophy. For influential discussions of shame, see Bernard Williams, *Shame and Necessity* (Berkeley: University of California Press, 1993); Martha C. Nussbaum, *Hiding from Humanity: Disgust, Shame, and the Law* (Princeton: Princeton University Press, 2004) 172–221; and David Velleman, "The Genesis of Shame," *Philosophy and Public Affairs* 30/1 (2001): 27–52. The subtleties of guilt as a moral emotion may have been taken for granted or left primarily to psychoanalysts. A notable exception is in the writing of Herbert Morris, such as his *On Guilt and Innocence* (Berkeley: University of California Press, 1976); "Nonmoral Guilt," in *Responsibility, Character, and the Emotions*, ed. F. Schoeman (New York: Cambridge University Press, 1987); and "The Decline of Guilt," *Ethics* 99 (1988): 40–45. Other

Kant, Nietzsche, and Freud on Guilt

Immanuel Kant, the eighteenth-century German enlightenment philosopher, sets the scene in the modern world for the vigil of conscience. Under Kant, Socrates' dictum to "know thyself" becomes "the first command of all duties to oneself"— a highest-order duty to "scrutinize, fathom" your heart for rightness of conduct and purity of motive.[8] The self becomes both judge and judged: the spotlight is on *me*, on what *I* have done or failed to do, and not on others, neither on their actions nor their characters. But despite the focus on self-judgment, Kant is neither particularly interested in what from ancient times forward has been described as the "bite"[9] of bad feelings for doing wrongs nor in the fear of punishment that can prod us to do what is right. The absence is deliberate. Kant is concerned with the mature conscience. The attitude of that conscience is not punitive pain or fear, but respect or reverence in the sense of attention and submission (*Achtung*) to our own authority as moral legislators. Kant imagines us in awe of the capacity to issue laws to ourselves. This legal capacity is neither that of a despot nor capricious lawmaker, but of a just and fair lawmaker making law

---

treatments have been influenced by his work: see especially John Deigh, "All Kinds of Guilt," *Law and Philosophy* 18/4 (1999): 313–25; and Jeffrie Murphy, "Shame Creeps Through Guilt and Feels Like Retribution," *Law and Philosophy* 18/4 (1999): 327–44. For a symposium on Morris's work on guilt, see his reply: "Some Further Reflections on Guilt and Punishment," *Law and Philosophy* 18/4 (1999): 363–78. Other important discussions of guilt are in John Deigh, *The Sources of Moral Agency* (New York: Cambridge University Press, 1996), especially the chapters, "Love, Guilt, and the Sense of Justice," "Remarks on Some Difficulties in Freud's Theory of Moral Development," and "Freud, Naturalism, and Modern Moral Philosophy." See also David Velleman, *Self to Self* (New York: Cambridge University Press, 2006), especially the chapter "Don't Worry, Feel Guilty"; Sam Scheffler, *Human Morality* (New York: Oxford University Press, 1992), ch. 5; Gabriele Taylor, *Pride, Shame, and Guilt: Emotions of Self-Assessment* (Oxford: Oxford University Press, 1985); Richard Wollheim, *The Thread of Life* (Cambridge MA: Harvard University Press, 1984); and R. E. Lamb, "Guilt, Shame, and Morality," *Philosophy and Phenomenological Research* 43 (1983): 329–46.

[8] Immanuel Kant, *The Doctrine of Virtue*, ed. M. J. Gregor (Philadelphia: University of Pennsylvania Press, 1964/1797) 440. For more on Kantian virtue, see my *Making a Necessity of Virtue* (Cambridge: Cambridge University Press, 1997).

[9] On the history of this psychological feeling, see Margaret Graver, *Stoicism and Emotions* (Chicago: University of Chicago Press, 2007).

The Guilt They Carry

for self that can apply to others similarly situated. We are not free riders. Before our internal moral legislator, we stand ready, at attention, capable of following duty's call even and especially when it conflicts with our strongest self-interests.

This is one reason why we find little talk in Kant of moral distress of the sort that bites and gnaws, or of fear that goads and bullies. The idealized emotion we feel before genuine moral authority is far more dignified. Indeed when the subject of repentance comes up, Kant warns against a morality that is "cheerless, morose, and surly"—a self-punishment that becomes "self-torture." Beware of "hypocritical self-loathing" and the moral melancholy that detracts from the real work of morality, Kant warns.[10] True virtue ought to be cheerful and soar with the sublimity of respect for its law. But in all this, Kant doesn't appreciate that harsh self-judgment is not necessarily self-righteousness. It can be inseparable from empathy with those we harm and a sense of responsibility and duty of reparation even when the harm is not intentional, or intentional and warranted but no less loathed, as in just killing in war. Soldiers as inflictors of the horror of war often bear this kind self-judgment, complete with its bite and gnaw. It is not self-righteousness or of pious melancholy they are feeling. It is more a feeling of "moral remainder," as philosophers have called it, a reasonable reaction to being a human and of having humanity. The good soldier does not lose that humanity simply by donning his uniform.

We might think Freud can do better than Kant in recognizing the rationality of guilt felt for actions for which we are not, strictly speaking, in a juridical sense, culpable. And he does in some ways, but not entirely. Freud famously tells a developmental story, a "just-so story" of sorts, of how morality comes to be internalized as part of our personalities: Our conscience is the product of a childhood battle of sorts. As children we both want parental love and fear its loss and repudiation in punishment when we do wrong and "are found out." With moral growth and independence, we move that tension inside ourselves, into an internal representation of authority and regulation that stands over and above our ego or self; thus, the super-ego is born. Through that super-ego we become our own judges, vigilant and fearful of self-indictment. So Freud declares, "the super-ego" is

---

[10] Kant, *Doctrine of Virtue*, 485.

the Kantian "moral law within us."[11] Guilt, on Freud's view, is a kind of leftover tension from childhood;[12] its predominant feeling is fear of punishment and retaliation.

But despite the Kantian legacy, Freud does not really offer an account that internalizes the *moral* law. Indeed, he does not offer an account of *morality*. Moving parental or conventional authority from outside to in is not enough to ensure that internal authority and judgment is legitimate or really moral. We can bully ourselves and be harsh tormentors without justification, just as parents can be cruel or military leaders overbearingly harsh. What the move from outside to in *does* do, as Freud rightly insists, is set up "a garrison" whose watch is inescapable. That is, if childhood morality is about "being found out," then once an internal garrison is set up, "nothing can be hidden" from self, "not even thoughts."[13] Of course, Freud famously leaves room for the work of repression and self-deception. But we need to veil ourselves from ourselves precisely because we have become our own watchdogs. Still, without some clever philosophical patching up of his theory,[14] Freud cannot explain why some self-indictments from that watchdog have at their base guilt that is more rooted in morality than in just the bullying of a harsh super-ego. Nor does he really seem to appreciate how very thin the wedge can be between the two. This is at the heart of understanding "the personal guilt" that Major John Prior carries with him.[15]

Accident Guilt

The guilt, as Prior explains, is the result of an accidental fratricide[16] in 2003 in which twenty-year-old Private First Class Joseph Mayek was killed.

---

[11] Sigmund Freud, "New Introductory Lectures," in *The Complete Psychological Works of Sigmund Freud*, SE, vol. 22, trans. J. Strachey (London: Hogarth Press, 1955) 61, 163.

[12] For example, Sigmund Freud, "Civilization and Its Discontents," in *The Complete Psychological Works of Sigmund Freud*, SE, vol. 21, trans. J. Strachey (London: Hogarth Press, 1955) 123.

[13] Sigmund Freud, "Civilization and Its Discontents," 125.

[14] See David Velleman, "A Rational Superego," *Philosophical Review* 108 (1999): 529–58.

[15] From an interview with John Prior, the author, 27 September 2006.

[16] It is worth noting that "fratricide" in the context of war, unlike "suicide" or "homicide," does not have intent implicit in the word. It typically implies "accidental,"

Prior, who was then commander of the Charlie Company, 6th Infantry, First Armored Division, was tasked to provide security around the U.S. Army headquarters just after the fall of Baghdad. Private Mayek was taking up his post when a Bradley blast ripped through his face. He had been standing no more than a foot in front of the muzzle. Prior reconstructs the scene. He is calm, but he is eager to lead off the interview with the accident: "I lost a soldier, which was extremely traumatic," he says without hesitation. He narrates every detail precisely, the way a person who has relived the scene over and over does:

> One of the Bradleys misfired. It was on the front gate, and had a malfunction and it took off a third of his face. It was as if an ice cream scoop just scooped out his face. ...He survived the initial blast, if you can believe it. We were in the medic tent with him. It was one of the most traumatic things I have ever seen in my entire life. To literally see someone's face completely scooped out, to see just the very bottom part of his jaw working...he couldn't see, couldn't hear, couldn't scream. ...I mean he had no eyes, obviously. No face. I can only imagine the terror, the fear, the pain he was in. He obviously couldn't breathe because he had no nose or mouth to take in air. ...It was one of the few times in my life I've really cried—tears just streaming down my face because I'm watching ten people work over this kid. ...It was an unbelievable thing to see. ...It is one of those images that will be in your head until you die....

If Prior's immediate response to the incident was marked by the bracing viscerality of his trauma, his further reflections suggest the struggles of a conscience racked with guilt and in an ongoing tug-of-war with his rationality. He continues,

> The aftermath of that was the guilt of the situation because I'm the one who placed the vehicles; I'm the one who set the security. Like most accidents, I'm not in jail right now. Clearly I wasn't egregiously responsible. But it is a comedy of errors. Any one of a dozen decisions made over the course of a two-month period and none of them really occurs to you at the time. Any one of those made differently may have saved his life. So I dealt with and still deal with the guilt of having cost him his life essentially. ...There's probably not a day that doesn't go by that I don't think about it, at least fleetingly.

"blue on blue," "friendly fire." For a gripping exception, see the movie *In the Valley of Elah*, DVD, dir. Paul Haggis (Burbank CA: Warner Independent Pictures, 2007).

The malfunction, as Prior explains in lay terms, had to do with a faulty replacement battery. When the Bradley's ignition was turned on, the replacement battery in the turret failed to shut off current to the gun. Prior had authorized the replacement after consulting with his maintenance team and after a thorough reading of the manuals. The replacement was a Marine battery, the only one available at the time for a Bradley. It had the same voltage as the original one, but different amperage. The amperage, they learned too late, was all-critical. Army manuals now prohibit the use of that Marine battery.

Prior was formally investigated by the military and ultimately exonerated. By the standards of the legal and moral community, he is not guilty in the sense of culpable or at fault. Yet he carries guilt and holds himself responsible. "On a personal note, I definitely felt tremendous personal guilt over it because of the placement of the vehicles and…the decisions made. I felt very personally responsible." He speaks of a "comedy of errors," but a tragedy of errors is closer to his experience. "I knew that clearly it was an accident," but "I kept wishing I had made other decisions." When he says he doesn't hold himself as "egregiously responsible," he means that it wasn't a careless blunder. But he still doesn't think of himself as fully, morally cleared.

In a very important way, Prior's guilt is not irrational. We understand it and admire him for it. We would think less of him as a commander, ready to lead his troops and have them follow, if he viewed what happened as just an accident, only remotely connected with his own choices. The guilt, perhaps, is reparation for harm done. It records something morally significant, something that marks his deep connection to his troops and his moral accountability to them, and to himself. It is not just a response to the fact that he was *causally* implicated. He feels *morally* implicated. Still, for all its reasonableness, the guilt oversteps moral accountability, even for a commander responsible for his troops and tied to them by the "sacred bands" that form in war. Prior's anguish needs to be alleviated in some way.[17] What happened *was* an accident, a *flukishly unlucky* accident, and one in which he is causally implicated, but not morally. This is a kind of case

---

[17] As Robert Roberts commented insightfully on this chapter, "The *moral* therapist has to walk a fine line between respecting a patient's character and alleviating anguish." Guilt is rational, he noted, too, in that it depends upon construals, though not standard judgments subject to strict standards of what is veridical.

where, surprisingly, we don't get much guidance from Freud. It is a case where we hold ourselves morally responsible for bringing about bad consequences we couldn't reasonably expect or prevent.[18]

Nietzsche has just this kind of case in mind when he says, "bad conscience" (his hyperbole for *subjective* guilt) doesn't grow in the soil where you would most expect it—such as in prisons where there are actually "guilty" parties who should feel remorse for wrongdoing. Rather, it is often a "question of someone who…caused harm," someone who causes a misfortune for which she is not really responsible. He appeals here to the earlier philosopher Spinoza for support: The "bite of conscience" has to do with an "offense" where "something has gone unexpectedly wrong here"; it is not really a case of "I ought not to have done that."[19] Personal agency is implicated in the accident, though involuntarily through ignorance. Guilt is felt, but there is no wrongdoing for which we can be held morally or legally guilty.[20]

Melanie Klein, a student of Freud and pioneering child psychoanalyst (and founder of the object relations school of psychoanalysis), elaborates the point in terms of the dynamic and lasting influences of childhood morality. To the notion of offense or harm, she adds the element of empathy. Our

---

[18] On this notion, see Thomas Nagel's seminal discussion of moral luck: *Mortal Questions* (New York: Cambridge University Press, 1979) 24–38. For the notion that moral luck highlights the idea of our personal agency as "impure," in the sense of requiring resources of character to meet the combination of choice *and* fortune in life, see Margaret Urban Walker, "Moral Luck and the Virtues of Impure Agency," *Metaphilosophy* 22 (1991): 14–27.

[19] Friedrich Nietzsche, *On the Genealogy of Morality*, ed. Keith Ansell-Pearson, trans. C. Diethe (Cambridge: Cambridge University Press, 1994) 59–66.

[20] The philosopher Bernard Williams has coined the term "agent-regret" to refer to the feeling often felt when a person is "casually" (though not morally) responsible "in virtue of something one intentionally did," in his *Moral Luck* (New York: Cambridge University Press, 1981) 20–39. But to my mind, a notion of regret, even *agent*-regret, doesn't adequately capture what is actually felt. It does not capture the despair or depth of the feeling of guilt, nor, as I indicate below, the empathic identification with victim so common in war. Nor does it capture the first-person aspect of the moral feeling: I see myself as morally implicated and need to make repair. It is not just that I should take responsibility because I am part of the causal chain. Guilt, it seems, is rational to feel on such occasions precisely because it is a response to this more robust moral involvement. I thank Elisa Hurley for discussion here.

principles of guilt are rooted in notions of harm and injury and not principally, *contra* Freud, fear of retaliative punishment. More significantly, the guilt is inseparable from empathic love for those we hurt, however hard the mind tries to keep separate and pristine ("split," in her terms) what we love from what we have damaged.[21] The "bite" of guilt comes from our recognizing that what we love we may destroy, often unwittingly. In the case of the young child, Klein envisages a primal drama between love and hate of the parent, and empathy and reparation for fantasies of destruction. Of course, guilt of the kind Nietzsche and Klein point to—focused on harm, often unintended, and a harmed victim, with whom we empathize—is certainly not the only kind of subjective or personal guilt. But the conception helps make sense of the kind of guilt Prior carries, and that which many other military men and women carry as the emotional fallout from decisions made in the fog of war, under stress and urgency, and often with non-optimal information. An illustration from Greek tragedy helps to further sharpen the contours of this kind of guilt.

Doing "Unwittingly the Will of the Beast"

Tragic errors (what Aristotle calls *hamartiai* in his *Poetics*) teach us that we are vulnerable to misfortune incurred through our own fallible agency. If "I made other decisions," Prior says, it wouldn't have happened. Yet he knows he took due care in making that choice. Aristotle's own favorite example is from Sophocles' *The Women of Trachis*. The botched choice is this: Deianeira is unaware that the "charm" she uses to woo back her husband Heracles is, in fact, a lethal substance that, when applied, literally eats away at its victim. In her case, perhaps she should have known better: the potion was a gift to her from the centaur Nessus. As he ferries her across the River Evenus to meet her new husband Heracles, the centaur puts lustful hands on her. Deianeira cries out for help and Heracles heeds the call, killing Nessus with his bow and poisoned arrow. In his dying moments, Nessus concocts a potion from the poisoned blood of his clotted wound for Deianeira.[22] It is a

---

[21] See Melanie Klein, *Love, Guilt, and Reparation and Other Works 1921–1945* (New York: Delta, 1977); also her "Our Adult World and Its Roots in Infancy," *Human Relations* 12/4 (1959): 291–303; and "Some Reflections on the *Oresteia*," in *Envy & Gratitude and Other Works: 1946–1963* (New York: The Free Press, 1975) 275–99.

[22] I thank Paul Woodruff for helpful comments on the play.

love charm, he tells her, to be used should Heracles' love ever wane. Wane it does while Heracles is at war, and he sends back home a new war bride as proof. It is just this "erotic diversion" that Deianeira aims to cancel with the potion.[23]

Deianeira, it seems safe to say, was duped; Prior was not. Deianeira did "unwittingly the will of the beast."[24] But it was, after all, a beast seeking revenge for being rejected. She should have suspected his motives. Even after the disaster, she focused not on the likelihood of that revenge, but on her own defense, on how she followed the beast's instructions to a tee; there were no "egregious" missteps here: "I neglected none of the instructions that beast the centaur explained to me. ...I kept them like an inscription on bronze that cannot be washed away. And I only did what I was told to do."[25] Even so, in her case and certainly in Prior's, there is ample space between full moral responsibility and the kind of luck where a person is more victim than agent.[26] Neither Deianeira nor Prior was picked up and blown along by the wind, as Aristotle might put it, forcibly moved by external forces. Rather, the impetus comes from within, from choices and actions performed voluntarily. Still, these choices have unexpected, heinous results that those who made the choices could not readily foresee. Each does awful things unknowingly, fallibly but not necessarily culpably. They feel tremendous guilt and regret. In Deianeira's case, she takes her own life when she discovers what she has wrought with her hands.[27]

"Regret" for these kinds of tragedies is, in fact, too light a word, not close enough to remorse and too close to the kind of regret we feel about

---

[23] See Bernard Williams, "The Women of Trachis," in *The Sense of the Past* (Princeton: Princeton University Press, 2006).

[24] Sophocles, *The Women of Trachis*, trans. David Green and Richmond Lattimore (New York: Washington Square Park, 1967).

[25] Ibid., 680ff. As these quotes suggest, there may be some culpable ignorance here, though Sophocles does not press the point too hard: Deianeira, after all, must remain a tragic character for whom we have sympathy.

[26] For a discussion of *hamartia*, see Stephen Halliwell, *Aristotle's Poetics* (Chapel Hill: University of North Carolina Press, 1986); also see Nancy Sherman, "Virtue and *Hamartia*," in *Essays on Aristotle's Poetics*, ed. A.O. Rorty (Princeton NJ: Princeton University Press, 1992).

[27] She acts with her own hand, but was fooled. Perhaps Prior, too, feels a bit betrayed by the manuals.

inclement weather. Philosophers of late have worked hard to beef up the notion.[28] But even the philosopher's term of art, "agent-regret," just doesn't capture the kind of feeling Prior experiences. The sheer weight of guilt—its heaviness, its identification with the victim, and the assertion of the need for repair—is what Prior feels. It is not just that things turned out badly and he happens to be involved instrumentally. It is that he stands indicted before himself and must make reparation. There is a perceived moral element to what he has done. To call it "regret" is to miss that.

After the fratricide, Prior and his first sergeant wrote a letter to Mayek's mother. For some time after, he tells me, she continued to send care packages to the company with letters. "Oh, it was terrible," said Prior. "It was horrible." The letters weren't "just very matter of fact—here's what we did today; it was more like a mother writing to a son." For this mother, Prior and his company became the son who was no longer. "It was her way of dealing with the grief. ...I had a responsibility to try to give back." Allowing himself to feel that mother's grief, so intimately, was part of his reparation.

He gave back, but held back, presumably, the graphic image of Mayek's suffering. The agony was simply too hideous, undeserved, and unrelieved to share with a mother. Prior told me that in watching Mayek's last moments, he wished he would die quickly, so his torture could end. In *The Women of Trachis*, Sophocles does not spare us the details of Heracles' final torment. This man of mythic labors, whose body once subdued so many, is now eaten away by a "ruthless, devouring malady" that never leaves him "without torment." The pain sears like "sharp points brought to burning heat."[29] His only relief is a quickened, but horrific demise: to be burned alive on a funeral pyre, a gruesome task he delegates for his son to oversee, instructing him, as he is laid on the pyre, to set a "steel bit in my mouth" to "hold back the shriek."[30] In point of fact, there is no holding back, Sophocles teaches (and Prior knows well), on the uncompensated physical agony humans can undergo as the result of mistake.

---

[28] Marcia Baron may be getting at a similar point when she speaks of remorse (as distinct from agent-regret) in her "Remorse and Agent-Regret," in *Midwest Studies in Philosophy*, ed. P. A. French, T. E. Uehling, and H. K. Wettstein (Notre Dame: University of Notre Dame Press, 1988).

[29] Sophocles, *Women of Trachis*, 840.

[30] Ibid., 1260.

The Guilt They Carry

Luck Guilt and Betrayal

Guilt like that which Prior experiences is the moral cost of making choices. Other kinds of battlefield guilt may also seem, at first blush, irrational, but less so upon further inspection. In fall 2005 I met with two small groups of Marine and Navy officers recently returned to the United States Naval Academy from Iraq.[31] I never specifically asked about guilt, nor did the soldiers touch the feeling by name. Yet it was there at every turn.

One kind of guilt that surfaced in the interviews is a variant of survivor guilt that I will call "luck guilt." Several Marines felt that by being in Annapolis, and no longer in combat zones, they had been the recipients of "undeserved" luck. They spoke of needing to return to their brothers and sisters in arms. The guilt is a kind of empathic distress for those still at war, mixed with a sense of solidarity and anxiety about betraying that solidarity. For some, abrupt ruptures from units exacerbated the guilt.

Major Mooney, an intelligence officer, was part of a lead battalion that on 23 March 2003 took catastrophic losses in an attack in Nazaria, Iraq. Eighty were killed and nearly another eighty were wounded in one day. The attack came just after a rescue operation in which the same battalion pulled out the dead and wounded from the freshly ambushed convoy of the 507 Maintenance Company (made famous by Jessica Lynch's story). Two months later, in mid-May, the battalion was ordered back to Nazaria for peace and stability operations. The troops were jittery about returning to the site of so much carnage. "I remember driving into this city from the north this time, almost flinching, bracing as we were going down Ambush Alley, because I remember the last time I was in it. ...[we were] still seeing the charred marks on the road where we lost amtraks [amphibious tractors]—catastrophic kills where every Marine in that amtrak was killed in action." Soon after a

---

[31] The first was a group of Marine majors who had become company officers at the academy: J. R. Clearfield (infantry), Michael Mooney (reconnaissance), Daniel Healey (infantry), Jerry Rizzo (aviation), and Mary Beth Bruggeman (combat engineering). Some had fought in the siege of Baghdad; others served in intelligence; still others oversaw security at medical units, working to ensure safe landings for helicopters carrying the wounded. In the second group were more senior Marine and Navy officers: Lt. Cdr. Tom Webber and Lt. Cdr. Irv Elson (both chaplains), Col. Robert Durkin (infantry), and Col. John Rupp (aviation). Several of those in this group were at the time of the interview resident at the Naval Academy's Ethics Center, now known as the Stockdale Center for Ethical Leadership.

battalion-wide memorial service on the very fields where Marines had fallen, Mooney got orders to report immediately to the naval academy. He left behind his regiment who would sail back slowly to the states. He was put on a commercial, not military, flight, sitting next to civilians who simply occupied a different world than he did.

The rupture with his unit is palpable, but so, too, the expectation that, as a Marine, he should be able to just carry on:

> I didn't have the same experience or opportunity as the other Marines leaving the combat zone. I had orders to report to the Naval Academy. I had to get here very quickly or I wasn't going to be able to execute those orders. It was around May 15…[s]o as my unit was backloading, moving down to Kuwait, I had caught a plane, got shuttled down to Kuwait City, and was thrown on a British Airways flight. Seven hours after being in Iraq, I was in Frankfurt, Germany, sitting in a first class lounge. It was very surreal. Trying to actually look at the porcelain toilets—'cause the last time I had taken a shower was I think March the 7th—and then 10 hours after that I was meeting my family and my wife-to-be…in Reagan National, which was also very surreal. There wasn't a decompression time. …Basically, I just had to start at the Academy…It was a very interesting dynamic being transitioned so quickly…boom, boom, boom.

When I ask him if he was able to manage with the transition, he answers, without pause, "Yes, ma'am." But seconds later he reveals the true weight he bears: "Just for me, personally, I don't think there's a day goes by that I don't think about those times, just because of the accomplishments we achieved and the incredible loss of potential for the Marines, even though I didn't know them personally. Just seeing and being present when the Marines were being pulled out of the amtraks…" He says he "reflects back" often on the "lost potential," his restrained words for the grief he feels for those he saw die far too young in Nazariah.

Mooney talks about the horrific with steel-like comportment. He carries his feelings tightly inside. But there is unspoken guilt that he is in tranquil Annapolis while others continue to fight. He is ready to go back and he is preparing his new wife for that reality: "I say you've got to prepare yourself for this because after sitting here in Annapolis for three years, after wonderful air conditioning in Annapolis, while my brothers and sisters have been out on their second and third tours…you need to come to come to grips with [the fact] as indicated that I'm going to be away for awhile."

The Guilt They Carry

Mooney's guilt while at home, separated from comrades in battle, recalls that of another young officer, Siegfried Sassoon, the British World War I officer and poet. Against the wishes of his doctor, the eminent Freudian-inspired physiologist and anthropologist, Capt. W. H. R. Rivers, Sassoon returned to the trenches out of profound mix of love and guilt and a sense of futility at his war protest. He experienced his separation from his troops as at once abandonment and banishment.[32] To return to the front line might well be a kind of "death," he writes in his memoirs, but it is also "my only chance of peace."[33]

> I am banished from the patient men who fight.
> They smote my heart to pity, built my pride.
> Shoulder to aching shoulder, side by side,
> They trudged away from life's broad wealds of light.
> Their wrongs were mine; and ever in my sight
> They went arrayed in honour. But they died—
> Not one by one: and mutinous I cried
> To those who sent them out into the night.
> The darkness tells how vainly I have striven
> To free them from the pit where they must dwell
> In outcast gloom convulsed and jagged and riven
> By grappling guns. Love drove me to rebel.
> Love drives me back to grope with them through hell;
> And in their tortured eyes I stand forgiven.[34]

Another poem, "Sick Leave," concludes with the battalion whispering softly to Sassoon, "When are you going out to them again? Are they not still your brothers through our blood?"[35]

---

[32] See Paul Fussell, *Siegfried Sassoon's Long Journey: Selections from the Sherston Memoirs* (New York: The K. S. Giniger Company, 1983). For a trilogy of novels based on Sassoon's life, see Pat Barker's Regeneration trilogy: *Regeneration* (New York: Penguin, 1992); *The Eye in the Door* (New York: Plume, 1993); and *The Ghost Road* (New York: Plume, 1995). For further discussion of this, see Nancy Sherman, *Stoic Warriors: The Ancient Philosophy Behind the Military Mind* (New York: Oxford University Press, 2005) 157–62.

[33] See Fussell, *Siegfried Sassoon's Long Journey*, 138.

[34] Ibid., 140. The poem is "Banishment."

[35] Ibid., 141.

"Brotherhood" is often an unanalyzed term in war. It speaks to attachment, a new family, and the trust in being able to count on another to cover your back. It is, to say the obvious, a gendered term: the masculine profession of war is precisely what the more inclusive "brothers *and* sisters in arms" is meant to counter; the brotherhood of arms is what some desperately wish to keep pure.[36] They want the profession of arms to remain free from the taint of women. Yet Sassoon, writing almost a century ago, implies that the brotherhood he has in mind involves "mothering" activity at its core—including caregiving, profound emotional love, and a willingness to die as if for your own child.[37] Those traditional "mothering" roles have always been part of a cohesive, effective army.

Sassoon's guilt is complex, but it is, in part, the luck guilt of a survivor. "Survivor guilt" (a specific kind of luck guilt) is itself a relatively new term, but the phenomenon is not. The term, when introduced into the psychiatric literature in 1961, referenced the severe guilt felt by survivors of Hitler's genocide of European Jewry. Those who survived the genocide felt they were the "living dead"; they carried the unconscious belief that "merely remaining alive was a betrayal of the dead."[38] Strictly speaking, survivor guilt is not rational guilt, for surviving the Holocaust, or surviving battle, our theme, is not typically because a person has deliberately let another take his place in harm. To be sure, it may be like that. Achilles' guilt over the death of his beloved war comrade, Patroclus, is perhaps one of the earliest

---

[36] See, for example, James Webb's controversial article, "Women Can't Fight," on women in the military http://www.washingtonian.com/articles/people/jim-webb-women-cant-fight/ (accessed August 9, 2012). Webb was teaching at the Naval Academy at the time of the article. His article was a response to Congress's 1975 authorization for women to attend service academies; eighty-one women graduated from the Naval Academy in 1980, many of whom were incensed by Webb's article. When I taught at the Naval Academy in the late '90s, the article was still widely discussed, and criticized, notably by Paul Roush, a retired Marine colonel and then professor in the leadership, ethics, and law division.

[37] See Virginia Held, "Feminism and Moral Theory," in *Women and Theory*, ed. F. E. Kittay and D. T. Meyers (New Jersey: Roman and Littlefield, 1987) 111–28. I thank Patty O'Toole for pointing out this connection to me.

[38] See Lawrence Friedman's discussion of William Niederland and Arnold Modell in his "Towards a Reconceptualization of Guilt," *Contemporary Psychoanalysis* 21 (1985): 501–47.

records we have of a soldier's survivor guilt. And in this case, Patroclus was killed, to reconstruct the moment, because Achilles refused to fight and Patroclus took up Achilles' shield and armor and did battle for him. What Achilles wants more than anything is to undo the original switch, to trade places, to suffer the harm and endure the death himself: "My spirit rebels—I've lost the will to live. The man I loved beyond all other comrades, loved as my own life—I've lost him."[39] He can't undo the switch and he feels profound guilt.

But the guilt of surviving war buddies, or of not being exposed to exactly the same lethal dangers, is not always or typically like this. It is often a matter of dumb luck that a soldier makes it out alive, and tragic luck that others do not. And yet many who have that good luck feel that it is a betrayal of those who don't—a betrayal of solidarity. It is not unlike what is sometimes felt in a family when one sibling does well and another does not. The child who succeeds may feel guilty, experienced as if the distribution of goods is based on a zero sum game: to do well means she has deprived, in some non-innocent way, her sibling of limited goods. Psychoanalyst Arnold Modell describes aptly this kind of guilt. There is "in mental life something that might be termed an unconscious bookkeeping system, i.e., a system that takes account of the distribution of the available 'good' within a nuclear family so that the current fate of other family members will determine how much 'good' one possesses. If fate has dealt harshly with other members of the family the survivor may experience guilt."[40] Soldiers, as a result of tight unit cohesion and solidarity, may have similar unconscious thoughts—that the cost of their good luck is another soldier's bad luck. To be lucky is to deprive a buddy of comparable good fortune. Though they do no wrong, they blame themselves as a way of sharing the ill fate. Sharing the evil is a way to negate the awful sense of betrayal.

As a form of guilt, survivor guilt (and more generally, luck guilt) points the blame inward and pins moral responsibility on self, though there is not even the causal involvement that characterizes accident guilt. Still, feeling guilty, in general, puts oneself at the center of the story. It is a way of

---

[39] Homer, *The Iliad*, trans. R. Fagles (New York: Penguin, 1999) 18.105, 94–96.

[40] Arnold Modell, "The Origin of Certain Forms of Pre-Oedipal Guilt and the Implications for a Psychoanalytic Theory of Affects," *International Journal of Psychoanalysis* 52 (1971): 337–46, as quoted in Friedman, "Towards a Reconceptualization of Guilt," 501-547.

repossessing moral agency and control, however much we overextend the orbit of our actual dominion. We do so unconsciously to make intelligible a terrible thing that has happened and claim agency in a chaotic world. Not surprisingly, that overextension may lead to good effect: in the case of the military, strong feelings of solidarity and fidelity mobilize fighters. Sassoon's luck guilt, like Mooney's implicit guilt, is part of the cohesion of the fighting cadre. But still, the guilt itself is an awful burden to the individuals who privately bear it. And it is a burden that persists long after war, as soldiers know and civilians don't often fully appreciate.

Major Daniel Healey, another Marine I interviewed that morning in Annapolis, was the commander of a rifle company in Iraq in the early years of the war. Healey was in charge of over 200 Marines, most who had just joined his unit shortly before what he refers to as "the race to Baghdad." Only two in the entire unit were combat veterans, both from twelve years earlier in the Gulf War, where they had served as junior Marines. His job, he tells me, is to build trust and faith in those whom he does not know personally or have time to train himself. He has to cultivate "empathy," he says, know his troops implicitly, however different their levels of training and experience from his own.

It is hard to overestimate the gravity of the command responsibility he feels, and that is a part of many commanders' sense of responsibility and guilt: he must prove himself and convince his troops to trust him as a competent authority. He has to rely on those who know him to convey the decency and wisdom of his command to those who don't. Some of those he does not know will have joined his command just minutes before battle. "I felt like my entire life had prepared me for that moment," he explained of the responsibility. "For me, I took it as a particular challenge because I had the potential of having to write to their parents, saying that they had died under my command." Stalin's famous remark is worth recalling here: "One death is a tragedy, a million deaths is a statistic." To Healey, as commander of 200, individual or aggregated death on the battlefield is never just a statistic: "I was thirty-seven years old, I was a father of three, and I had been in the Marine Corps for seventeen and a half years," begins Healey.

> I was leading people who had been in the Marine Corps for five months and were eighteen years old. So in many ways, although it was my first time going into combat, I truly feel that everything I've done up until this point has prepared me for this. And I had to make sure—I made a constant effort to look for, to try to understand how those young Marines'

experience was not necessarily mine. How I was responding to something—how well-prepared I was, was not necessarily how well-prepared they were. It's called empathy…[a]nd as a commander, as a leader, you really have to put a lot of energy into that. Because you're busy, it's very easy to just overlook. Because you're genuinely busy, not because you don't want to. It takes effort.

Healey does not speak of losses, but like Mooney, he alludes to the unfair burden other Marines are shouldering while he has been in Annapolis. "You got twenty-year-old Marines over there for the third time while we've been here trying to be in touch, but not much being asked of us personally." Like Mooney, Healey is trying to get back to a unit that will go overseas. "There are so many people out there who have had to reach so much deeper than we have and for so much longer and so many more times."

The unspoken guilt that Healey or Mooney feels is different from Prior's: neither is triggered by events that lead to a tragic death. Rather, theirs is a more generalized kind of guilt rooted in omission rather than commission. In leaving the war zone, they have let others take their place. Their guilt or moral anxiety is experienced as if a betrayal. Admittedly, this is an interpretation made outside a clinical setting. I am in no position to plumb the depths of their souls, nor pretend to do so. But the point I am trying to make is as much conceptual as psychoanalytic: guilt is a part of the battlefield that often goes unrecognized. And while its genus may be single—about apparent transgressions against others for which an individual indicts himself and seeks reparation—its shapes are myriad.

Are these feelings misplaced or marginal cases of guilt in so far as they do not track objective culpability? Should we minimize them, as some philosophers might urge, and spotlight instead clearer cases of what we might think of as rational guilt or rational remorse? This would be a grave mistake. The conception of guilt and its phenomenology, like that of all emotions, includes the rational and the irrational and the many imperceptible degrees in between. Proper emotions are not just the sanitized ones, responsive to our best reasoning, as the Stoics famously insist. Rather, they include the full array of what we feel. They are real by virtue of mere fact that they are felt. This is important not just in treating pathology, but in understanding the nature of emotions themselves and the psychic reality they can express. For soldiers, who often feel all too alienated from those who do not fight or bear directly the costs of war, it is essential that their subjective experience of war be understood and their feelings accepted and given due consideration.

The Guilt of Collateral Damage

But what of cases where wrongdoing is not so easily ruled out? In particular, what of guilt feelings that arise from killing civilians, where civilian deaths are part of the "collateral damage" of attempts to discriminate legitimate from illegitimate targets? This, I suggest, is a kind of guilt different from accident guilt or luck guilt. Yet it shares with them a similar theme. Even if limited collateral damage in war is widely regarded as permissible within just war theory, those who incur it do not always live with it easily.

Marine Col. Bob Durkin commanded a battalion just south of Baghdad in the Sunni Triangle during Operation Iraqi Freedom II. He recalled how "emotionally upset" his Marines became when Iraqi children were injured or killed when cars ran the "trigger lines" at vehicle checkpoints. In some cases, elaborated Lt. Com. Irv Elsten (a Navy rabbi), families would be put on the hood of a car, followed by a pick-up truck with armed Fedayeen (Ba'athist loyalists) intent on running the checkpoint. If the injuries or deaths were of an adult male whom they suspected was a suicide bomber or a woman who might be concealing explosives under a large burka, his Marines, Durkin said, would "generally fluff it off and justify it to themselves, rightly or wrongly." They would reason counterfactually, "even if I couldn't find out, it *coulda been* this or *coulda been* that." But when children were involved, "there was a dramatic psychological difference." The soldiers would immediately become "visibly upset when they killed children." In the case of a badly hurt child, "they would go out of their way to try calling in medevac aircraft to get the kid out to the hospital." It was just different, he said, when kids were involved. The soldiers were more vulnerable. They couldn't shake what they had done.

One way to think about this is psychoanalytically, with a twist. The sight of the helpless, injured child may throw the Marine back to an image of himself, as once, not so long ago, a child dependent on adults for protection and survival. In that child's world, adults are supposed to construct sound moral order.⁴¹ They are the moral legislators. This is true for the Marine in a special way. The combatant in an urban counterinsurgency war is never just a war fighter but also a policeman and peacekeeper. He is tasked to fight but also to help create a sustainable, civic order. The dual role is never easy: when to be a policeman and when to be a fighter is often a tough fielder's choice; the rules of engagement don't always settle the matter. Yet the wish to be the good cop, who can restrain his fire when innocent children's lives are at stake, is part of what Durkin's Marines must feel profoundly.

Checkpoints make vivid the moral ambiguity in war and the anguish of killing civilians caught in the crosshairs of war. Security checkpoints are in place to help sort out combatant from noncombatant, threat from non-threat. But as these Marines attest, the opportunity for mistake is great. After the heat of battle, with time to reflect, soldiers often struggle to make sense of what they have done.⁴²

This is the force of a remark Lt. Com. Webber makes: "It is a hard thing to gun down innocent people." He is not talking about Marines who kill out of malice. Nor is he talking about causing collateral damage impersonally, in the way that air strikers do. What he has in mind is a specific case he knows well, that of Sgt. Rob Sarra of Illinois, who, speaking about his experience in Iraq on a PBS television special, claimed he shot an innocent woman on 26 March 2003. Webber worked with Sarra while in Iraq and then again after they returned home for a few months until Webber was transferred to another unit.

Sarra's case is wrenching. It was reported in detail in the *Chicago Tribune*.⁴³ It is the early days of the war. Sarra was a part of a convoy of armored vehicles in the push toward Baghdad. According to Sarra's war

---

⁴¹ Here I am indebted to comments by Paul Schwaber at a seminar I gave at Yale, March 2008.

⁴² As Lt. Co. Tony Pfaff noted just after returning from Iraq in summer 2006, not all checkpoints are well advertised. And even when they are, some local drivers may not be used to them. Others may run them out of fear of Americans, or in defiance of "occupiers," or simply because they are teenage boys out for a joyride. Given all the ambiguity, a commander may want to have in place fairly explicit rules of engagement precisely "to limit moral culpability their guys have to buy."

⁴³ Louise Kierman, "A Son Confronts the Aftermath of War" (2 July 2004) http://www.chicagotribune.com/features/health/chi-0407020125jul02,0,5055328.story?page=1 (accessed January 5, 2010).

journal entry for that date, a woman walked toward the assault vehicles ("amtracs," as the Marines call them). The Marines shouted at her in Arabic to stop.

> So she's walking and walking and walking…I'm like, OK, we've had reports of suicide bombers, she's wearing all black, she's carrying a bag under her arm. One of two things is going to happen. Either we drop this woman—either she's going to stop or we'd better drop her or she's going to blow up and kill a bunch of guys. …So she's walking. She's walking. She's walking. I perceived her as a threat. You know what, I've got a shot. Two shots. The first one, I think I missed her. Second one, I saw her buck. And then the Marines from the other amtrac opened up on her. And I was the only guy in my platoon to fire. And she hit the ground and when she hit the ground, there was a white flag in her hand, a piece of white flag in her hand. And I was like, "Oh my God."

The general lines of Sarra's account are corroborated by Marine official reports.

Given the perceived threat the woman presented, the shooting was regarded as within the rules of engagement. Furthermore, the official report concluded that even though the woman was killed by Marine fire, it was most likely the fire from the platoon in the second amtrac that caused her death. Yet this far from settled the question in Sarra's own eyes of his moral responsibility and guilt. Sarra was irreversibly shaken by his experience, and despite counseling and rest, was unable to resume his position as platoon guide. He returned to the States and eventually was given an honorable discharge from the Marines.

There is a final perspective to bring into the conversation. Col. John Rupp is a Marine Corps aviator who sees war from the relatively safe distance of a F-18 cockpit. He is part of the interview group in Annapolis who has been quiet until the very end: "All the baggage that comes with combat—stress, anxiety, fear—is directly related to the proximity of the action. And all the baggage that comes after the war is, I think, directly related to the proximity. Aviators, because they are in a jet that's above the fight, that's sometimes thousands of feet above the fight, don't necessarily get the full impact of what they're doing like a ground officer or infantryman would."

Rupp is insulated by distance, and feels almost the guilt of it before these ground troops. He doesn't see the faces, the child's or the adult's or the woman wearing the big bhurka. He is focused on targets and non-targets.

He is not being callous. The gut, moral experience of war is just different for him than for his colleagues on the ground.

For these Marines, the intimacy of indirect killing may simply cancel out other judgments about its permissibility. Indeed, empirical moral philosophers have argued that even if we generally think it is morally alright to cause harm as a side or collateral effect when the overall benefits are great enough, in cases where that harming is "up close and personal," we are less likely to think it morally permissible.[44] We might speculate, given the testimony we have heard, that when a child is harmed or killed, the act seems to cancel out permission in an even more visceral way.

There is a more general lesson as well. And that is that in experiencing certain kinds of guilt, soldiers try to reclaim a sense of personal agency and moral autonomy minimized by putting on a uniform and marching in step as part of a cadre. They take personal responsibility for what they have done, even if that responsibility exceeds what they can in fact do. In so doing, they reaffirm their own humanity in fighting war.

---

[44] There is a body of empirical studies suggesting that we may mentally represent in an unconscious and hardwired way—as a part of some deep "moral grammar"—a significant moral difference between directly harming an innocent in a way that uses them as a mere means and causing them harm as a foreseen side effect; for discussion, see John Mikhail's philosophical computational model of double-effect dilemmas in his "Universal Moral Grammar: Theory, Evidence, and the Future," *TRENDS in Cognitive Sciences* 30 (2007): 10. However, other empirical moral philosophers have argued that we register the incurring of indirect harm differently when it is up close and personal. Joshua Greene's work may be particularly relevant to the above checkpoint cases; see his "The Secret Joke of Kant's Soul," in *Moral Psychology: The Neuroscience of Morality: Emotion, Disease, and Development*, ed. W. Sinnot-Armstrong (Cambridge: MIT Press, 2008). fMRI studies may suggest that our limbic systems step in here in a way in which they do not for action at a distance. I thank Rick Waugaman and John Mikhail for discussion here.

5

Uncovering the Hidden Values about Values Assessment: Assessing Student Dispositions in Teacher Education[1]

Susan Malone, Emilie Paille, and Kelly Reffitt

According to the National Council for the Accreditation of Teacher Education (NCATE), the guiding principal and goal of the teaching profession is student learning. This guiding principal is so important that NCATE emphasizes it in their first standard requiring that teacher candidates possess sufficient knowledge, skills, and professional dispositions necessary to help all students learn. The knowledge, skills, and dispositions should be evident in the institution's conceptual framework, in addition to being assessed by the institution.[2]

NCATE defines professional dispositions as "the professional attitudes, values, and beliefs demonstrated through both verbal and non-verbal behaviors as educators interact with students, families, colleagues, and communities."[3] They require the inclusion of two specific dispositions, fairness and the belief that all children can learn. Many teacher preparation programs in the United States use the agency's definition of dispositions in order to meet the accreditation standard. Based on the institution's mission, other professional dispositions may be added, and these dispositions are articulated in the institution's conceptual framework.

---

[1] Originally presented by Susan Malone and Emilie Paille, "Uncovering the Hidden Values about Values Assessment: The First Steps Towards Meaningful Assessment of Dispositions," presentation to the American Association of Colleges of Teacher Education, New York NY, 26 February 2007.

[2] National Council for the Accreditation of Teacher Education, "NCATE Unit Standards in Effect 2008," http://www.ncate.org/Standards/NCATEUnitStandards/UnitStandardsinEffect2008/tabid/476/Default.aspx#stnd1 (accessed August 18, 2012).

[3] National Council for the Accreditation of Teacher Education, "NCATE Glossary," http://ncate.org/Standards/NCATEUnitStandards/NCATEGlossary/tabid/477/Default.aspx#P (accessed August 18, 2012).

Uncovering the Hidden Values about Values Assessment

The following is an account of the Tift College of Education's experience in developing an assessment of the professional dispositions of teacher candidates. What is most salient about this process is the set of often unexamined assumptions that complicate the process of reaching real consensus on professional standards and values, especially as those standards and values manifest themselves in assessment. This complication is about more than inter-rater reliability, although that is a related concept and certainly has important implications for the validity of assessment results.

Reaching a true consensus about why we assess, what we assess, how we assess it, and what we do with the assessment results is a challenging process for several reasons. One is that human beings are inconsistent, not always responding to the same phenomenon in the same way. Another reason is that our subjective realities interfere with objective assessments. Additionally, while we may use the same language, we bring to the table different, usually unarticulated, assumptions about the concepts represented by that language. Nowhere is this challenge in developing consensus more evident than in the issues surrounding the assessment of professional dispositions.

Sockett argues that the dispositions valued by a professional community, as well as the community's responses to the development of professional behaviors, are determined by the primary moral perspectives of that community.[4] Likewise, Tift faculty approached the *assessment* of dispositions from the argument that how we assess dispositions, how we interpret assessment instruments, and how we ultimately use assessment results are similarly informed by philosophical perspectives. This approach is consistent with the one advocated by Dottin that ties the assessment of professional dispositions to a unit's conceptual framework; he calls for "continuous analysis of relationships among beliefs, relationships between beliefs and actions, and relationships among actions."[5] It is in the process of analyzing these relationships that faculty may inadvertently discover the lack of consensus among their beliefs, and this discovery can lead to the

---

[4] Hugh Sockett, ed., "Character, Rules, and Relations," in *Teacher Dispositions: Building a Teacher Education Framework of Moral Standard* (New York: AACTE, 2006) 926.

[5] Erskine Dottin, "A Deweyan Approach to the Development of Moral Dispositions in Professional Teacher Education Communities: Using a Conceptual Framework," in Sockett, *Teacher Dispositions*, 45.

desired reexamination of the framework that guides and binds them together as a professional community. Finally, the principles Diez presents to guide the practice of assessing dispositions "make the invisible visible," the necessity of making criteria used in assessment "public and explicit," so that the process has "moral meaning for teacher educators and for their practice."[6]

Developing the Dispositions Assessment

The faculty encountered no significant difficulties in articulating the dispositions they valued or in generating a list of descriptors for those dispositions. See Table 1 for the original list of dispositions. These dispositions were based on the existing conceptual framework, recommendations from the assessment committee, and standards from Interstate Teacher Assessment and Support Consortium (InTASC), a coalition of state education agencies, higher education institutions, and national education organizations committed to educational reform of teacher preparation, teacher licensing, and ongoing professional development.[7]

Table 1. Professional Dispositions of Teacher Candidates

Respect
    Values self and others
    Is considerate of others
    Values diversity
    Exhibits tolerance
Responsibility
    Is reliable and trustworthy
    Accepts consequences for personal actions or decisions
    Prepares for classes/meetings/group work/instruction
    Demonstrates ethical behavior
    Maintains confidentiality of students/colleagues
Flexibility
    Adapts to change

---

[6] Mary E. Diez, "Assessing Dispositions: Five Principles to Guide Practice," in Sockett, *Teacher Dispositions*, 49.

[7] Council of Chief State School Officers, "The Interstate Teacher Assessment and Support Consortium,"http://www.ccsso.org/resources/programs/interstate_teacher_assessment_consortium_%28intasc%29.html (accessed August 18, 2012).

Uncovering the Hidden Values about Values Assessment

    Is open to new ideas
    Deals appropriately with less than ideal situations when necessary
    Maintains a positive attitude when necessary changes occur
Collaboration
    Supports teamwork
    Shares knowledge and responsibilities with others
    Accepts feedback from others
Reflection
    Self-assesses knowledge/performance
    Demonstrates accurate self-analysis regarding own strengths and weaknesses
    Uses constructive feedback
    Assesses situations accurately
Commitment to Lifelong Learning
    Engages in professional development activities
    Is committed to the profession
    Models and promotes lifelong learning
    Has enthusiasm for the discipline(s) he or she teaches and for the process of learning
Belief in Teacher Efficacy
    Demonstrates a belief that all students can learn and that he or she can influence student learning
    Is willing to take risks
    Views the work of an educator as meaningful and important
    Maintains emotional control and responds to situations professionally
Additional Disposition Added:
    Communication[8]
    Engages in socially appropriate behaviors
    Is able to read social situations
    Understands nonverbal communication
    Responds in socially appropriate and professional ways
    Negotiates place
    Maintains engagement with others (i.e., colleagues, peers, parents, students)

---

[8] This disposition was later changed to social intelligence with minor changes to the disposition descriptors.

The faculty agreed to pilot the dispositions assessment with the conditions that the assessment would not be "high stakes," the assessment committee would develop an assessment policy, and they would implement the existing rating scale used in their portfolio assessment—that is, "Proficient," "Developing," "Unacceptable," and "Not Able to Rate."[9] In addition, they agreed on the process, meaning that all faculty would assess all candidates in all education courses every semester. The process would be modified as necessary, based on experiences and data from the initial semester.

Problems became evident as the data were examined and as the faculty were asked to adopt a policy. An ad hoc committee was formed and charged with examining the assessment process and proposed policies, analyzing results to identify patterns, studying related literature on dispositions assessment, and finally making recommendations to the full faculty. The committee developed and used an effective strategy to help the faculty confront the disparate values and assumptions that were undermining the attempts to reach real consensus and blocking any commitment to an assessment policy. At a monthly faculty meeting, professors anonymously indicated agreement or disagreement with a list of statements designed to clarify understandings of the purpose of various components of the disposition assessment. Results were tallied immediately. See Table 2 for the Values Statement Exercise.

The results, both startling and informative, made it clear that, although the faculty shared a common conceptual framework, worked toward the same goal of preparing teacher candidates, and used a common vocabulary, they did not share common concepts and understandings. With the *lack* of consensus explicitly confronting them, faculty were then ready to begin the process of developing a fair, equitable, and meaningful assessment that provides a vehicle for shaping the growth of teacher candidates. The ad hoc committee made the following recommendations: the addition of an eighth disposition category, communication; changes to definitions of ratings; the adoption of a growth model versus a deficit model with a document clearly articulating the college's philosophy of assessment; and revisions to the proposed policy with due process for students.

---

[9] More recently, the assessment committee recommended and the faculty approved a new rating scale for the assessment of dispositions and the indicators for the instrument were revised to be more behavioral. The ratings changed to "Always," "Usually," "Needs Improvement," "Not Satisfactory," and "Not Able to Observe."

Table 2. Values Statement Exercise

Agree	Item	Disagree
26	Educators are always in the process of moving toward ideal professional attitudes and behaviors.	5
11	Moving toward an ideal behavior should earn the evaluation "proficient."	17
14	When a teacher candidate finishes a TE program, he or she will be at some particular point in developing professional dispositions. The candidate should be operating at a proficient-level category on each to be deemed ready to teach.	15
3	It is negative to have less than proficient ratings on a dispositions scale.	28
6	The evaluation that a student receives on a dispositions rating says more about the assessor than about the person who is assessed.	22
3	The evaluation that a student receives on a dispositions rating says more about the program than about the person who is assessed.	26
10	As each student begins a TE program, his or her dispositions, by virtue of beginning as a teacher candidate, will be developing.	11
5	Everyone in entry-level classes should be rated as "developing."	25
5	Students' dispositions are "proficient" unless they demonstrate otherwise.	22
3	"Developing" is a negative evaluation.	28
9	Disposition assessment is a net to stop students from further advancement in their professional programs.	19
31	Disposition assessment is to make visible the dispositions we believe we desire our teacher candidates (and ourselves) to possess.	0

Relevance and Implication for Action

What did the institution learn from implementing a dispositions assessment? Primarily, it is relevant to and carries implications for policy, because the concept of policy assumes all stakeholders are using the same language and have common understandings of the concepts that are the foundation for the policy. Such consensus allows for common application of the policy. Faculty could have given lip service to this truth prior to the piloting of their dispositions assessment but did not anticipate the discrepancy in understanding until informed by the data, nor were they aware of the vast differences of philosophy among them until confronted by the responses to the values statement exercise. Quantitative evidence from practice was used to put a draft policy on hold, because this policy could not have been applied consistently or fairly. In addition, quantitative evidence brought to light the vast differences of opinion and of philosophy among faculty. The journey the institution took, with the intent of coming to common terms, reaching agreement on how to administer the assessment instrument so that the outcomes could be trusted and its follow-up would be equitable, would lead towards exemplary practice—at least for the time being. Later, especially with the addition of new professors, the faculty would need to revisit their philosophical differences, the change in assessment ratings, and the use of the dispositions assessment in order to shape teacher candidates' individual professional growth.

An institution attempting to assess something as value-laden as professional dispositions must take systematic steps to ensure a fair, equitable, and meaningful assessment process. The developers of such a process should assume that disparate values and understandings lie beneath a common language and take steps to uncover, examine, and work through the different perspectives held by their faculty. The necessary discussions strengthen the shared vision of the professional community and must occur with any assessment that is to be administered widely and that will result in policy that has a positive impact on teacher candidates.

Part II: Professional Character and Professional Formation

6

Professionalism and Vocation Across the Professions

William Sullivan[1]

Let me begin by thanking the organizers of this event for the invitation to be part of such an extraordinary initiative. It is rare in our day for an entire university to focus its attention on its educational mission as a common project. The topic, "Professionalism and Vocation Across the Professions," is particularly important for reasons that I will enunciate in just a few moments. But first I want to compliment you individually and collectively on the seriousness of your purpose and the thoroughness of your organization and arrangements. It is a pleasure for me to join you.

Social science tells us that the key to that mysterious electricity we call "morale" lies in the ability of groups and organizations to sustain a common focus of attention. Doing so requires crafting forms of regular and significant interaction. Such interactions, if they are to be sustained—and sustaining—must take on regular patterns. They must become ritualized forms of communication that help bring into being at that moment, as well as further, the values that they seek to achieve. This is the secret of good classes, good sports and cultural events, good conferences. However, it is hard for us, formed as we have been by a culture that disdains "mere ritual," to keep hold of this elementary social fact. (That is one of the contributions of the social sciences: to rescue us from our thrall to obvious but false nostrums of our time and place.) In fact, far from being the window-dressing, it is in all domains of human activity just these events of mutual engagement that generate the élan that makes possible high achievement.

---

[1] We did not ask the author to prepare a paper for publication in connection with his keynote address at the 2005 symposium. However, after this book project was conceived in 2009, we edited the text of the keynote address he had sent us. This editing included adding material in note 5 drawn from the Q&A session following the keynote address as well as references in notes 10-12 to various works published subsequently. We are grateful to the author for graciously agreeing to proceed in this manner so that this collection could include all the important contributions to our project's development.

Accordingly, I intend for my remarks this evening to heighten some of the central themes that your "Professionalism and Vocation Across the Professions" project has taken up. But it will be tomorrow's conversations that will matter. So, I have organized my reflections to try to set up a context that can be sustained, deepened, and expanded in your work tomorrow.[2]

I will proceed in simple format. First, I want to address the big issue of professionalism—what it is and why its renewal matters so much, and what role higher education needs to play in its renewal. Second, I will describe in broad outline the salient findings of the research in which I have been engaged for the past five years at the Carnegie Foundation for the Advancement of Teaching in the Preparation for the Professions Program. Here the central idea I want to emphasize is the metaphor of the three apprenticeships as a new way of understanding and analyzing what goes on in professional programs and schools. Third, and finally, I will take up one of the most important challenges facing professional education: the problem of *rebalancing* the three apprenticeships. I will contrast two strategies for achieving this rebalancing. I will call these the additive versus the integrative strategies, and end by arguing for the importance of the integrative approach, while sketching briefly some of the implications of taking this approach seriously.

I. Professionalism: What It Is and Why It Matters

A. Civic Identity as the Core of Professionalism

To become a professional is not only to join an occupational group. It is to assume a civic identity. The core of professionalism is that by functioning as lawyer, engineer, doctor, accountant, architect, teacher, pharmacist, or nurse, an individual carries on a public undertaking and affirms public values. With this identity comes a certain public status and authority, as is granted both by custom and the profession's social contract, but professionalism also means duties to the public. Chief of these duties is the demand that a professional work in such a way that the outcome of that work contributes to the public value for which the profession stands.

---

[2] For a more detailed treatment of these themes, see William M. Sullivan, *Work and Integrity: The Crisis and Promise of Professionalism in America*, 2nd ed. (San Francisco: Jossey-Bass, 2005).

The larger public seems instinctively to understand this. There is widespread expectation that professionals should be accountable beyond the measure of profit and loss, because the professional ethic rests upon a fiduciary basis. Amid the general outcry over the revelations of fraud and malfeasance as the U.S. financial bubble exploded in 2002, the sharpest outrage was directed at the law and accounting firms. Quite correctly, both officials and the public at large saw the leading lawyers and accountants of those organizations as guilty of an insolent repudiation of public trust. They therefore judged these professionals corrupt and so more odious, if not more reprehensible, than mere business leaders of companies like Enron and Worldcom. Like hypocrisy, moral outrage is premised upon accepted standards of value.

The ideals bound up with professionalism have been only imperfectly realized in any professional field, but the persistence of these, at least in the form of aspiration, is noteworthy. "Professions are defined," writes the historian Sheldon Rothblatt summarizing a large literature, "by an ethic of service. All agree that education, whether apprenticeship or science, has been the central feature of professional identity."[3] Equally true, the professions are highly skilled occupations with a distinctive corporate form of organization. But they are more than this. In their corporate organization they represent a project for bringing into the capitalist marketplace the spirit of public service. In professions, the claims of public safety and welfare have established a beachhead squarely within the realm of self-interested market transactions. The structure of professions embodies the proposition that capital, specifically human or intellectual capital, ought to be treated as a public trust rather than an absolute individual possession to be traded upon without regard for the consequences to others. Consequently, the professions are organized so that individuals must submit to the corporate organization in order to acquire their specialized skills and, equally important, can only benefit personally from the employment of this "human capital" by applying it according to standards that are established and, in aspiration at least, monitored for the public benefit. Of all job categories, professionals have traditionally shown the greatest degree of involvement in their work, along with the greatest attachment to its intrinsic rewards as opposed to income

---

[3] Sheldon Rothblatt, "How 'Professional' Are the Professions? A Review Article," *A Comparative Study in Society and History* 37/1 (January 1995): 195.

and status. In many ways, the professions have indeed provided models of "good work."

B. A Contract with Society to Sustain Public Goods

Professions operate within an explicit contract with society as a whole. In exchange for privileges such as monopoly on the ability to practice in specific fields, professions agree to provide certain important social services. In exchange for the privilege of setting standards for admission and authorizing practice, professions are legally obliged to discipline their own ranks for the public welfare. The basis of these contracts is a set of common goals shared by the public and for which different professions undertake responsibility. So, medicine, nursing, and public health are chartered for the maintenance and improvement of society's health, just as education exists to promote the goal of an educated citizenry, law to secure social justice, or engineers to ensure safety.

These are public values. In economic parlance, they are public goods, meaning that they are values from which all benefit and which depend on everyone's cooperation, but to which no individual market actor has a strong incentive to contribute. The professions are publicly chartered to make it their primary concern to sustain such public goods. They are, therefore, in an important sense public occupations even when they work outside government or publicly supported institutions such as schools and universities. In theory, though ambiguously in American practice, the professions' natural ally is government, in its vital function as the guardian of citizens' common values.

C. Professional Vocation

The modern professions were the products of the creative period of institution-building that occurred around the turn of the twentieth century. They grew up with the modern industrial society of the past century. A century ago, both Britain and the United States felt the impact of a reforming generation seeking new careers that could be "callings," at once addressing social needs and providing vehicles for meaningful individual contribution to society. The burst of new professions, such as social work and journalism, were one result, along with the expansion and greater opening up of the traditional learned fields.⁴ While the value of having a calling is still accepted today, it is seen mostly as applicable in very restricted spheres. So, apart from the directly religious sense of calling, it is widely understood that both in the arts and in science, contributions of value require nothing less than the whole of a person's life and devotion. However, in its inception, the modern notion of the professional was concerned with finding a new way to institutionalize the idea of vocation.⁵

II. The Critical Role of Professional Education: The Three Apprenticeships

To sustain that project, to reinvigorate a truly civic professionalism, requires that professionalism establish sites from which it can develop and spread, creative nuclei of cultural renewal within the several professional communities. The movement of professional education into the university a century ago was a crucial part of the larger effort to establish the modern professions on a public and socially responsible basis. Then the project was to raise standards and improve the technical competence of basic practice. That effort has been largely successful. Today, however, the big need is to recover the *formative* dimension of these large and impressive educational enterprises. Every field confronts the challenge of providing an apprenticeship that includes theoretical knowledge and practical know-how. But each profession must also, if it wishes to survive and contribute to the greater well-being of society, lay a foundation for a lifetime's identity and solidarity as a member of the profession. The need of our time is for professional schools to provide their students with a preparation for

---

⁴ For the American context, see Robert M. Crunden, *Ministers of Reform: The Progressives' Achievement in American Civilization* (New York: Basic Books, 1982).

⁵ One of the most worrisome trends in recent decades is the tendency of the most successful practitioners in several professional fields, such as medicine and law, to move off the charts economically. The professions and professional education will be in serious trouble if they are unable to address the potentially corrosive effect of such external rewards on the intrinsic goods of the practice and on the practitioner's commitment to public service and sense of calling. Indeed, as we have seen in the case of accounting, a serious diminution in the sense of public spirit and public purpose likely will lead to a dilution of the privileges of self-governance and to increased governmental regulation and bureaucratic control.

professional life that integrates cognitive learning and practical skills with judgment and a commitment to the profession's particular public mission.

A. The Academy's Current Emphasis on Intellectual Training

The kind of imagined professional preparation we are seeking would have to reckon with the tensions and complexities that beset the effort to educate professionals. From the perspective of the student, professional school is the entry portal to a world that, while attractive in imagination, is in practice likely to be initially alien, perhaps even threatening or hostile. Whatever its faculty may imagine, for the student the school represents the profession, in both senses of the word. The knowledge and skills expected by faculty (and later by board or license examiners) is the profession, for practical purposes. Therefore, it matters a great deal just what is put forward as significant and obligatory through the medium of requirements, subject matter, and modes of assessment. Faculty whose loyalty is mostly to their academic discipline, for example, may convey to students more about what is required to succeed as a future professor than as a practitioner. Together with the forms of pedagogy, these expectations form the wider or "hidden" curriculum.

Seen from the student's perspective, professional school functions as a kind of apprenticeship to the profession. By teaching and example, the faculty initiates and guides beginning students into the mysteries of their guild. Too often, however, the students' experience teaches that the main point is to display some knowledge or deploy some problem-solving skill as demanded, without occasioning much thought about how these apparently arbitrary kinds of knowledge and skills are supposed to come together in the full range of professional performance. This is the potential drawback of schooling as a way to train practitioners: the reduction of learning to performance on demand rather than training for mastery of a domain.

Particularly in the early phases of professional training, however, performance as a student is the critical bar against which novices are measured, and it is academic professionals who do the measuring. Yet, while professional practice draws upon such theoretical knowledge, and often contributes to its development, it is wider and deeper than the predominantly cognitive emphasis of academic culture. Historically, professions have relied upon apprenticeship carried out by practitioners to inculcate these broader dimensions of competence and perspective. Accounting, for example, continues to demand practical experience as part of the requirements for full certification. However, when the professions moved most of their training into the academy a century ago, they introduced into professional preparation a tension between the values of academic training and those attached to the traditional apprenticeship.

A century ago, professions such as law and medicine made university attendance mandatory at just the time that the European university model of training professionals through formal academic programs was enjoying great prestige. Academics whose loyalties were primarily to their disciplines came to insist that "pure" theory had to precede any mingling with the contaminating aspects of actual practice, including the substantive—but not "scientific"—commitments of the professional fields to values and goals. The most famous and influential model of this viewpoint, the 1910 Flexner Report on medical education, decreed two years of "basic sciences," taught in the academic mode, as the necessary rite of passage into later clinical training. Other fields have followed that model almost universally.

At the same time, the rise of positivism to ideological ascendancy in the American academy helped legitimate these trends. Positivism held that only scientifically verified claims can count as knowledge. It thereby sharply separated factual, empirically based knowledge from claims about aesthetic, religious, or moral value. Only the former was to be the proper concern of academic disciplines. However, as we have seen, professional practice and identity are necessarily shot through with evaluative and normative standpoints. This not-so-subtle clash also worked to downplay the importance of apprentice-like relations, and so of the community of practitioners, in professional training.

The result of the tension between the cognitive focus of the academy and the more holistic concerns of the practitioner community has, in virtually every field, been a legacy of unequal attention and divided loyalties. Professional education has become divided into specialized areas, separating the cognitive from the practical and the ethical dimensions.[6] These intellectual separations have, in turn, become embedded in

---

[6] In an important sense, what the university does best and what the professions most need are antithetical to each other. The university advances knowledge by dividing it, and for university faculty the route to advancement lies very often through increasing specialization, especially specialized research (as opposed to teaching). By contrast, almost by definition practitioners have to be good at synthesizing and integrating knowledge, skills, and an understanding of people and situations.

institutional divisions, in what is taught, by whom, and in what kind of setting.

The master trend spawned by the positivist impulse of the American academy has been ever greater emphasis upon the intellectual training in which academics take pride. This has had the sometimes unintended effect of separating cognitive development from the kind of moral formation that was long the focus of professional apprenticeship organized by practitioners. Moving professional training into the university setting has sharpened the focus on cognitive skills, with resulting improvements in all fields. Yet, it also has narrowed and divided the focus of much professional education, creating a major tension between the accelerating advance of cognitive knowledge and the need to integrate these advances with the other essential dimensions so as to form genuine professional identity.

B. The Need to Rebalance the Academic, the Practical, and the Socio-Ethical Apprenticeships of Professional Preparation

The disaggregation of the cognitive, practical, and ethical dimensions in professional education can be conceptualized, and is experienced by students, as three relatively separate, even freestanding, kinds of "apprenticeship" or ways of entering the profession—the academic apprenticeship (focused on cognitive or intellectual knowledge), the practical apprenticeship (focused on skill or practice), and the socio-ethical apprenticeship (focused on identity and purpose).

The first apprenticeship, as we have seen, is focused on the cognitive demands of the academy. Today's professional education tends to emphasize the values of the modern academy. It weights academic credentials over practical competence, academic success over apprenticeship experience, and expert knowledge over professional identity. In order to achieve integrated competence for practice—the goal of our attempted imaginative reconstruction—the preparation we are seeking would have to shift the balance among these three areas.[7]

Such a rebalancing would likely have several of the classic features of traditional guild training. In today's context, induction into the craft of the

---

[7] Although the relative emphasis among the three apprenticeships in professional education varies across different professional fields, professional educators in all fields recognize the need to bring them into closer association with each other.

guild would require incorporation of the modern academic forms of knowledge and assessment. It would also need to tie this first, academic apprenticeship more closely to the practitioner's perspective and concerns. The setting of the first apprenticeship is the school, while the workplace is necessarily involved in "clinical" and "practical" training. This second apprenticeship corresponds to the guild's tradition of training the journeyman.

Throughout these two interrelated phases, the unique set of attitudes and perspectives typical of the guild would be held out as both demands and as aspirations. Here, there is need for strong cooperation between the academic and practitioner wings of each domain. Auditing of publicly traded corporations, for example, is mostly done by a few firms. Since certification requires "on-the-job" training, which is typically carried out within these firms, the effective education of accountants depends upon a proper alignment between the academy and the culture of the firms in order to succeed.

The final aim of professional preparation, now as in the past, is shaping the future practitioner as a member of a specific community of practice, integrating learned competence with educated conscience. This provides the substance of the third apprenticeship: the formation of the requisite perspective on work and the self that marks a genuine professional. Achieving this end will require a rethinking and consequent rebalancing of these three aspects of existing professional education: the academic curriculum, the introduction to practice skills, and formation of professional identity and social responsibility. Each of these "apprenticeships" exhibits its own distinctive kind of teaching methods. Each demands, and at its best develops, different kinds of learning abilities in students.[8] But they need to be thought out together in order to provide the basis for a more coherent experience, one that is clearly oriented toward the ongoing development of future practitioners by cultivating an appreciation that really there are no purely technical solutions and that all real solutions involve the entire range of knowledge, skills, and professional responsibility or moral commitment.

---

[8] Psychologists tell us, for example, that learning about and learning to act as someone in role draw on very different cognitive and emotive capacities.

III. Rebalancing the Three Apprenticeships

A. *The Additive Versus the Integrative Strategy*

How, then, might we go about envisioning such a "rebalancing" of the apprenticeships? How to imagine a reform program that seeks to ensure that not only practical training, but professional commitment and identity, emerge from the relative eclipse they have suffered from our laudable enthusiasm for science and cognitive prowess? The usual academic response, upon discovering that some area of knowledge has been slighted, is to "add requirements." I will call this familiar approach the additive strategy. It has been the particular focus of many professional school-accrediting bodies. It is not a wrong response in principle. However, as I will try to show, it is often counterproductive in practice. That is because the additive strategy rarely gets to the heart of the problem, which is not only the relative imbalance among the emphases of professional school curricula, but the isolation in which each of the kinds of knowledge and experience represented in the three apprenticeships is typically taught and learned.

To take an example, consider briefly the conclusions reached in the past decade by a study of training in legal professionalism carried out by the prestigious American Bar Association. To quote the 1996 ABA Professionalism Committee Report:

> Providing additional classroom coverage of professionalism issues will not be an easy task. Law school curriculum reform is a tedious and often frustrating task and seems to work best when modest changes are made at the margin by adding one or two additional courses. If the proponents of the need for increased law school training in ethics and professionalism are right, however, an effort equivalent to that which led to the increase in clinical legal education in the 1970s and the increased emphasis on skills training in the 1990s is required. The aim of this effort should be to elevate the twin concepts of the practice of law as a public service calling and the development of the capacity for reflective moral judgment to the same level as legal knowledge and traditional legal skills. This is indeed an ambitious goal.[9]

---

[9] ABA Section on Legal Education and Admissions to the Bar, *Teaching and Learning Professionalism, Report of the Professionalism Committee* (1996): 15.

Efforts to add new requirements are almost universally resisted, not only in legal education, but in professional education generally. This is for good reason that there is always too much to accomplish in too little time. Sometimes this problem becomes so acute that the only solution is to extend the time allocated to training. In engineering, for example, current debate centers on the question of whether the master's rather than the bachelor's degree should be the entry-level credential for the field. Extending the duration of training is a radical solution, however, and certainly not one that would appeal to law school administrators, faculty, or students.

This additive strategy of educational change assumes that increasing emphasis on the second and third apprenticeships will reduce time for, and ultimately weaken the first, or cognitive, apprenticeship. When academic values and goals are pre-eminent, this assumption implies that each of the apprenticeships is actually freestanding. Thus, the second and third apprenticeships can be strengthened only to the point at which they might begin to encroach on the first. However, this is not only a practical problem of too much to accomplish in a limited amount of time. It is also a conceptual and pedagogical problem. In essence, the additive strategy assumes that the first apprenticeship is sufficient in its own terms. We just need to find ways to beef up the second and third without disturbing the first.

We want to endorse a different strategy, which we will call *integrative* rather than additive. Something like an integrative strategy has, in fact, begun to emerge recently in discussions of legal education. The core insight behind the integrative strategy is that effective educational efforts must be understood in holistic rather than atomistic terms. For law schools, this means that, far from remaining uncontaminated by each other, each of the three apprenticeships takes on part of its character from the kind of relationship it has with the others. So, in the standard model, in which the first apprenticeship as expressed in the Socratic classroom dominates, the other two apprenticeships are each tacitly thought of and judged as merely adjuncts to the first. That is why adherents of the additive strategy resist the idea that all three are critical, that they are inseparable, and that all three will be strengthened through their integration. In the emerging model, by contrast, law schools are employing simulated or real-life clinical settings to teach lawyering and to familiarize students with the roles, skills, and activities that lawyers actually perform on behalf of clients, such as representation, counseling, advocacy, and negotiation.[10]

This emerging model in legal education is similar to the problem-based learning that is central to professional education in the health field.[11] It is not a total substitute for theoretical study, but by directly connecting theoretical knowledge about the law and about how it should function in society to settings in which students are experiencing what it is like to be that kind of professional, it offers the potential to transform the nature of the cognitive apprenticeship itself.[12]

B. Taking Integration Seriously—The Professions and the Liberal Arts

Today's professions face not only changing domains of knowledge, but shifting fields of practice within a dynamic and often confusing society. Therefore, the horizons of the professions need to be broad. Practitioners must be able to think critically about their own situation and that of their field in relation to its defining purposes. The institutions of professional education must both model and challenge their students to genuine agency

---

[10] See William M. Sullivan, Anne Colby, Judith Welch Wegner, Lloyd Bond, and Lee S. Shulman, *Educating Lawyers: Preparation for the Profession of Law* (San Francisco: Jossey-Bass, 2007).

[11] See Molly Cooke, David M. Irby, and Bridget C. O'Brien, *Educating Physicians: A Call for Reform of Medical School and Residency* (San Francisco: Jossey-Bass, 2010); and Patricia Benner, Molly Sutphen, Victoria Leonard, and Lisa Day, *Educating Nurses: A Call for Radical Transformation* (San Francisco: Jossey-Bass, 2010).

[12] Another striking example of an integrative strategy comes from clergy education in Jewish and Christian seminaries utilizing four distinct kinds of pedagogies—pedagogies of interpretation (the disciplined analysis of sacred texts), pedagogies of contextualization (understanding the social, political, personal, and congregational conditions that affect the reception and application of those texts), pedagogies of performance (developing the skills of preacher, counselor, liturgist, and congregational leader), and pedagogies of formation (inspiring and shaping students' pastoral identities, dispositions, and values)—in order to enable students to place themselves within a disciplined way of life and service, that is to say, within the professional context, in graduated doses over time. See Charles R. Foster, Lisa E. Dahill, Lawrence A. Golemon, and Barbara Wang Tolentino, *Educating Clergy: Teaching Practices and Pastoral Imagination* (San Francisco: Jossey-Bass, 2006). For integrative strategies in the professional education of engineers, see Sheri Sheppard, Kelly Macatangay, Anne Colby, and William M. Sullivan, *Educating Engineers: Designing for the Future of the Field* (San Francisco: Jossey-Bass, 2009).

as experts and as citizens. To complete our thought experiment, we need to imagine integrating a critical yet engaged standpoint into the guild's particular sense of knowledge, craft, and attitude. To preserve the professional social contract, we need to bring the perspective of the aware and critical citizen into the formation of the members of the community of practitioners. The opposing pulls of specialized expertise versus the broad sympathies needed for active citizenship define this crucial third "apprenticeship."

Adequate professional preparation must reconceive the traditional concern with professional ethics and social responsibility to mean the capacity to think as a citizen, to judge from the standpoint of social justice and the public welfare. Without this ability, even good intentions may not prevent a slide into dereliction of duty, as accounting's problems demonstrate. This means that professional judgment has to be open to the expanding horizon typically associated with education in the liberal arts. From its roots in the Greek and Roman classics, the best liberal learning has urged upon students the perspective of the reflective yet engaged citizen, one who seeks to understand the world in order to take a responsible part in it.

American professional schools, uniquely, have long demanded evidence of competence in liberal arts disciplines either as prerequisites or as collateral studies. This provides an opportunity to broaden the scope of professional training. A broad education in the arts and sciences is valuable for professional preparation precisely in order to understand relationships among the disparate domains of knowledge and social institutions as these affect professional practice. These concerns define the civic dimension of professional preparation.[13] Something of this spirit can be heard today in renewed interest in leadership training and public service as part of professional preparation. Professionals who have not only served their professional domains, but have worked to reorganize their fields to better meet public need, or serve in civic and public capacities, stand as examples of this important, if relatively neglected, dimension of professional aspiration.

---

[13] The need to analyze and understand the complex social environments and systems in which both practitioners and those whom they serve find themselves has become extremely clear in medicine and nursing, but it is also clear in such areas as teaching and the law.

IV. Conclusion

The final aim of professional preparation, then, includes both individual and social dimensions. The great promise of the professions has always been that they can ensure the quality of expert services for the common good. The professions have also opened to individuals the possibility of a form of self-actualization as workers, as citizens, and as persons. They offer the hope of a career in which one's livelihood is good for others as well as oneself, that it can be a contribution to the progress of society. Professional education needs to aim at making a good beginning in that project. To do so, it must ask again, in a way suited to our times, the radical questions about its purpose and means. Educators of professionals have a special relationship to their domain, their students, and their society. They stand at the crucial interface between the inheritance of their field and the needs of the times. Their highest calling—and most exciting pedagogical challenge—is to ensure that the connections are made in the developing minds and hearts of future practitioners. It is making those connections that, above all, will fulfill the civic promise of professionalism.

7

Forming Professionals and the Quest for Common Ground in the University

William May[1]

To prepare for my visit to Mercer University, I requested and received a great deal of information about the university's self-understanding. The packet of materials made me realize that you were going through huge changes as an institution, including a change in your relations to the Georgia Baptist Convention. I read documents about a set of projects concerning higher education and the professions launched under such banners as the Mercer Commons, a Center for Faith, Learning, and Vocation, and the Quality Enhancement Plan Concerning the Engaged University Learning Together. In particular, I received materials relating to your symposium last year on "Professionalism and Vocation Across the Professions," led by William Sullivan of the Carnegie Foundation, including his keynote address and his book entitled *Work and Integrity*.[2] Finally, I read the volume entitled *The Baptist Summit* containing the collection of addresses by your past and current presidents, R. Kirby Godsey and William D. Underwood, and by your distinguished chronicler, Walter P. Shurden, author of *The Baptist*

---

[1] We did not ask the author to prepare a paper for publication in connection with his keynote address at the 2006 symposium. However, after the idea for this book was conceived in 2009, we prepared an edited transcript from the videotape of the keynote address and this paper was developed based on that transcript. We are grateful to the author for graciously agreeing to proceed in this manner so that the collection in this book could include all the important contributions to our project's development.

[2] William Sullivan, "Professionalism and Vocation Across the Professions," *supra* chapter 6; and also Sullivan's *Work and Integrity: The Crisis and Promise of Professionalism in America*, 2nd ed. (San Francisco: Jossey-Bass, 2005).

Identity.[3] I was impressed by the quality of the writing in all of these addresses.[4]

Clearly you are opening up new ground here with consequences for the professions and for the university. Nowhere is this more obvious than in your choice of the metaphor "common ground" as the description of what a university should be about and your discussion of professionalism and vocation across the professions as they figure in the quest for common ground. In this lecture I will attempt to explore contending notions of common ground and then explore some of the barriers and opportunities the professions pose in reaching it.

I. Common Ground in the University

A. Historical Development: From Sacred Canopy to Training Ground

The nineteenth-century Protestant liberal arts college often looked to scripture as supplying a kind of sheltering sacred canon, a common ground, in educating the young. In the course of time, the sacred canon in such colleges extended beyond scripture to include the "greats," as it were, the *auctores* of the West: Plato, Shakespeare, Milton, Wordsworth, and perhaps also Locke, Jefferson, and the Federalist Papers. Education should be broadening (through an array of required distribution courses) but also traditioning. The college served as a kind of *in loco parentis,* in the sense of handing on the past, honored as a valued past, a heritage or legacy. To this end the president of the college or university often taught the senior course in ethics. This may have meant, of course, that ethics was not so well taught, the president being a busy person, but the symbolism was obvious. Instead of ethics falling to the responsibility of a young assistant professor teaching the course as a technical specialty within a large array of courses, no less a person than the president taught ethics as the crown of the educational experience. Education pointed students, enlarged by their experience away

---

[3] Walter B. Shurden, *The Baptist Identity: Four Fragile Freedoms* (Macon GA: Smyth & Helwys, 1993).

[4] *The Baptist Summit at Mercer University January 19–20, 2006: Three Addresses by R. Kirby Godsey, Walter B. Shurden, and William D. Underwood* (Macon GA: Mercer University Press, 2006).

from home, toward the goal of self-realization, of becoming well-rounded selves in the setting of family, church, workplace, and citizenship.

Colleges afforded students the chance to escape from the small towns their parents led and to grow up in a social setting that resembled the towns of their origin. Education helped broaden their intellectual horizons and provided them with an antidote to the narrowing and restrictive tendencies of life in a small town. The enlargement of their sensibilities helped prepare them for a more spacious leadership role in the towns to which they would return. On the whole, the consensus the liberal arts college presupposed fostered a sense of vocation that embraced more than the graduate's job. The ideal of well-roundedness correlated with a vocation that included additional responsibilities as a spouse, parent, citizen, and participant in voluntary communities. Liberally educated graduates would reflect a *pleroma* of shared values that let them play out a variety of social roles within the setting of the common good. So went the ideal.

Tellingly, the twentieth-century university differed from the nineteenth-century college in that it increasingly restricted the scope of its responsibility to its educational mission, which it also redefined. It largely shed its responsibility for the student's personal and social life, renouncing the role of *in loco parentis*. This renunciation fit into its general orientation to the future rather than the past. While the liberal arts college initiated students into the community and culture of their birth, the university now prepared them for the economic and organizational identities they would assume on their graduation. Education orients less to origins than to destination, not to past tradition but to future possibility. To this end, the intellectual ideal of education was no longer the well-rounded, but the skilled self—that is, the professional.

Massively, the professions, beginning with the Carnegie reforms in medical education, moved into universities—medicine, law, ministry, engineering, accounting, business, and many more. Coordinately, the intellectual focus of the university also shifted from inquiry about received values to the acquisition of factual knowledge that would equip young professionals in the making to seize the future. With an almost priestly asceticism, Max Weber put it to academics to shed their values as they pursued factual knowledge in the classroom. Weber put it most sternly and vividly: Do you want to be a teacher or a leader, a pedagogue or a demagogue? Leave your values out in the cloakroom, along with your hat and coat, before you enter into the classroom.[5] Because values are merely subjective, arbitrary, spongy matters of preference, they cannot figure in what the professor imparts objectively as knowledge in the classroom. In effect, education can only focus on helping students acquire a factual knowledge base and the skills attached to that knowledge base that will equip them for their futures.

On the American scene, the shift of education from a rural past to an urban future served an immigrant nation well. For example, at the beginning of the twentieth century, both sides of my family immigrated to this country: one side from Scotland and the other side from Poland. Education let immigrants coming to this country prepare for a more promising future than was available to them in the stringencies of Europe, or in the penury of a ghetto, or on a family farm. The university offered students not so much a *sacred canopy*, but a *training ground* that would equip young people to enter into the slipstream of modern power with professional credentials. In effect, the fashionable objectivism of the modern positivist university prepared for an energetic, but morally uncriticized, careerism on the part of students.

Unfortunately, this view of the role of the modern university offered too diminished a view of human intelligence. It reduces the mind to the work of purely analytical, technical, and instrumental intelligence. The intellect can tell you how to go from here to there, but it cannot address the critical question as to whether the "there" is worth getting to. It cannot pose the critical question of ends, goals, values, because these are all simply matters of subjective, arbitrary preference. In effect, intelligence diminishes from critical to merely operational intelligence, from substantive to merely technical reason. The university can turn out people who will be effective technicians for the world as it is, but the university cannot help young people determine morally the ends they should pursue.[6]

---

[5] Max Weber, "Science as a Vocation," in *From Max Weber, Essays in Sociology*, ed. H. H. Gerth and C. Wright Mills (New York: Oxford University Press, 1958) 146 and 151 [paraphrase].

[6] William Sullivan, in his lecture last year, sought to compensate for this problem by distinguishing between three apprenticeships in professional education oriented to cognition, skill, and ethics. See his "Professionalism and Vocation Across the Professions," *supra* chapter 6. In my judgment, he too quickly identified the cognitive side of the university with merely analytical/technical intelligence, which thus required him to

The next moment in higher education, the so-called "free university," was a child of the counter-cultural movement of the sixties and seventies. It protested against the intellectual and moral authority of both the parent and the expert. It oriented neither to the past of the nineteenth-century liberal arts college nor to the future goals of the twentieth-century university. The Vietnam War discredited the future societal goal of a military victory, and the movie *The Graduate* exposed and rejected the personal future proposed by the available Mrs. Robinson and the plastic Promised Land offered by the drunken friend of the graduate's father. Students at the time self-consciously described themselves as the "now generation"—celebrating neither the past nor the future, but the present.

In my judgment, the revolutionary force of protest against authority by this counter-cultural movement can be exaggerated. When its force was spent, it left the liberal arts college, the modern research university, and its professional schools still intact, with all their achievements and defects still in place. So where do we stand now, especially this institution, as it thinks about its earlier heritage and its accomplishments as a modern university turning out students with negotiable professional skills?

B. Beyond the Positivist University

1. Back to the Christian University as a Fortress? A first possible response would be to attempt to recover by several means the hegemony and dominance of a Christian university—for example, by insisting on a profession of faith as a condition of matriculation for students and as a prerequisite for being a faculty member. This solution would not, in fact, return to the spirit of a liberal arts college that enlarges horizons; it would take the oxygen out of the air by reacting to a larger culture experienced solely as threat.

The common ground would serve neither as a sacred canopy nor a training ground, but as a *fortress*, a castle with a moat around it, securing an embattled institution that lacks self-confidence. Such an institution would be defined less by what it loves than by what it fears. The embattled would seek

---

separate out three distinct apprenticeships including the moral. If, however, one takes into account the full range of the work of intellectual inquiry, then one has to connect intellectual inquiry itself with the question of ends, goals, and values, and the self's own moral formation.

an arsenal providing them with a stockpile of certainties, rather than engage in a faith deepened through understanding. I see the power of fear and the loss of self-confidence in this project as a serious and central problem.

2. *The Christian University as a Representative University and an Engaged Campus*. Nicholas Wolterstorff, who was a theologian at Calvin College before moving to Yale University, suggests a second possible response. He calls this second alternative a "representative university." Such a university would recognize and substantially fund its Christian heritage by exposing students to the tradition in its intellectual vitality, but it would also recognize that the institution and its students live in a pluralist society. It would not signal either directly or silently that, unless you are a Christian, you cannot teach here. Instead, it would want to see surface in the institution a range of views, "representing" the main traditions, whose presence would allow the university to be a part of the wider dialogue going on in the culture at large. It is important that students be exposed to this larger dialogue. Otherwise, one is simply asking students to disappear into an enclave where they would purportedly shut the doors, close the windows, and turn off their iPads. Consequently, one wants to admit into university life faculty members and students with diverse backgrounds, traditions, intellectual commitments, and vitalities.

However, this alternative clearly differs from the naked Weberian ideal of the value-free university. It would drop the modern masquerade of the so-called neutral research university that excludes the presence of any and all traditions within it—except, oddly and ironically enough, the positivist tradition of neutered inquiry. That is the curious twist of the positivist outlook—it holds that we are not going to have any tradition present except the positivist tradition. Curiously, in the name of tolerance, this tradition does not tolerate the presence of any traditions in the room except those that have gone through a kind of anti-fungal foot bath before entering the classroom. In this way, one purportedly eliminates particular traditions except one's own.[7]

---

[7] When I started the Department of Religious Studies at Indiana University, a public university, I thought it made little sense to include as members of the faculty experts in the history, psychology, and sociology of religion, but to exclude theologians in the mix. In discussions with my dean, I argued that a religious studies department should include, among others, some people who draw on the intellectual vigor of religious traditions. Otherwise, one curiously claims that a department can have experts *on* Thomas Aquinas or

Getting back to Mercer, the vision of a "representative" university acknowledges that an institution with a Christian heritage functions within a religiously and culturally pluralist society. It should allow for and encourage intellectual and cultural diversity. A representative university would support engaged dialogue across some intellectually significant traditions. It would call for intellectual vigor, but also the proprieties of civility and thoughtfulness in two senses of that term: reflectiveness and considerateness. This view of the university moves beyond the images of a *sacred canopy*, a *training ground*, and a *fortress*. In their place, why not revisit and explore an old term that would define the university's common ground as a *campus*? It is an interesting word. The Latin refers to "an open space." In military parlance, a campus is an open space where battles are fought, but in this case, one would recognize that it is better to marshal arguments than troops. Can such a space offer common ground?

3. *The Deepening of Faith through Engaged Dialogue.* As a campus, the representative university offers an open space that engages various traditions in the culture at large, even as it sustains a specific tradition of its own. It supports and affirms its specific tradition, but it does so with self-confidence rather than with the fearfulness of a fortress. Some might argue that such a university justifies itself solely on the grounds of tactical necessity—that is, Christians are stuck with a pluralist society and, therefore, they should invite it in to avoid being cut off from the larger culture in which they live. Others would more persuasively argue that there are positive warrants, beyond tactics, for the Christian tradition to recognize and value such dialogue in the course of deepening faith. Augustine was neither the first nor the last theologian to discover a deepening of his understanding, as he debated with the Manichaeans and the Platonists. At less exalted levels, most of us discover in the course of time that a tradition is not simply umbilically transmitted and received. All of us go through a period of distancing from a tradition even as we appropriate it. Students can discover that they need to look at their own parents, and brothers and sisters, and themselves, with the eyes of a stranger in the course of recognizing more deeply who and what they are. Far from being disloyal to identity, such distancing can be a pathway to the deepening of identity.

Moses Maimonides, but these distinguished thinkers could not themselves be part of such a department. That approach seemed to me a strange act of self-impoverishment on the part of the modern university.

II. Seeking Common Ground Across the Balkanized Professions?

A. Balkanization and Its Discontents

The project at Mercer University also seeks common ground by generating specific discussion of professionalism and vocation across the professions. This is an interesting and bold, even astonishing, move. At first glance the terrain seems unpromising. The professions themselves, for all practical purposes, have balkanized. Far from providing the way to common ground, they often behave like a group of Balkan states barely on speaking terms with one another. The field of professional ethics itself in the modern university has broken up into a series of subspecialties, such as medical ethics, legal ethics, and journalism ethics, each attached to one of the great professional schools into which the larger world of the university is divided. Until very recently, the university has not offered studies cutting across the stand-alone professional schools. Was it not Robert Hutchins who said something to the effect that the only thing that unifies the modern university is the heating plant? Flagship universities, such as Harvard, operate on the financial principle of every tub on its own bottom. That offers a strange picture, a flagship as a series of tubs, economically *and* intellectually.

Meanwhile, in the world beyond the university, the professions deal somewhat suspiciously with one another. Doctors dread the lawyer's intrusions on malpractice issues. Business leaders miss the good old days of the handshake and view lawyers as a latter-day evil. Professionals of every stripe are often dismissive of academics in their ivory towers and clergy in their steeples, and they are particularly nervous in coping with journalists who hemorrhage the intellectual authority of professionals by handing out information on medicine and law to lay readers in the society at large. Such balkanization has produced nothing so bloody as the Croatians versus the Serbs, but professionals are exceptionally wary of one another, with little intellectual and moral exchange across the borders in the academy.

B. Commonalities Among the Professions

The balkanizing of the professions is intellectually unfortunate because it has obscured the great similarities among the professions that deserve study. I will highlight only a few commonalities explored at greater length in my book, *Beleaguered Rulers: The Public Obligation of the Professional*.[8]

1. *The Societal Role of Professionals.* First, in a society like ours, modern professionals are effectively *rulers*—not necessarily individually, but collectively. We transmit power today largely on the basis of knowledge, which is chiefly acquired at a university. By going to a university today, one has a better chance of moving into the slipstream of modern power. Because knowledge is so empowering, parents breathe a sigh of relief when their children receive that degree. Physicians have the power to heal (which is perhaps the most striking contrast between life in the eighteenth and the twentieth century), scientists and engineers and industrialists have the power to reshape the earth to serve human extravagance, and business leaders exert a power unmatched by most nations on the face of the earth. However, while professionals rule the world, they also perceive themselves as *beleaguered* rulers. In public conversation, professional groups often seem triumphalist, but privately they blurt out their anxieties: they feel under pressure, assaulted, under siege, harassed, and insufficiently appreciated.

2. *The Public Responsibilities of Professionals Marginalized.* Feeling beleaguered, professionals often obscure for themselves another important commonality—their public responsibilities: "What do you mean by saying I am a ruler? I am busy pressing ahead simply to make the cut, to get the job done that will move my family into the best neighborhoods, the best suburbs, the best second homes, the best cemeteries." Professionals fixate on their struggle to get ahead, and the public responsibilities that go with their power tend to fade. The ancients defined tyranny as the wielding of public power for purely private purposes. Modern professionals hardly think of themselves as tyrants, but they often wield a huge public power to pursue only their own private goals.

(a) *The Sense of Professional Calling.* In effect, professionals tend to lose or marginalize the important commonality of being a professional: a sense of calling. I was helped on the subject of calling by William Perkins, a great English Puritan who was influential in the American scene. Perkins defined

---

[8] William F. May, *Beleaguered Rulers: The Public Obligation of the Professional* (Louisville: Westminster John Knox Press, 2001).

a calling as "that whereunto God appointed us to serve the common good."[9] In the language of the philosophers, we might say God is the efficient cause—God does the calling—and the common good serves as the final cause. So understood, a calling describes the temporal extension of love or service. Christians are called, not simply to perform occasional acts of charity as impulse prompts them but to a life of extended service in the temporal sphere. This sense of service to the common good carried over into the speech of Roscoe Pound, the former dean of the Harvard Law School, who referred to the essence of a profession as "pursuing a learned art as a common calling in the spirit of public service."[10]

However, when Pound offered those words, this sense of calling had already deteriorated into the modern notion of a career. Instead of being called by God to serve the common good, I am called by my SAT scores and MCATs or GREs to serve my own ends and purposes. One should not dismiss the importance of one's own ends and purposes. The task of earning a living usually serves more than the self's own interests. It helps provide for others, send children to college, and support good causes. But a calling is more than a career. It professes a service that transcends a simple marketplace exchange. A career without a sense of calling is merely a car, if you will, an automobile, a self-driven vehicle through life, that carries one out into the public thoroughfares toward one's own private destination. Service to the common good fades from sight.

(b) *Reasons for Seeing a Profession as a Calling*. Why should we conceive of professions like nursing, medicine, accounting, law, engineering, mathematics, education, the ministry, political leadership, business, labor leadership, and so forth as a calling? First, the religious heritage of the West so interprets a profession. A society needs more than the frantic, self-interested activity of the marketplace to hold it together. Second, modern professionals, such as accountants, financiers, and engineers, wield a huge public power with impacts, for good or ill, on workers, suppliers, and neighbors; on the water we drink, the air we breathe, and the schools to which we send our children. It is passing strange that the university would

---

[9] William Perkins, "A Treatise of the Vocations or Callings of Men with Sorts and Kinds of Them and with the Right Use Thereof," in *Puritan Political Ideals*, ed. Edmund Burke (Indianapolis: Bobbs Merrill, 1965) 36.

[10] Roscoe Pound, *The Lawyer from Antiquity to Modern Times* (St. Paul: West Publishing, 1953) 5.

hand out all this knowledge-based power to professionals and yet be silent on the question of its responsible uses. Third, the society at large, from the humble to the mighty, has made a huge social investment in the forming of professionals. No student can go through a modern university and think of himself or herself as a self-made man or a self-made woman. As one zigzags one's way through college or professional school, one depends upon so many who have invested in one's formation—the janitors who clean the johns, the secretary who makes the institution hum, the deans and the president and the provost who have worried about the bottom line, the faculty members who have shaped the emerging professional-to-be, and the research traditions that allow the teachers to do that shaping. Huge investments from centuries past, tuition monies, the gifts of patrons, and funds from state legislatures have helped to set the table. Professionals do not spring out, unbeholden from their own foreheads. They owe service to the common good.

3. *Common Marks of the Professional: Intellectual, Moral, and Organizational.* Despite their differences from one another, professionals bear three common marks. Intellectually, professionals profess a body of knowledge; morally, they profess this knowledge on behalf of someone, either to individuals or to agencies that minister to common human purposes and needs; organizationally, they band together collegially as they serve human need. Three virtues correlate with these intellectual, moral, and organizational marks: *practical wisdom, fidelity,* and *public spiritedness.*

Since the professional body of knowledge must be applied to a range of human need, the professional needs *practical wisdom* in discerning and responding appropriately to the concrete circumstances of the patient or client. Such lawyering, doctoring, and nursing entail more than the mechanics of applied science; they are arts, not just applied science. (Teaching, too, is an art, although that fact often tends to get obscured in the letters of recommendation one receives from graduate schools in the course of building a department. One hears much about the candidate's grades in courses but little about his or her skill in the art of teaching.)

The virtue of *fidelity* correlates with the moral mark of the professional. While professionals earn their daily bread by their labors (it would be a species of angelism to deny this fact), the professional exchange must also rise above the marketplace transaction in two ways: it must be disinterested rather than self-interested, and it must be transformational rather than transactional. It must not merely give the patients or clients what they want, but address their deeper needs.

Finally, the virtue of *public spiritedness* correlates with the organizational mark of a professional. Because professionals today usually work with others in the setting of a large-scale institution, tensions can develop between the natural mode of organization for professionals, which is collegial—a peer relationship—and the setting in which they work, which is hierarchical. Hierarchy obtains in the hospital, the law firm, the corporation, and in the university as well. The academy features instructors, adjuncts, assistant professors, associate professors, full professors, and heads of department, as well as deans, provosts, presidents, and boards. Everybody is layered somewhere between the ham and the hard cheese. The power of the hierarchy in controlling pay and promotions can sometimes obscure a larger responsibility to public good.

Public-spiritedness also requires some measure of quality control of the good being offered. Am I my colleague's keeper? This is a serious problem for Americans because we want to be liked by the people with whom we work. For example, when I was at Indiana University, the dean complained to me one day that he could not get a negative tenure decision out of the English department. They always punted the problem up to him. The law steps in for medical cases but not usually for academic malpractice. We know that a bad doctor can kill you. However, a bad teacher just bores you to death. There seems to be less at stake in the academic setting. Clearly we must deal with the problem of professional quality control since a society gives professionals a monopoly in the exercise of power.

Since professionals serve a fundamental or high good, such as health, justice, education, and the like, the virtue of public-spiritedness requires that professionals and the society work to make this good accessible to all. The United States struggled through the entire year of 2009 with the problem of access to medical care, and even with the passage of legislation, opposition continues in 2010 and 2011. (The Gospel of John [5:2–9] records that powerful passage about the invalid by the side of the healing pool of Bethzatha who has been there for many years without access to the pool. We have the most advanced healing pool in the world, but we have had forty-five million people who have not had access to the healing pool through insurance and another thirty million people underinsured.)

III. The Mission of the University in Forming Professionals: Cultivating Intelligence, the Professional as Citizen, and the Professional as Teacher

Heretofore, professional education has tended to emphasize the training of technical intelligence at the expense of developing critical intelligence. However, critical intelligence is vital in all professional performance. Professional education in medicine, for example, needs to ask: what is the end of medicine? Is it simply to fight against disease and death, or is it to heal? If it is the former, then textbooks tend to organize around high-tech battles against diseases. They tend to downplay preventive medicine or, until very recently, the tasks of pain management, palliative care, and the hospice alternative to the hospital. If it is the latter, then the profession will have a very different sense of how to handle educational and budgetary issues. Or, what is the end of the law? Is it primarily to maintain law and order as an alternative to the brawl in the streets, or is it to achieve justice? Order and justice are both fundamental, societal human goods. However, an overemphasis upon order may discourage criticism of the law and the claims of justice that might lead to a reform of the legal system. Again, what is the end of business? Is it to maximize profits, which tends to exclude all other considerations, or is it to achieve economic performance at a profit? Or what is the end of engineering? Is it to conquer nature, or is it to work with nature? In America we have tended to look on engineers as conquerors, as nature's adversary rather than as nature's advocate. The harsh natural environment in America, as compared with the more temperate climate in Europe, tended to invite this more combative understanding of technology. Immigrants settling in Northern climes welcomed central heating systems in a hurry and the extractive industries that fueled them. The intemperate heat of the South similarly led to the extravagant defiances of air-conditioning. Cumulatively, these solutions have taken their toll on energy resources and required us to rethink the role of the engineer serving as nature's advocate rather than nature's adversary.

In forming young professionals and all its students, the university needs to take its aim at cultivating the citizen—that is, the art of acting in concert with others for the common good. This goal links to the first. Critical intelligence asks whether the "theres" are worth getting to. This means raising all those liberal arts questions: what are our appropriate ends, goals, and values of the society at large and the professions in particular; and what are the fitting and appropriate means to those ends? These are intellectual questions, but they are also crucial to the formation of the citizen.

Finally, the university needs to form professionals as good teachers of what they know. If the name of the game in medicine, for example, is not simply therapy and intervention, but also preventive medicine, rehabilitative medicine, and terminal care, then teaching patients to alter their habits is a significant component of being a physician. What is the name of the game in law? Is it merely litigation? Or is it also counseling the client to keep him out of litigation in the first place? Counseling is the functional equivalent of preventive medicine in the practice of the law. What is the name of the game in politics? Here I am reminded of the tragedy of Jimmy Carter's presidency. I happen to think that his basic policies were good, but he was not, at that stage of his life, a very good teacher to the nation. In a democracy today, leaders do not rule by the bark of command and the grunt of obedience, but by persuasion. Athens rather than Sparta provides the template for professional authority.

IV. University Teaching and Moral Formation

This lecture concludes by addressing two matters relevant to teaching and moral formation—first, a series of contending metaphors for understanding the task of teaching; and second, some thoughts about promoting curricular development in this area.[11]

A. Metaphors for Teaching in the Area of Moral Formation

1. *Engineering or Manufacturing*. The model or metaphor of the teacher as engineer presupposes that teachers have a preconceived goal or plan and achieve this goal through their skill in shaping students to their end. The teacher acts as an efficient cause, turning out a product or contriving experiences for the student that will maneuver the student towards a predetermined design.

This metaphor of manufacturing fails at three points. First, the student is a self-determining creature, not a piece of material, a lump of iron, a drop

---

[11] The author presented the material in section IV.A. as part of his concluding observations at the end of the first day of the symposium. However, it was originally intended to be included in his keynote address at the beginning of the symposium.

of mercury, or a plank of wood, upon which we can impose a form or devise a use. Second, the metaphor distinguishes too sharply between the process and the product. We can distinguish the watchmaker from the watch he or she makes, but a bonding occurs between the teacher and student in the course of the process that contributes to the development of both.[12] The teacher is engaged in the student's learning process and, by virtue of this engagement, becomes a learner in the relation. Teachers undergo changes in their understanding of their own subject in the course of teaching it. This is part of the student's gift to the teacher. Third, the metaphor of manufacturing also overlooks the element of freedom in the midst of bonding, for in handing over a valued tradition to the keeping of others, we hand it over into their freedom. That is why one cannot simply say, "Here is the product, and here are the manipulations I made to produce this product." The root of the word "tradition" connotes handing over.[13] Traditioning in education means handing on, handing over into the freedom of others. While we can talk about evaluating the product, it is hard to control what is going to come out of the other side if we would really understand what goes on in tradition.

2. *Inculcating or Indoctrinating*. The second model or metaphor is that of inculcating or indoctrinating. Whereas the engineering or manufacturing metaphor regards the student as a finished product, the inculcating or indoctrinating metaphor regards the *truth* as the finished product and the student as the receptacle for that truth. The student receives the truth as a substance, a fluid or a solid body to be injected, infused, or digested. Teaching based on this metaphor quickly alienates students (often especially the best students) from both the tradition and the teacher. The resisting

---

[12] The power of bonding led me to oppose the legal enforcement of contracts in the case of surrogate motherhood. Treating surrogate motherhood as a commercial case of buying and selling overlooks the power of bonding in the process of gestation. Delivering a baby into the hands of another differs from delivering a refrigerator at someone's door. While I do not oppose surrogate motherhood as such, I opposed treating it as a legally enforceable contract. One cannot separate the process of gestating from the product issuing from it. The bond is strong and calls for the element of gift in the eventual conveyance of the baby to another. The bond in the classroom is less powerful, but an element of Eros obtains in the relationship.

[13] Our words for "treason" and "betrayal" share the same root: to hand over into the hands of what seems to be an enemy.

student develops spiritual lockjaw, a kind of gagging, when subjected to such inculcation or indoctrination.

3. *Training.* The third model or metaphor is the one discussed earlier, the notion of training.[14] This athletic and military metaphor works nicely for teaching at the lower levels where students must form good habits.[15] Training helps at professional schools in preparing professionals to be competent technicians, but not so well in empowering the professional to be an effective teacher of what he or she knows. Moreover, it is insufficient in helping the student to develop wisdom in discerning the ends, goals, purposes, and values to which habits must be oriented.

4. *Parenting or Dirt Farming.* A fourth model or metaphor is that of teaching as parenting or dirt farming. To this day, the academic calendar has tended to follow the agricultural year. Generative metaphors sprinkle through our vocabulary: seeds in the earth, dirt farming, and seeds of light; the seminar in teaching, the seminal mind, the seminal teacher, the seminary. When we started the Center for Ethics and Public Responsibility at SMU, my patron Cary McGuire rightly wanted us to put on big public conferences. We were a start-up organization needing to announce our arrival. But I also felt that the center would not succeed unless it also tended to the nurturing of organic growth. We needed to provide assists and events for faculty and students that you might not see if you were to put a camera on them, but that would lead to long-term growth. Although you might not see these changes if you were to put a camera on them, this seeding would make the difference in the enduring culture at SMU.

The metaphor of parenting moves in the same direction. In our high-pressured, competitive, and meritocratic society, parenting orients, not to accepting the child as she is, but pushing her toward what you want her to be. Anxious parents tend to drive their children towards performance and results in a highly competitive world. But, of course, this approach to parenting overlooks the other side of parenting. The role includes accepting

---

[14] *Supra,* section I.A.

[15] I came very late to the appreciation of good habits in life. I wish I had sent a dog through training school before I had children! That would have been helpful because I had read too much Kierkegaard and too little Aristotle. I did not realize that a very important feature of my responsibility as a father was to provide a structured setting in which my children could develop habitual responses to quotidian situations in their lives. I do not mean to dismiss the importance of training at all.

love, not simply transforming love; it entails savoring the child for what he or she is, not simply pushing the prodigy toward maximal accomplishment. The latter, alone, turns parenting into engineering or manufacturing a product. And, of course, such parents let themselves in for a let-down. In the muddle of things, parents can fall into the good-cop/bad-cop routine. One parent does not usually do both jobs well. So, one parent pushes, and the other accepts. In parenting as in teaching, one needs to recover some of the modesty of the dirt farmer who tills the ground, broadcasts some seeds, and prays for a little sun and rain. One does one's best while conceding, and perhaps even thanking God, that much, and perhaps even the most important, work lies beyond one's power to mess up or to guarantee. These considerations lead to:

5. *A Final Metaphor.* The job of teaching resembles structurally the role of Joseph in the Holy Family. Joseph is not at the heart of the story. He certainly is not central to the action. In fact, he is cuckolded by the Holy Ghost. But he sticks with Mary, buys the tickets to Egypt, and makes himself generally useful. So, the teacher—when teaching really works—should be cuckolded by the blackboard, the text, the laboratory experiment. A third party takes over as the student gets engaged. The heretofore indispensable teacher begins to fade. Also, like Joseph, the teacher can watch a few seeds of light take hold, and grow, and expand, and also like Joseph, he or she can take delight, without envy, because it is a privilege to see this happen.

B. *Promoting Curricular Development in the Area of Moral Formation*

I noticed that Bill Sullivan addressed two alternatives in curricular development bearing on moral formation: additive and integrative. The additive approach would introduce particular additional courses dealing with moral development; the integrative approach would address moral formation in many different courses.[16] Unless the latter approach leads to a masterful, overall design, I am more inclined to see it as offering a "leavening," rather than an integrative experience for faculty members and students. To this end, the Center for Ethics and Public Responsibility at Southern Methodist University set up a funded program in which faculty members could apply for a modest summer grant to prepare a curricular unit or course in ethics or professional ethics. But we did not just send

---

[16] See Sullivan, *supra,* note 6, at 110-112.

winners a letter awarding the grant. In addition, we arranged an entry meeting with them in the spring and then, again, an exit meeting in the fall. These meetings provided a seminar-like setting in which those awarded a grant would share what they were doing with a larger group, including colleagues of their choosing as well as others invited by the center.

This ritual of entry and exit meetings proved very important. In my experience, university curriculum committees do not provide faculty members with a substantive, collegial experience. They are basically janitorial or they operate like border patrols. They serve the institution bureaucratically in that they keep the curriculum pruned and avoid catalogue creep with the addition of too many overlapping courses. But they do their work without offering much meaningful, substantive discussion. Our ritual of entry and exit meetings, independent of the actions of a curriculum committee, fostered intellectual exchange among faculty members on the subject of ethics as it bore on their disciplines and lines of inquiry. The grantees and colleagues across the years begin to develop a true *collegium*.

There are two main benefits to this "Leavening Approach," applied more broadly to a university's sense of its research/teaching. First, it encourages scholarship to enter into the public domain. Consider what usually happens when a faculty member goes on a sabbatical leave. Most faculty research in a university tends to be private, whereas teaching is a public act. The faculty recipient happily gets relieved from the public act of teaching and goes on sabbatical leave, fantasizing about all she will get done on the research project, now that she is free of students. But then, she soon misses the amphetamine kick of the classroom, her body undergoes metabolic changes, and she does not get much of the work done. When she is back at the university teaching again, the project slides onto the back burner of private worry time and, at length, turns cold. Universities ought to structure things more collegially and encourage faculty members to present their work in public forum for colleagues at the close of a sabbatical with the aid of deadlines. It would enhance the chances of completing a project and it might enrich and leaven faculty discussion.

A second benefit of this circle of collegiality is that it would help break the mindset of faculty members who usually assume, when they write, that they write solely for experts, the gatekeepers in their field, who, of course, reside elsewhere. These distant gatekeepers control job offers elsewhere and even tenure and promotion in their home institution. Consequently, the social vector of most academic writing is reflexively filial. It orients *upward* to the gatekeepers in one's field. The only alternative is *downward*, the sometimes dismissive act of popularizing. The university needs to recover the intellectual tradition of writing *outward* and *over* to an intelligent audience of inquirers. In writing this way, academic writing will begin to recover the intellectual tradition of the Renaissance essay. Machiavelli did not write *The Prince* for the gatekeepers of political science. He wrote it for princes. Indeed, many of the great classics follow this social vector of *out* and *over*. Writing for inexpert but intelligent colleagues in one's own institution would help leaven the intellectual and moral life of our universities.

In similar spirit, the Maguire Center for Ethics and Public Responsibility gave grants to students to do summer internships in non-profit institutions. (Most students otherwise would have had to take conventional jobs to help out on their university expenses, but those jobs would not usually help them break out of the limits of their moral imagination and experience.) Once again, we asked for entry and exit interviews, a setting in which students could learn from one another before and after their experience. The preparation and the particulars of their reports were often moving. Moreover, incidentally through the process, they got some practice in the skill of teaching, a skill that, in its own way, if this lecture is correct, would figure as important in their professional lives ahead.

8

"God at Work": A Reflection on Vocation

John Dunaway

Answering the call of our Creator is "the ultimate why" for living, the highest source of purpose in human existence. ...Calling is the truth that God calls us to himself so decisively that everything we are, everything we do, and everything we have is invested with a special devotion and dynamism lived out as a response to his summons and service.[1]

"God at Work." If we believe that we are indeed called by God to our professions, then he is intimately involved in the tasks about which we busy ourselves daily, from the mundane to the more elevated. Each of us needs to surround our work area with at least an imaginary strip of engineering tape with the words "God at Work" inscribed on them as a reminder.[2]

My own understanding of vocation is primarily a function of my personal faith, and therefore, it is deeply informed by the Judeo-Christian worldview. However, as director of the Mercer Commons, I consciously attempted to make it accessible to those of all faiths, as well as the non-religious. Many of us involved in what the Lilly Endowment called the Theological Exploration of Vocation found Frederick Buechner's definition to be worded in broad enough terms to be almost universally applicable. For him, vocation means "the place where your deep gladness meets the world's deep need."[3] Even those who cannot relate to talk of a caller from whom the call originates can buy into the notion that higher education, at its best, must be an exploration of one's life purpose. And that central purpose that gives

---

[1] Os Guinness, *The Call: Finding and Fulfilling the Central Purpose of Your Life* (Nashville: Word Publishing, 1998) 4.

[2] I owe this "God at Work" idea, as well as the engineering tape, to Miroslav Volf, who spoke to the program directors of Lilly's Program for the Theological Exploration of Vocation on the topic at a conference several years ago in Indianapolis. He actually brought the yellow tape to the conference and gave us each a length of it.

[3] Frederick Buechner, *Wishful Thinking: A Seeker's ABC* (San Francisco: HarperSanFrancisco, 1993) 119.

to us a sense of identity and to our actions a sense of direction is necessarily a matter of matching personal giftings and motivations with service to others.

Several years ago I read a paper at the South Atlantic Modern Language Association's annual convention on the notion of vocation among French writers. The French have always acknowledged writers as *maîtres à penser*. And individual French writers have often found the discovery of their vocation as a writer to be the watershed experience of their lives: Pascal's *nuit de feu* (23 November 1654); Rousseau's enlightenment upon learning of the Dijon Academy's writing competition on the value of civilization and the arts; Descartes's day-long philosophical reverie in a stove-heated room where he intuited his famous *cogito ergo sum*; and my favorite story of vocation among French writers, Marcel Proust, the greatest French novelist of the twentieth century, who remained a dilettante, an obsequious social-climber, and a profound disappointment to his family until only about ten years before his death, when he discovered his deepest identity as a writer. This quest for one's deepest, truest self is at the heart of the search for vocation.

* * *

Professional students are often so career-driven and so narrowly focused on negotiating the successive hurdles that stand between them and their dreams of professional success that they may not expect their teachers to lead them in exploring the meaning of vocation. Yet, as William Sullivan suggests in *Work and Integrity*,[4] they would be well advised to consider such questions, or else they may end up in a short few years profoundly unsatisfied with the degree of fulfillment their careers afford them. And we who teach undergraduates are well aware of how many pre-professional students come into our classes with equally unexamined tunnel vision.

We may be able without too much of a stretch to distinguish between vocation and careerism, but it is a subtler distinction when we come to vocation as opposed to ambition. And, lest we become too self-righteous about our students, we must face our own less than noble motives. My early

---

[4] William M. Sullivan, *Work and Integrity: The Crisis and Promise of Professionalism in America,* 2nd ed. (San Francisco: Jossey-Bass, 2005).

dream of becoming a publishing scholar at a great research university was probably a socially scripted version of a success track that appealed to my own personal ambition. In a similar vein, Brian Mahan's book[5] starts with the case of the senior who tells him that she's been accepted by Yale Law School but has decided to go into the Peace Corps instead. He offers it as a classic example of diametrical opposition between idealistic vocation and socially scripted role models for personal fulfillment. The student's choice turns out to be regarded by her peers as a totally incomprehensible scandal, so taken in are they by the scripted story of success. Mahan uses Tolstoy's *The Death of Ivan Ilyich* as an example of pursuing a "prefabricated envisioned self." Ivan's life is so inauthentic and so wrapped up in the scripted role he has adopted that the voice of his soul asks him three times, "What do you want?" and he is never able to answer.[6]

Mahan rightly points to a seemingly prevalent symptom of the socially scripted roles that we often accept in place of vocation. He calls them "moments of invidious comparison." My moments of invidious comparison were times when I envied others' good fortune, because it resembled the scripted ambitions I had appropriated for myself. All these moments made me feel that life wasn't fair, that I was not receiving my just desserts. I tried to dismiss them by telling myself (and my wife) that those things weren't really that important to me. Yet there was still a feeling of discontent in the back of my mind that I was unable to argue away. I was finally able to face those tendencies toward invidious comparison thanks to a conference for Christian faculty in 2002, where University of Virginia economist Kenneth Elzinga spoke on the topic of what motivates us as academics. I was deeply convicted of my own egoism when he talked about how we academics seem to long for recognition, honors, awards, fame, and yes, even money, rather than being motivated to serve our God, our students, and our colleagues.

I daresay all of us have at one time or other proclaimed to the world that we chose our profession out of a desire to seek knowledge. We enjoyed the pursuit of learning. The academic life may not be the best path to wealth and fame, but it does offer great personal fulfillment. Saint Bernard of Clairvaux, a man whose pursuit of truth was certainly guided by purity of spirit, can help us examine our own professional motivations. James Sire

---

[5] Brian J. Mahan, *Forgetting Ourselves on Purpose: Vocation and the Ethics of Ambition* (San Francisco: Jossey-Bass, 2002).

[6] Ibid., 98.

quotes him as follows: "There are many who seek knowledge for the sake of knowledge: that is curiosity. There are others who desire to know in order that they may be known: that is vanity. Others seek knowledge in order to sell it: that is dishonorable. But there are some who seek knowledge in order to edify others: that is love [caritas]."[7]

Ideas do have consequences. Students do pay attention to us, sometimes when we least expect it. The university is perhaps the one most powerfully placed institution in society for social change. Colleagues, this responsibility is never to be taken lightly. If my contention is true that higher education really should be about finding one's life purpose, one's calling, then we must never allow narrower concerns to crowd that purpose out of our classrooms.

Further Reading on Vocation

Robert Coles, *The Call to Service: A Witness to Idealism* (Boston: Houghton Mifflin, 1993).

John Marson Dunaway, ed., *Gladly Learn, Gladly Teach: Living Out One's Calling in the 21st-Century Academy* (Macon GA: Mercer University Press, 2005).

_____, "The Ultimate Why: My Calling as a Christian Professor," *Southern Baptist Educator* 49/3 (2nd quarter 2005): 4–7, accessible online at http://www.baptistschools.org/Educator/Educator2005-2ndQtr.pdf\.

Os Guinness, *The Call: Finding and Fulfilling the Central Purpose of Your Life* (Nashville: Word Publishing, 1998).

Douglas V. Henry and Bob R. Agee, eds., *Faithful Learning and the Christian Scholarly Vocation* (Grand Rapids MI: Eerdmans, 2003).

Michael J. Himes, *Doing the Truth in Love: Conversations about God, Relationships, and Service* (Mahwah NJ: Paulist Press, 1995).

Brian J. Mahan, *Forgetting Ourselves on Purpose: Vocation and the Ethics of Ambition* (San Francisco: Jossey-Bass, 2002).

J. P. Moreland, *Love Your God with All Your Mind: The Role of Reason in the Life of the Soul* (Colorado Springs: NavPress, 1997).

William C. Placher, *Callings: Twenty Centuries of Christian Wisdom on Vocation* (Grand Rapids MI: Eerdmans, 2005).

Cornelius Plantings, Jr., *Engaging God's World: A Christian Vision of Faith, Learning, and Living* (Grand Rapids: Eerdmans, 2002).

---

[7] James W. Sire, *Habits of the Mind: Intellectual Life as a Christian Calling* (Downer's Grove IL: Intervarsity Press, 2000) 216.

James W. Sire, *Habits of the Mind: Intellectual Life as a Christian Calling* (Downer's Grove IL: InterVarsity Press, 2000).
Gordon T. Smith, *Courage and Calling: Embracing Your God-Given Potential* (Downer's Grove IL: InterVarsity Press, 1999).
Miroslav Volf, *Work in the Spirit: Toward a Theology of Work* (Eugene OR: Wipf and Stock, 2001; 1st ed. Oxford University Press, 1991).

9

Answering the Call to Service:
Vocation and Professional Identity

Timothy Floyd

Although we often talk about them together, professionalism and vocation certainly are not synonyms—but they are related. Perhaps it is helpful to see them as two sides of the same coin. Professionalism deals primarily with the social, with our public and communal obligations—that is, with *externals*. Vocation concerns the other side of this coin, the *inner* life of the professional. I understand Bill Sullivan to be saying that professionalism cannot survive unless individual professionals are motivated by an ideal of service.[1] At its core, professionalism is about service, about subordinating personal needs or goals. Professionals must not be motivated primarily by external goods such as money, power, and status. Thus, in the law, for example, we refer to fiduciary obligations, which require one to subordinate one's own interests to the interests of another.

A sense of vocation, then, can supply the motivation to transcend narrow self-interest, to subordinate the self in an ideal of service.

* * *

The concept of vocation has its origin in religious language and concepts. The idea of calling has deep roots in the Jewish and Christian traditions. The God of the Bible is one who speaks to individual persons and calls them to specific tasks. Indeed, throughout the Bible, God calls particular persons: God called Abram out of the land of his kindred to go to the land of Canaan; out of the burning bush, God called to Moses to go to confront Pharaoh; on the road to Damascus, God called Saul of Tarsus. Drawing upon this biblical concept, Christians have traditionally used the terms "calling" or "vocation" to refer to the work or activity that God desires and makes known for a

---

[1] See chapter 6 in this volume.

person to do.² When used in this sense, calling is a peculiarly personal issue. Specific individuals are called for specific purposes. While vocation is personal and unique, I believe that it is also universal: all persons have a destiny—a unique calling.

Last evening, Jack Sammons and I discussed how vocation in modern American usage retains some of the sense of being called to a task or mission by someone or something external to ourselves. But it also has come to imply a need for self-reflection, for exploration into our own unique giftedness. There is a paradox here. Vocation is essential to transcending self-interest. But I submit to you that we best transcend selfishness, that we learn to subordinate self to service, by looking more deeply inside ourselves. Discerning that call to service requires a focus on ourselves.

John Dunaway referred to the definition of vocation offered by theologian and novelist Frederick Buechner.³ In all of his writing over several decades, Buechner has consistently emphasized the need to listen to our lives. Once called upon to state in a few words the essence of everything he had been trying to say both as a novelist and as a preacher, he said: *"Listen to your life.* See it for the fathomless mystery that it is. In the boredom and pain of it no less than in the excitement and gladness: touch, taste, smell your way to the holy and hidden heart of it, because in the last analysis, all moments are key moments, and life itself is grace."⁴ If we listen to our lives, we just might find that God is present in even the hardest and most hair-raising events in our lives, calling us to rise beyond the narrow interests of self, and offering possibilities of new life, of healing, of fulfillment.

* * *

Getting back to Buechner's definition of vocation, Buechner defines vocation as "the place where your deep gladness meets the world's deep need." ⁵ This

---

² For historical reasons, Catholics tend to use the Latin-derived "vocation"; Protestants tend to favor the Germanic/English "calling." I think the two are entirely synonymous, and I will use the two interchangeably.

³ See *supra* p. 134 in this volume.

⁴ Frederick Buechner, *Listening to Your Life: Daily Meditations with Frederick Buechner* (New York: HarperCollins, 1992) 2 (emphasis added).

⁵ Frederick Buechner, *Wishful Thinking: A Seeker's ABC* (San Francisco: HarperSanFrancisco, 1993) 119.

definition insists that we can find work that makes a contribution to the world's need and also brings deep personal fulfillment. Or, as Parker Palmer puts it in his book, *Let Your Life Speak: Listening for the Voice of Vocation*, vocation "must begin—not in what the world needs (which, after all, is everything), but in the nature of the human self, in what brings the self joy, the deep joy of knowing that we are here on earth to be the gifts that God created." [6]

We find our callings by claiming authentic selfhood, by being who we are, by discerning and using the gifts God has given us. As Palmer puts it: "The deepest vocational question is not 'What ought I to do with my life?' It is the more elemental and demanding 'Who am I? What is my nature?'"[7] Those questions of core personal identity require us to listen to our inner voice. Ignoring the inner voice, or dividing our soul from our role, is ultimately destructive. Vocation as listening to the inner voice, however, offers the hope of uniting our deepest aspirations with the reality of work, the possibility of "living divided no more," of combining soul and role. As Palmer describes the journey toward wholeness at the core of authentic vocation:

> From the beginning, our lives lay down clues to selfhood and vocation, though the clues may be hard to decode. But trying to interpret them is profoundly worthwhile—especially when we are in our twenties or thirties or forties, feeling profoundly lost, having wandered, or been dragged, far away from our birthright gifts. ...Our deepest calling is to grow into our own authentic selfhood. ...As we do so, we will not only find the joy that every human being seeks—we will also find our path of authentic service in the world. True vocation joins self and service.[8]

For those who are concerned that this call to listen to your inner voice is self-indulgent, I am not saying, "If it feels good, do it." But I am saying, if after giving certain work in the world a fair shot, and engaging in honest and searching introspection, it does *not* feel good, don't do it. Let me give an example: I have been blessed to know and work with a remarkable group of professionals, lawyers who dedicate their careers, their lives, to defending

---

[6] Parker Palmer, *Let Your Life Speak: Listening for the Voice of Vocation* (San Francisco: Jossey-Bass, 2000) 16–17.
[7] Ibid., 15.
[8] Ibid., 15–16.

persons in death penalty cases. Of course it is difficult work—the stakes are enormous, the emotions are raw, you are often dealing with people at their worst, and there is little external reward in terms of money or prestige (indeed, quite the opposite). I have discovered that the ones who are most successful, who thrive in this work over time, have an inner joy and fulfillment. I have also observed others who do not last in this work—it is not for everyone. All are committed intellectually, philosophically, morally, to the cause of death penalty defense. The difference is that some feel a deep personal fulfillment. They are called. How do we know they are called? Not because they have an intellectual commitment to the cause, but because they have a deeper fulfillment in doing this work.

* * *

Discerning our call is not easy. Not all of us hear a voice coming from a burning bush, are blinded by a light on the road to Damascus, or even hear a still, small voice calling in the night. Sometimes, even when we believe we are most attuned, all we perceive is silence. At other times, listening for God's call in our lives feels like a great struggle. Perhaps that is why the story of Jacob wrestling all night with the stranger resonates powerfully with many of us.

I also do not mean to imply that discerning vocation is an individual matter, to be discerned alone, in isolation. Although vocation is always in one sense personal and unique, we are made for communion with each other—and our friends, family, and colleagues can be rich, even essential, resources for testing the nature of our perceived calling.

And that brings us back to why we are here. As educators of professionals (as mentors to these apprentices), we have a unique opportunity to help them as they begin the journey of vocational discovery, as they begin to form their own professional identity. At least in my own profession, helping students learn skills of self-reflection and self-awareness, encouraging them to reach into the personal, to pay attention to their souls, has not been a part of our curriculum and pedagogy. Nor have we focused on developing connections and relationships with others, including professional mentors. If we are serious about the third apprenticeship—the formation of professional identity—we must find ways to encourage self-reflection and awareness, and to encourage students to form relationships.

10

Reform and Formation:
Revisiting the Role of Liberal Education

Peter Brown

> A liberal arts education creates citizens: people who can think broadly and critically about themselves and the world.
> —William Deresiewicz[1]

The curricula and credentials of modern professionalism had their origin in the reformed American universities of the late nineteenth century. From Colonial times, the model of liberal education in American colleges had been the seminary, with emphases on ancient languages and classical and biblical texts as well as on logic, mathematics, theology, and philosophy. The German model of scientific research and graduate-level instruction in the professions was introduced in the United States with the founding of the Johns Hopkins University in 1876 and of its school of medicine in 1893. Women, modern languages and literatures, the sciences, the arts, and disciplinarily based departments and majors soon followed at the undergraduate level, while the Ph.D. became the *de rigueur* professorial credential in the disciplines and doctoral or master's degrees the normative credential for admission to the professions (JD, DPharm, MBA, MDiv, etc.). Unlike the European university system, however, the new American research university retained an ideal of liberal education, requiring an undergraduate degree for admission to degree programs in medicine and law or completion of broad general education programs in the case of bachelor-level professional programs like nursing or engineering.

This expansion of the means and purposes of liberal education in the era before World War I has been matched by an analogous expansion in the

---

[1] William Deresiewicz, "Faulty Towers: The Crisis in Higher Education," *The Nation* (23 May 2011) www.thenation.com/article/160410/faculty-towers-crisis-higher-education# (accessed August 18, 2012).

post-World War II era, as social access to college has dramatically expanded, vocationally oriented undergraduate majors have increased in number and popularity, and the humanities have deconstructed the canons of judgment and authority that were the backbone of the liberal arts. These changes have led to repeated calls for the reform and reinvigoration of liberal education, most notably by the Association of American Colleges and Universities (AAC&U). The AAC&U's watchword over the past decade is that professional success and effective citizenship in the twenty-first century will require that "all practical education be liberal" and "all liberal education be practical." Or, as glossed by Stephen Weiss (former managing director of Neuberger Berman LLC), "more big-picture thinking in the professions and more real-world application in the liberal arts and sciences."[2] This suggests three related questions: What is liberal education today? Is it still the foundation of the American university? How would a reformed liberal education affect professional formation? The cross-college initiative documented in this book offered Mercer a unique opportunity to raise these questions for itself—in conversation with some of the most thoughtful national critics of American higher education.

One deep theme that emerged from this discussion is education *against the grain*, education that resists the flow of American culture. For example, William Sullivan insists on the professional's responsibility for public goods beyond the services for which they are paid: "[the professions] represent a project for bringing into the capitalist marketplace the spirit of public service."[3] Likewise, in arguing for seeing a profession as a calling, William May observes that "[a] society needs more than the frantic, self-interested activity of the marketplace to hold it together."[4] Both May and Sullivan detect a decline in this sense of professional calling and blame it in part on "the positivist tradition of neutered inquiry,"[5] which "sharply separated factual, empirically based knowledge from claims about aesthetic, religious, or moral value."[6] As Max Weber argued almost a century ago, the

---

[2] Debra Humphreys and Anthony Carnevale, "The Economic Value of Liberal Education," The President's Trust (2010) www.aacu.org/leap/presidentstrust/talkingpoints.cfm (accessed August 18, 2012).

[3] See Sullivan, p. 103 in this volume.

[4] See May, p. 124 in this volume.

[5] Ibid., p. 120 in this volume

[6] Sullivan, p. 107 in this volume.

predominant cultural forces of the modern world are reductive rationalizations: of value to cost-benefit calculation, of knowledge to scientific objectivity, and of action to technocratic efficiency. *Teaching against the grain* means resisting these cultural forces, insisting to the contrary that there are important intellectual, professional, and religious values that evade calculation, that there are modes of intellectual inquiry that engage these values, and that there are intellectual callings that challenge the civic, corporate, and academic powers that be. In the often somewhat self-mocking, but nonetheless seriously intended, rhetoric of a past generation of Mercer leaders, including Joseph Hendricks, Tom Trimble, Ray Brewster, and Ted Nordenhaug, we are called as teachers to prophesy against the powers and principalities that are the false idols of the age.

What has this resistance meant and what might it mean at Mercer? And how do critics like Sullivan and May point us forward?

Liberal Education at Mercer

The key to resisting powerful trends is having a standpoint from which to launch a critique or set sail in an alternative direction. Over the past five decades, the College of Liberal Arts (CLA) at Mercer has evolved a rich and heterogeneous array of points of resistance to the cultural flow. This sometimes contentious diversity has perhaps obscured the functional similarities of these counter-cultural moorings. I will briefly describe six of them that seem to me to distinguish liberal education at Mercer.

(1) To the occasional bewilderment of some of our sister schools at Mercer, CLA has maintained—in principle and often in practice—a purist approach to mathematics and science as liberal disciplines where "why?" is as important as "how?" This mirrors a purist approach to liberal education in general, seen as a broad familiarity with the generative questions and methodologies of the disciplines. Thus, "critical thinking" is the one outcome of liberal education universally embraced by CLA faculty. (This has sometimes meant that the introduction of more problem-based and skills-oriented programs has been resisted as "pre-professional." Others of us argue that critical thinking becomes practical wisdom only when it gains purchase in the complexities of real-life judgments and decisions.)

(2) & (3) Since 1968 and the establishment of the Experimental Freshman Program (EFP) and its several descendants at Mercer, a sometimes persnickety insistence on excellence and rigor in student work in the disciplines has often been arrayed against the "grab-ahold" provocations of

interdisciplinary seminars where the students' own opinions are the focus of critical pressure. But both of these approaches, as different as they are, stand against the prevailing idea of consumerist catering to students' expectations. The one insists that students must raise their sights and suffer the frustration of trying to meet demanding standards. The other tries to wake students up, disrupting the spiritual comforts of an anodyne automatism.

(4) Civic engagement, whether as volunteerism, service-learning, or social advocacy, has become a hallmark of the Mercer experience, prized for its transformative potential. The experience of otherness within a context of empathy, care, and concern can displace students from their self-satisfied quasi-sophistication and push them toward a systemic radicalism, where "why?" again emerges as the key question. The admission of Sam Oni in 1963—breaching the color barrier—has become iconic for Mercer as a community, and Mercer on Mission—with its service-learning projects in developing countries—has become our signature undergraduate program.

(5) Mercer's singular Great Books Program had its rise in Ted Nordenhaug's query in early September 1981: "How can we expect our students to be liberally educated if their teachers aren't?" Two weeks later, over twenty faculty met in the faculty lounge to begin reading *The Iliad* together. The Great Books Program was the brainchild of the same faculty who had a decade before thrown the general education curriculum in the trashcan in favor of a radical focus on contemporary social topics in EFP (for over a decade, completing three sections of EFP satisfied all general education requirements). This time, the general education curriculum was displaced in favor of a chronological, naïve reading of the classical works of dead white males. Student opinions were still the focus, but this time they were to be disturbed by the cultural strangeness of ancient texts, the premise that some truths transcend the cultural moment, and the demand "Show me where that is in the text." Needless to say, many experts in secondary literatures at Mercer were disturbed by this amateurism and its disregard of scholarly standards, reprising the local culture wars of the 1970s.

(6) Finally, the pervasive cultural anomie that motivated several of these reformers at Mercer had its deepest origin in a Barthian theology of radical freedom and radical doubt, whose touchstone was Paul's Galatians 3:28—"There is neither Jew nor Greek, there is neither slave nor free man, there is neither male nor female. For all are one in Christ Jesus" —and whose watchword was Luther's "Sin bravely!" In the face of God's otherness, even your conscience—much less any other aspect of your human identity—

should not become your idol. We are addressed in sin and grace from a Beyond that shatters false idols, no matter how culturally prized. This vertical dimension or daunting intimation of a new heaven and a new earth makes us strangers in a strange land—exiles with an unknown destiny we must fulfill. This uneasy standing-under is certainly not identical with the aims of liberal education at Mercer as I have outlined them here, but it has been a deep motive behind their evolution for at least three generations of faculty leadership.

The Role of Liberal Education within the University

The 1980s and early 1990s were years of great change and turmoil at Mercer. New professional schools of medicine, engineering, business, education, and theology were established, and two liberal arts campuses (Tift College in Forsyth and the College of Arts and Sciences in Atlanta) were closed. These decisions split the trustees, financially damaged the university and the College of Liberal Arts, and arrayed the College of Liberal Arts faculty against President Kirby Godsey and the board of trustees. A vote of no confidence in the president passed by one vote in the newly established faculty house of delegates. A generation of CLA faculty was lost as financial exigency loomed, and the status of the college in the university was diminished. In a subtle shift of language, CLA ceased to be the "heart" of the university and became its "cornerstone." The edifice raised on the reputation of that cornerstone now depends on these new professional schools and, in particular, the Atlanta campus and regional centers for enrollments and revenues.

Many of these changes mirrored changes in universities across the country, as liberal arts enrollments dropped and professional degrees proliferated. But the vehemence of the dispute at Mercer, together with the pervasive sense on the part of CLA faculty of a betrayal of vision and fiduciary responsibility, has made liberal education the university's *bad conscience*, so to speak. At one point, the plan was to convert CLA into a service unit of the university, offering general education courses for the professional schools along with a few high enrollment majors. A provost *de jour* in the late 1980s dismissed CLA concerns with a cavalier, "If you don't like it here, go somewhere else. It's just a job." However, this philistine approach to our calling as professing professionals jarred faculty members across the university. Mercer's greatest assets are teaching faculty who see molding students as a vocation—not just a job. The College of Liberal Arts has no monopoly on such faculty. From the School of Medicine to the College of Continuing and Professional Studies, most faculty have a strong sense of mission with their students and a deep sense of responsibility to their professions. What is shaky is their sense of "for what"? As market forces and bureaucratic rules increasingly reduce professionals to technicians for hire, professional formation at Mercer continues to focus primarily on knowledge and skills, failing to shape the professional character required to go against the grain of a reductionist culture.

Professional Formation at Mercer

Sullivan and May help us understand in a deeper, structural sense why liberal education is the contemporary university's bad conscience. It represents the professional schools' failure to ask "why"? May charges professional education with focusing on training technical intelligence rather than on developing critical intelligence: "Critical intelligence asks whether the 'theres' [of the professions] are worth getting to. This means raising all those liberal arts questions: what are our appropriate ends, goals, and values of the society at large and the professions in particular; and what are the fitting and appropriate means to those ends?"[7] Likewise, Sullivan argues that "changing domains of knowledge [and] shifting fields of practice" require that "[p]ractitioners must be able to think critically about their own situation and that of their field in relation to its defining purposes. ...This means that professional judgment has to be open to the expanding horizon typically associated with education in the liberal arts."[8] Both May and Sullivan connect this critical shift in perspective to professionals' responsibilities as citizens, "the art of acting in concert with others for the common good"[9] or "the capacity...to judge from the standpoint of social justice and the public welfare."[10]

Sullivan and May summon us to a liberalized conception of professional formation. Rather than it being the professional's duty simply to serve members of society, it is the professional's duty to challenge, summon, and transform society. Rather than simply being technicians at the beck and

---

[7] May, p. 127-128 in this volume.
[8] Sullivan, p. 112-113 in this volume.
[9] May, p. 127 in this volume.
[10] Sullivan, p. 113 in this volume.

call of civic and corporate authorities, professionals should be leaders shaping civic and corporate society toward genuinely public and humane goods. What would it mean to take these idealized conceptions of professional identity seriously as important elements of professional education? Must all practical education be liberal, as the AAC&U insists? How far are Mercer's professional schools willing to incorporate liberal education within professional education? How bad is their "bad conscience?"

And, to raise a second huge question, to what extent is the College of Liberal Arts willing to make liberal education practical enough that pre-professional students can see themselves and their futures in its counter-cultural resistances to the technocratic rationalization of life? Must we reform liberal education as well? Is it too much to expect our students to make the jump from a (more or less) coolly intellectualist liberal education to a civically responsible professionalism? Or, to put it in terms of "bad conscience," could it be that critical thinking taught in the abstract at the undergraduate level actually lends itself to the dissociation of technical training from civic responsibilities at the professional level?

Thus, our conversation leads us up to the brink of a rapprochement that would make liberal education the real conscience of the university—not its heart, not even its cornerstone—its *conscience*. Do we see the beginnings of a vision of liberal arts graduates with their hands prepared to change the world and professional graduates with their hearts set on change? Head, hands, and heart are Sullivan's three apprenticeships: "a preparation for professional life that integrates cognitive learning and practical skills with judgment and a commitment to the profession's particular public mission."[11] We have all the right pieces. Can we put them together at Mercer in a way that revitalizes liberal education and strengthens professional training?

---

[11] Ibid., pp. 105-106.

11

Confronting the Three Apprenticeships

Jack Sammons[*]

There is so much that is good and valuable in what Bill Sullivan said to us last night in the keynote address that one is hesitant to be critical—but critical we must be, for a criticism of his "three apprenticeships" understanding of professional education seemed to have emerged from the exercises today, despite the fact that everyone, myself included, appeared to be in agreement with his description of the problem with professional education and fully supportive of his efforts to address it. I think the criticism can be simply stated: even with a heartfelt plea for an "integrative approach" to the "three apprenticeships," his acceptance of a perceived division of professional education into the apprenticeships works against his overall purpose and reveals something of a misconception about how professional education works in practice. Essentially, what he has done is tell us to integrate something that is already *necessarily* holistic in *all* its aspects by telling us that there are parts that should be put back together by connecting each more closely to the others. Rather than this, I think what is needed for professional education, a need that emerged from our discussions today as I heard them, is a better understanding of what we mean by "professional education": what we mean by the "cognitive," as he uses this

---

[*] I would like to express to Mark Jones my deep appreciation and heartfelt gratitude for putting together the events in the Professionalism and Vocation Across the Professions Project and so much of this book. Mark has doggedly insisted for years now that members of the various faculties of the university advance beyond the parallel play to which they typically confine themselves. To this challenging task, and to the task of offering practical wisdom as a central pedagogical theme for the professions, Mark has been called. Like so many who are called, he was not naturally gifted for the task—Mark is more the scholar than the organizer—but he has become gifted in the doing. Thank you, Mark, for all this and especially for your friendship. Some good Aristotelian should warn you, however, that the gift of perfect friendship should not be offered to those, like me, who are not your equal in virtue.

term to distinguish the first apprenticeship; by "skills," the term used to distinguish the second; and by "professional identity," the distinguishing feature of the third, which Bill says requires the professional to act as an "engaged citizen." This understanding, an understanding of what we are already doing, is one that more directly confronts the positivism that Bill says, rightfully I believe, is one of the primary reasons behind the professional pedagogical problem he describes so well. So, simply put, the argument is that there are not three apprenticeships, and the perception that there are is the misunderstanding that needs to be addressed directly.

I want to start meandering towards this understanding with a brief reminder about something else that was said last night and a small clarification: Craig McMahan began our program praying for a blessing upon the professions, which, he said, "are extending God's care to the world." I will come back to this later on. Following Craig, Bill Sullivan started his speech with a description of the professions. It was a good one about social contracts, responsibility for public goods, and so forth, which, as good as it was, risked giving the impression that the professions were somehow meant to be as they are, rather than giving us the more honest description of them, one to be found in his book as having evolved from very particular, very contingent, and very historical traditions.[1] I very much doubt that the professions can be neatly distinguished from other practices using the distinctions Bill offered to us last night, at least at the margins and perhaps well beyond these. But defining the professions turned out not to be very important to anything we were talking about today, for the subject of those conversations was not "professions" really, but practices. A culture can sort out for itself which of its many practices it wants to treat as professions—that is, those to which it wants to give special status along with special responsibilities. And, in fact, Peter Brown's discussion group this afternoon saw this point almost immediately, talked about it briefly, and moved on.

So it was practices, as opposed to professions, to which we spent much of the day applying Bill's primary analytical tool of thinking about the education of our students through a cognitive apprenticeship, a skills apprenticeship, and an apprenticeship of professional identity, all of which,

---

[1] William M. Sullivan, *Work and Integrity: The Crisis and Promise of Professionalism in America,* 2nd ed. (San Francisco: Jossey-Bass, 2005).

he says, need to be more closely related. But I think everyone in the room last night listening to Bill's descriptions of the apprenticeships—probably including Bill—from the perspective of his or her own practice knew intuitively that the imagined distinctions among these apprenticeships are not going to be very sharp in practice. Given this, perhaps others wondered, as I did, if one profession could have a whole lot to say to another about these issues that would be relevant and meaningful. An overarching conception of what these distinctions consist of surely would not be of much help in addressing them within a particular practice. If we take law as our example, the particular virtue of the good lawyer—a central virtue, it seems to me—of seeing both sides of any honest dispute cannot truly be apportioned out to any of these apprenticeships without doing great harm to the virtue. Bill, I am reasonably sure, would be in complete agreement with this. But, if so, then it seems that the suggestion of moving an apprenticeship called the "cognitive" closer to one called the "skills" only exacerbates the problem. I am sure there are virtues that work this way in other practices, but it would not be for me, as a lawyer, to say what these might be. This is, of course, the problem we encountered with Bill's approach in a nutshell, but let me see now if I can move it out of its small container a little farther for better observation.

Practical Wisdom As Character Ideal of the Practice

There is something far more important behind Bill's analysis, and more central to it than he lets on, for what seems to lie behind his call for better integration within the three apprenticeships model is an Aristotelian conception of practical wisdom as a defining virtue—one that can, without too much harm to Aristotle or to any practice, be applied to all true practices. It is this virtue, practical wisdom, that can stand against viewing professional education as divided up into apprenticeships; stand against thinking of the knowledge of the cognitive apprenticeship as impersonal; stand against thinking of the techniques of the skills apprenticeship as "mere" techniques divorced from the teleologies of the practices in which they are techniques; and stand against a conception of the character required (or, for Bill, the "professional identity" of the third apprenticeship) as itself somehow separated from the practice—this time as Bill has recommended—in what we might think of as yet another apprenticeship, the one of the "engaged citizen." And this is what much of our conversations today have been about, or so it seems to me.

Confronting the Three Apprenticeships

Aristotle's virtues, especially this central one of practical wisdom, require not just a teleology (as, I think, all knowledge does), but a particular teleology of character. For the practices, this means the virtues require a character ideal of the practice, one that the practitioner seeks to become in his or her practice and, as he or she does, provides most of the motivation for virtuous behavior within the practice. It is this good—an internal good carried by the practice—that makes the practice a true practice more than anything else we might say about it. If you are with me on this, and willing to join me in thinking of Bill's analysis as really Aristotelian at its core, you can see that a recognition of the holistic nature of professional education is to be found by asking a rather straightforward question: Is the education of the practitioner, in all its forms, well grounded in the practice itself, especially in the relationships that constitute that practice? We can accomplish this grounding by asking of all our teaching a further question: Does this teaching move the apprentice towards the ideal of character of the practice? In simpler terms, am I as a teacher moving this person towards being a good X (with "X" being whatever practice you are in, e.g., a good lawyer, a good doctor, a good nurse, a good teacher, a good liberal learner, and so forth).

The Holistic Nature of Our Teaching

Now, it may seem to you that in insisting that we ask this question, I have already moved into Bill's third apprenticeship of professional identity, but the point here is that I have not; the point is that such thinking can never be, and in reality has never been, separated from any aspect of professional education. We are always answering this question in all of our teaching, whether we are conscious of this or not. To think that we are not is to accept what I will call here the positivist's mistake of thinking that there is a clear distinction between fact and value, a mistake that makes a mockery of the very idea of a practice.

There are many to whom we could turn to make this point. I will turn here to Michael Polanyi because, I think, his version of this, with just a little bit of twisting on my part, is the closest to the issue of professional education.[2] Let us start with the knowledge taught in the cognitive

---

[2] Polanyi is a very accessible writer and he has been made even more accessible for us in an excellent book by Mark Mitchell titled *Michael Polanyi: The Art of Knowing* (Wilmington DE: ISI Books, 2006) [hereinafter, Mitchell]. I will rely upon Mitchell here,

apprenticeship. Polanyi teaches that all knowledge is personal. This is true, in part, because all knowledge, including scientific knowledge, has a tacit dimension to it that requires "the constant integrating activity of the knower."[3] You might think here of how dependent a child's learning a language is upon the child's ability to integrate context into what is being taught. (The language analogy is a good one for our purposes because it applies across the board to all teaching, which is always, at least to some degree, a process of acquiring a language.) If, as Polanyi says, knowledge is rooted in a tacit dimension, then "all tacit knowing requires the continued participation of the knower, and a measure of personal participation is intrinsic therefore to all knowing."[4] But how can a new learner provide this participation? He or she does so, Polanyi argues, through what he calls "indwelling." The idea here is that the practical knowledge of any discipline always precedes all other knowledge the discipline may require, because practical knowledge is required for the integration that *all* knowing requires. How, then, can the student of a discipline practice its art before he or she has acquired it? By submission to an authority—specifically in our context, the authority of a teacher—and, thus, dwelling within the practice of the discipline through the teacher. "In order to share this indwelling, the pupil must presume that a teaching which appears meaningless to start with has in fact a meaning which can be discovered by hitting on the same kind of indwelling as the teacher is practicing."[5] If, however, "knowing is an art, and if learning an art requires dwelling in the practices of a master, then it follows that there must exist a tradition by which the art is transmitted."[6]

---

which I hope will encourage you to read the book as an introduction to Polanyi if you are not already familiar with his work. There is a wonderful short summary of Polanyi's work, placing it in the context of education and using it to examine the role of practical wisdom and the teaching methodology of case studies, in Paul Lewis, "Teaching to Form Character: A Polanyian Analysis of Practical Reasoning," in *Knowing and Being in the Intersection of Philosophical Traditions, Reconsidering Polanyi*, ed. Tihamer Margitay (Newcastle upon Tyne: Cambridge Scholar's Press, 2010) 80–95.

[3] Mitchell, 77.

[4] M. Polanyi, *Knowing and Being: Essays By Michael Polanyi*, ed. Marjorie Grene (London: Routledge and Kegan Paul, 1969) 152, cited in Mitchell, 77.

[5] M. Polanyi, *The Tacit Dimension* (Garden City NY: Doubleday and Company, 1966) 61, cited in Mitchell, 64.

[6] Mitchell, 64.

This reveals what Polanyi calls the "fiduciary framework" of all knowing, a framework that "can exist only in a social context rooted in a particular tradition into which members are inculcated."[7]

Notice an important implication here: the more tangible (think here of the detached knowledge of the positivist) the thing being taught is, the *less* real it actually is! Tangibility, since it never captures the true complexity of our knowledge of anything and always needs to be integrated in the act of tacit knowing, can never be a stand-in for the real. It is, instead, the "infinite richness of reality"[8] alone that deserves the title "real," and the process of coming to know something is, therefore, always open-ended and contingent. If this is true, however, then the positivist claim of a distinction between facts and values has disappeared, and (and this reveals much of what Polanyi was attempting to accomplish) "if…personal participation and imagination are essentially involved in science as well as in the humanities, meanings created in the sciences stand in no more favored relation to reality than do meanings created in the arts, in moral judgment, and in religion."[9]

There is one more point to be made before applying this to our context, and it is a point that takes us to the second apprenticeship of skills. For Polanyi, as I think you can readily see, all learning will occur within a multi-leveled reality of that which is being taught regardless of the practice. The higher level (higher in terms of the real, as he has described it) will govern the one below it, and the one below it will govern the one below it, and so forth. "Govern" is perhaps the wrong word, for what is meant here is that comprehending each level depends upon an understanding of the levels above it—either explicitly or, as is very often the case, tacitly—and the higher levels can never be understood as the sum of the parts of the lower ones, for each one below was already dependent upon the higher level. Each level, then, is a matter of what Polanyi calls "dual control"—that is, it is subject to its own rules, conventions, customs, and so on, and to those of the level above it. This is so because each level leaves some things indeterminate, things that are nevertheless essential to understanding that level.

---

[7] Ibid., 63.

[8] Ibid., 85.

[9] Michael Polanyi (with Harry Prosch), *Meaning* (Chicago: University of Chicago Press, 1975) 65, as cited in Mitchell, 100.

When reality is defined in these terms, so that at the highest level of our knowledge reality offers an "indefinite range of unexpected manifestations,"[10] the intangibles at the highest level (justice, beauty, morality, religion, etc.) suddenly appear as more real than the tangible at the lowest and—and this is important for us—necessary to understanding the tangible, necessary to considering it as real. All knowing, including all knowing within a practice, is embedded in just such a hierarchy.

Since the highest levels of a practice are always beliefs about what is real (and truth claims about those beliefs, which are themselves beliefs), they always provide the teleology towards which all learning within the practice moves and, in doing so, give meaning to all other levels. "Even the most elaborate objectivist nomenclature cannot conceal the teleological character of learning and the normative intention of its study."[11]

I have gone over Polanyi very briefly here with you to make a few very simple points, as you will see. Why bother, you might ask, if the points to be made are simple ones? The reason is that these simple points, I believe, mask a very different perspective on learning and our practices than the one now dominant in our culture. Polanyi, by taking on that culture directly, challenges us to reconsider what we think we know, and it is just such a reconsideration that is essential to our getting this professional education right—or so I believe.

What we have just said, through Polanyi, is that what is taught at the first apprenticeship in all practices *necessarily* "integrates" all learning within the practice, although we seldom notice that it does. All learning in the first apprenticeship is already holistic; it already not only presupposes certain skills of the second apprenticeship, but it also depends upon them for its meaning—and it is already teleologically driven towards the ideals of the practice. Initially, all this is provided by each of us through our students' trust that we are communicating honestly to them the fiduciary framework in which, and only in which, all that is taught makes sense.[12]

---

[10] Polanyi, *Knowing and Being*, 155, as cited in Mitchell, 112.

[11] Michael Polanyi, *Personal Knowledge: Towards a Post-Critical Philosophy* (Chicago: University of Chicago Press, 1958) 371, as cited in Mitchell, 108.

[12] I would like to offer an example of what I have said thus far and how it is different from what Bill Sullivan suggests. It is one that will be most relevant to law professor readers. Each practice, however, should have its own version of this example. First-year students in law schools typically are taught three or four or more basic courses—torts,

Confronting the Three Apprenticeships

Whenever we teach, we *always* are making a moral claim (or a truth claim, if you prefer, for only claims at that level can really be considered true if we follow Polanyi) on behalf of our practice. This is inherent in the act of teaching. We often seek to deny this, believing, for example, that at the lower levels we are only teaching knowledge of something called "facts," or knowledge of something called "skills" that have no moral implications and do not involve the personal for they can be used—it is up to the student, we

---

property, contracts, and criminal law most commonly—using the "case method" of instruction, an interactive reading of cases with each reading further refined by hypotheticals designed to test each reading and sometimes accompanied by a sequencing of cases in which a more refined rule emerges. This teaching, in accord with the argument in the text, is as much about professional identity (including the virtue of seeing good arguments on both sides previously mentioned in the text) and skills as it is about knowledge—more so, in fact. It is the primary shared shaping experience of lawyers, and the virtues it requires are central to any adequate understanding of what it means to be a lawyer. It is also, for all law students, a traumatic experience, for it offers the shock of knowing that certain practical skills, ones that are inevitably personal, must precede any understanding of the "rules" they thought they were there to learn. They have to become someone different (a different sort of reader, for example, but not just this)—we can call this a role if we want to, although the division between the role and self is never clear—before they can do what is being asked of them in these courses. This "role" includes within it a certain tolerance of ambiguities, contingencies, and an unspoken respect for that within the law that points beyond us. This teaching is "dual-controlled" in these ways. It is, I believe, the central moral moment in legal education and, thankfully, the theoreticians and policy mongers among us have had sense enough to leave it alone, never proceeding to the pedagogical conclusions of their own arguments. Now, the problem with this is that it is being abandoned. The forces at work in this come in part from those who divide professional education into apprenticeships, and for these the inherent mystery behind legal analysis just gets in the way of acquiring "knowledge" of the rules. These teachers typically abandon the traditional essays for testing and instead use multiple-choice questions, short answers, and so on to discover whether the students acquired the "knowledge" that was the real subject of the course. Others, seeing the tension in this, abandon the teaching method entirely. But in other part, the forces at work come from well-intended people like Bill Sullivan, who would assign the case method to the first apprenticeship and then urge us to integrate it with the other apprenticeships, which, in practice, means abandoning the case method and, I believe, risking losing that which is most important in it for professional educational purposes. Teachers who understand what they are doing in these courses do not need advice about "integration"; they need encouragement to explore the meaning of their teaching.

say; it is their choice—in many ways. This objectivism "seeks to relieve us from all responsibility for the holding of our beliefs."[13]

Notice, however, that the moral claim we make to our students, the only one that merits the trust they give us as teachers of a practice, is the one made, as I said, on behalf of our practice. When we get to the third apprenticeship, Bill wants to escape the responsibility we have to make a moral claim on behalf of our practices by shifting the moral claim, shifting the very ideal that defines the practice, to another practice, or, as I suggested above, yet another apprenticeship: the apprenticeship of the "engaged citizen." Whatever currency it may have had in times past, could there be a practice that offers less moral guidance of the sort he seeks and the sort our teaching requires? What could it possibly mean to say, for example, that whether or not a lawyer is to be considered a good one should be done with reference to citizenship, when the very issue that all lawyers always address in their legal arguments is the issue of our identity as a people? Surely, then, he does not really mean "citizenship," but, rather, uses the word to reference people who take into account in their work the interests of others and of the community, people who are not just self-serving, in other words. This, too, strange as it may seem, is deeply problematic as defining the moral standard for the good lawyer or the good doctor or the good accountant, and so forth, those professions, in other words, that morally obligate its practitioners to consider first the interest of those they serve. So, for example, to suggest that the good lawyer acts in the interests of the community is true only if we are willing to accept that giving a legal voice to everyone we can, including those who would destroy those values that we think of as defining us as a community, is nevertheless somehow good for the community. And even if we are willing to accept this, surely it is a moral claim more strongly made within the practice of law than the practice of being an engaged citizen. This is because, as a moral claim, it points towards a reality—specifically, a certain understanding of what justice requires—that transcends our community. Continuing with our example of legal practice, what Bill seems very reluctant to say is that the law can be understood only as in service to manifestations of justice that it believes to be true. What the practice of law seeks to do is uncover this justice for all of us within the mundane world of our legal disputes.

---

[13] Polanyi, *Personal Knowledge*, 323, as cited in Mitchell, 101.

Confronting the Three Apprenticeships

Could Bill's failure to describe the ideals of the third apprenticeship within the terms of the practices themselves, could his escape route of the "engaged citizen," reflect his own personal reluctance to abandon the security of the positivist's mistake he rejects? (If this sounds too personal, then you are part of the problem. It already was personal.) I hope he will be open to the possibility that this is the case, and if you agreed with him on this, I hope you will as well.

Let me go back now to the one question I said we need to be asking ourselves in all of our teaching: Am I as a teacher moving this person towards being a good X (with X being whatever practice you are in, e.g., a good lawyer, a good doctor, a good nurse, a good teacher, a good liberal learner, and so forth)? Now, of course, the difficulty here is in understanding the term "good." As I have just argued, it is not something that could be imposed upon the practice from the outside, however romantically or liberally tempted we might be to do this by reference to such vagaries as the "engaged citizen" or, and far more commonly, the "good person." It is instead something that is and has to be defined in an ongoing conversation within the practice itself about what it means to be a good X, and, and this is terribly important to what I have to say, this ongoing conversation *includes the one in the classroom*. All the conversations we have in the classroom—and here I mean *all* classes: basic classes, especially basic knowledge classes when you think this subject is not there; technical skills classes, especially technical skills classes when you think this subject is not there; statistics, mathematics, chemistry classes, for goodness' sake, when you think that the subject is not to be found in these; and so forth—have to be *haunted* by this "good X" hovering over the classroom in judgment of it, a judgment of both the teacher and the student that, in being judged together by it, unites them in the learning.

So, what we do in all of our classes, when we are at our best, is introduce our students to their appropriate voice within the very conversation that will define the thing they wish to become. It is circular, as many have noted, but not viciously so, and our task as teachers and as students is not to work our way out of the circle, but to work our way into it. Simple enough, right? So, why do we not do this, or if we do, why does it not work better? Why do we have to have conferences like this one, in other words?

Our Understanding of Morality and Self

There is much to be said, and much of it was said today in various ways, about the dominance of external goods—money, power, fame, security (the latter being the fundamental external good to which most others can be reduced), and so forth—that have corrupted our practices such that we hardly know any longer what they might offer against these external goods. For some practices and for many people (and for our entire culture, according to almost all economists), these external goods are the only remaining measure of success. As Tim Floyd reminded me last night, our mutual mentor, Dean Tom Schaefer, said that there is nothing wrong with lawyers and doctors that could not be cured by paying them like teachers and clerics. Yet the temptations offered by external goods have always been around. Why are they so dominant now? Why do they dominate practices now that were in times past *identified* by their avoidance of reliance upon external goods as measures of success? There is something going on here, something reflected strongly in each and every conversation I heard this afternoon. It was there in the background of our conversation in the morning, and in the afternoon it was brought to the fore. In one group it was a conversation about professional choice of clients and whether you could refuse service and things like that, and in other groups it took other forms. What is it? It is, I think, the recognition that what is at stake here—as you already have seen in our discussion of Polanyi—is nothing less than our understanding of morality and our understanding of the self.

As a matter of professional identity, professionalism means submitting oneself to the moral authority of a practice. As several groups noted, this authority is often expressed through mentors. Someone in one group said it is caught, not taught—a very nice way of saying it. This is, however, a problem. Submitting oneself to the moral authority of a practice is not something that those of us who were raised in the liberal tradition have any intention of ever doing, or so we pretend. We are just not going to submit ourselves to much of any moral authority that is not completely of our own choosing, especially the moral authority of our roles. (Now, we do this all the time, of course. The real prohibition is on public recognition that we are doing it or of thinking of ourselves in this way.) Our identities are not to be found in our work, so we believe, but within what we typically call our personal moralities and our private selves, which, we mistakenly think, are the foundations for the products of self-reflection that we then mistakenly call conscience. We do this because we all share the extraordinary conceit not only that we are good people who can stand in judgment of all of our social roles, but also that we know what it means to be good. I would like to assure you of something: I have no idea what it means to be a good person and I am not one. My own conscience, understood in these personal and private terms, changes dramatically after three beers, and I (and you) would be a fool to trust it.

To hold onto these identities of removed selves in which we have conveniently defined ourselves as very good, we divide our lives between personal moralities and role moralities, between private selves and public selves, and, once again, we have divided our world between fact and value by considering only the former as an object worthy of calling true. When we do this, we lose not only the integrated self, but also any conception of our practices that could make them something worth pursuing—worth being "called to," to use the right language for this. When we do this, the practices that *we have abandoned to the impersonal* are quite appropriately then described as constituted by a form of knowledge and of techniques that have nothing to do with who we are, because as mere techniques and impersonal knowledge, they can make no personal demands upon us.

In this, we remove our practices from the complexity, the contingency, and, yes, the tragedy of our lives so that we don't have to consider our complexity, our contingency, or our tragic nature. Another way of saying this is that we do this to avoid having to be authentic; we create a virtual self to avoid having to have a real self at all.[14] This, then, is a lie of convenience that we have made into a truth of necessity in order to preserve our conceptions of ourselves as above the fray of our own lives. It's exactly the opposite of Aristotle (and of Wittgenstein, Heidegger, Merleau-Ponty,

---

[14] In other words, by separating ourselves from our roles, we not only render the practices in which those roles are roles impersonal, but also lose the very selves we are seeking to protect. For the self that is now detached from that which it does—off stage we might say, to continue the metaphor, and looking in from the wings on something in which it "plays a part"—has abandoned the perspective that made it a self, that made it something entitled to be called "the personal" and the "person" something entitled to the revelatory value implicit in our use of that word. This detached self, because its perspective is that of an observer, literally cannot see the living and very human practice in which justice, in the case of legal practice, can be uncovered. Instead, something called "justice" can be examined only as a subjective standard that must be removed from that practice and, as such, nothing real.

Taylor, McIntyre, Hauerwas, Milbank, and of our own Polanyi, and on and on in what constitutes, I think, a counter-philosophical tradition within our culture). It is, in fact, a conception of the self that makes the practices, as we have been discussing them, quite impossible and Bill's educational reforms completely futile. You can't solve this problem by trying to make practices more human or more humane, as so many suggest, for the underlying problem is in the understanding of what being human or humane might mean.

Let me return then to Craig McMahan's prayer for us last night, the one with which I started these little polemical observations. The conception of our practice as "extending God's care to the world," which is what our practices honestly are, is not something from which you would wish to escape into a self, or avoid with a lie, or improve with something called the human, or think of in terms of the three apprenticeships, or judge on the standards of citizenship. It is not something in which the good to be done comes from you at all. It is one in which you are best described as a servant. This is a quest for self, as all good quests should be, but it is one in which you find that true self as you always do: by losing it.

Looking Forward

My guess would be that it will only be when practitioners, whatever their religion or lack thereof may be, are willing to listen to those like Craig McMahan, or Polanyi, or others that I heard here today who have the courage to ask us to see the world with very different eyes that we will have any chance of becoming good professionals, as strange and counterintuitive as this might seem to some.

Despite the good efforts of wonderful people like Mark Jones, who has worked tirelessly for us on the symposium and, in the process, motivated others to do the same—a task for which he was not gifted, but clearly called, and became gifted in the calling—I am not optimistic about our prospects for change or for institutionalization of the wonderful start Bill and Mark have given us here. If he is looking for outcomes, measurable or not, I hope that Mark will be pleased, and he should be, if we leave here today with a few new gadflies upon the riderless horses of impersonal knowledge and mere technique that our practices are rapidly becoming.

I think these gadflies might help in some cases; I *am* optimistic about this. I cannot be pessimistic about our practices when each day I face students who want, as much as they want anything, to be good at what they do, are eager to learn what being good at it means, and trust me to help. My students, like yours, I have learned, are at that point in their lives when they understand why Wittgenstein, who was a teacher like Cathy and Ann, a nurse like Helen and Pat, a philosopher like Peter and Dave's uncle, and an architect as well, always carried with him a worn piece of paper, rumpled up in his right coat pocket, with a line from Longfellow:

> "In the elder days of art builders wrought with greatest care each minute and unseen part for the Gods see everywhere."[15]

---

[15] Henry Wadsworth Longfellow, "The Builders" (1846) http://theotherpages.org/poems/longf05.html (accessed August 10, 2012).

Part III: Practical Wisdom in Practical Context

12

The War on Wisdom and How to Fight It

Barry Schwartz and Kenneth Sharpe[1]

We are very excited to be here. We thought that we were working in a vacuum, and it is incredibly gratifying to know, whatever comes of your project, that there is a group of people who take these issues very seriously. If everything breaks right, we may transform professional education, which certainly needs to happen.

I. Practical Wisdom in Professional Life

A. The Need for Practical Wisdom: Four Illustrations

Why do we need wisdom? One way to think about this is by considering four illustrations of wisdom in action in different domains of professional life:

---

[1] We did not ask the authors to prepare a paper for publication in connection with their keynote address at the 2008 symposium. However, after the idea for this book was conceived in 2009, we prepared an edited transcript from the videotape of their keynote address and this paper was developed based on that transcript. We are grateful to the authors for graciously agreeing to proceed in this manner so that the collection in this book could include all the important contributions to our project's development.

The authors delivered their keynote address jointly, using a tag-team approach. Barry Schwartz presented the material in the opening paragraph and in subsection I.A., section II., the opening paragraph of section III, and subsection III.A. 1–4. Kenneth Sharpe presented the material in subsection I.B., the first two paragraphs of subsection III.A., and subsection III.B. As indicated *infra,* note 16, the editors have reorganized the material in section III for the purposes of publication. In addition, the editors have incorporated certain material from the Q&A session following the keynote address in notes 11, 20, and 21. It also should be noted that note 17 refers to the authors' book, published subsequently.

1. *Physicians and Patients.* The first illustration comes from an article that Jerome Groopman wrote in the *New Yorker* several years ago.[2] Groopman is a distinguished oncologist at Massachusetts General Hospital, and we are largely going to be quoting him, or at least paraphrasing him.[3] So: You are Jerome Groopman, an oncologist, and you have just started treating Maxine, a thirty-year-old woman who discovered a pea-sized lump in her breast. Tests then reveal a malignant tumor and that the cancer has already spread to her spine and liver. Now, as she sits across the desk from you, accompanied by her parents and her fiancé, you have to tell her that, in all likelihood, she will be dead in two years. How should this conversation go? On the one hand, the canons of medical ethics—not to mention, more general moral principles demanding that we treat human beings with respect—require you to tell Maxine the truth. On the other hand, there are many different ways to tell the truth, there are many different truths, and your approach may determine whether this woman's last months of life are full of hopelessness and misery or whether she will have the strength to go through the rigorous treatment that awaits her with some measure of optimism.

So, you begin, or Groopman begins, by reviewing the facts—the size and location of the original tumor and the evidence of spread—but before complete hopelessness sets in, you quickly say that the cancer should be treated aggressively. "You stand a very strong chance of remission," you say. Now, your patient's mother responds with, "So, that means that she'll be okay?" And you realize that now you have to backtrack a little. You have to make clear that remission isn't a cure—that treatment may make the current metastatic deposits go away, but they will almost certainly come back in other places. Treatment is "palliative." But what does "palliative" mean? You go on: "We can knock down the cancer with drugs. Your bones and liver can heal. You can go back to living a normal life, and when [do you say 'when' or 'if'?] the cancer returns, we'll work to knock it down [do you say 'down' or 'out'?] again. Meanwhile, research may lead to new treatments that are far more effective than our current ones. So, at the very least, we are buying time."

Now what? You presented the best case, and their eyes are welling with tears. But you have to present a worst case also. You have to let the patient

---

[2] Jerome Groopman, "Dying Words: How Should Doctors Deliver Bad News?" *The New Yorker* (28 October 2002): 62.

[3] See ibid., 62–63.

know that the point may (or perhaps you should say "will") be reached at which treatments are no longer effective. You have to say this both because you owe your patient an honest assessment, and because she will likely face decisions about when to stop therapy. She should be thinking about this while she is still well enough to do so coherently.

Your patient seems satisfied. She doesn't seem to want to know any more. But then her fiancé chimes in. "What are the exact odds for a remission?" he wants to know. You look at him after stealing a quick glance at your patient. Does she want to know? Does she want this question answered? She doesn't seem to want to know. "Dr. Groopman says that there is every reason to think I'll go into remission." Does this comment let you off the hook? Or should you present the bald statistics that more than 50 percent of patients with this presentation die within two years? Should you find the gentle way of saying this that focuses on the positives—how young the patient is and how good her health is in general—on the principle that your patient would benefit both medically and psychologically from a little encouragement? And can you find a way to be encouraging without creating false hope? How well do the people sitting across from you understand statistics? How well do they know that "probable" does not mean "certain"? And that there is a distribution of courses to this illness, and at the tails of this distribution is a small number of people who die very quickly and a small number who live decent lives for many years? So, you choose not to answer the question directly, and instead deceive just a little by telling them how little statistics can tell us about any particular individual. You conclude by saying, "We need to plan for the best while acknowledging the worst."

All the while that you are having this painful conversation, you realize it is not just *what* you say that matters, but *how* you say it. If you hesitate too long before answering a bleak question, no matter how encouraging you are, they will think you are holding something back. If you are too upbeat in describing the most positive scenario, they will leave the office with unrealistic hopes. For you to pull this off, both the form and the content have to be just right. That's why a good doctor needs practical wisdom.

2. *Lawyers and Clients.* Here is the second illustration: the case of Mrs. Jones.[4] Mrs. Jones was a homeowner, a churchgoer, and a sixty-five-year-old, well-respected member of a lower-middle-class black community. After a minor traffic accident, she stopped to identify herself, but the other driver, a white woman, fled—and then called the police to report that Mrs. Jones was the one who fled. The police, without investigating, took the other woman's word for it. Even after the woman dropped the charges, the police insisted on prosecuting Mrs. Jones for leaving the scene of an accident.

A very young William Simon, now a very famous lawyer and professor, was asked by his law firm to defend Mrs. Jones. He knew she was innocent. She had been made to suffer both indignity and injustice. Simon planned to expose the racism of the police "through devastating cross-examination." He asked a friend with a lot of experience in traffic cases for help: dismissal on racism charges, he wondered? His friend rolled his eyes: not with this judge and this police department. And if Mrs. Jones lost—unlikely but possible—she would lose her license, she would be fined, and perhaps she would even face a jail term of up to six months.

The friend worked out a plea bargain with the prosecutor: to plead *nolo contendere* (neither admitting nor denying the charges); accept six months probation; apply to have the case sealed after a year; and Mrs. Jones's criminal record would disappear—no trial, no loss of license, no anxiety. Simon didn't like it. He felt Mrs. Jones deeply resented her recent abuse and a plea bargain would deprive her of any sense of vindication. But he presented it to her because he knew it was her decision. In court, before the trial, he laid out the plea to Mrs. Jones and her minister. They then asked his advice. "You're the expert," they said. "That's what we come to lawyers for."

And, this is Simon speaking: "I insisted that, because the decision was hers, I couldn't tell her what to do. I then spelled out the pros and cons…. However, I mentioned the cons last, and the final thing I said was, 'If you took their offer, there probably wouldn't be any bad practical consequences, but it wouldn't be total justice.' Up to that point, Mrs. Jones and her minister seemed ambivalent, but that last phrase seemed to have a dramatic effect on them. In unison, they said, 'We want justice.'" So Simon went back to his

---

[4] All Simon citations are from William Simon, "Lawyer Advice and Client Autonomy," in *Ethics in Practice,* ed. Deborah L. Rhode (New York: Oxford University Press, 2000) 165–76.

friend: "No deal. She wants justice." His friend stood for a moment in disbelief and then said, "Let me talk to her."

The friend laid out the same considerations. He didn't tell her what to do, but in making his presentation, he discussed the disadvantages of the trial last, while Simon had gone over them first. He described the remote possibility of jail at slightly greater length than Simon had, and he didn't conclude by saying it wouldn't be total justice. At the end of his presentation, Mrs. Jones and her minister decided to accept the plea bargain. As Simon said nothing further, that's what they did.

The principles of legal ethics told Simon that the client should have the autonomy to decide. And decide Mrs. Jones did. Twice. Differently. All it took was a sudden shift of frame: first a justice frame, then a criminal record frame. No attempt was made to understand Mrs. Jones's perspective. No effort was made to encourage reflection. Legal counsel was given in ten minutes just prior to walking into court.

3. *Teachers and Students.* The third illustration: grading papers.[5] This is something we encounter all the time. We suspect many teachers do. So, you are grading papers. You read one written by a student who is struggling to get a C. It's a B-/C+ paper. It is coherently organized, decently written, and evidences no major misunderstandings. But it is by far the best thing the student has done in your course. Then there is the paper by the smartest student in the class. She is effortlessly acing everything you throw her way. It is well written, clearly organized, and it demonstrates fine comprehension. It's a solid B+, perhaps an A-. But it lacks spark, it isn't very original, and it doesn't go very far beyond what has been said in class. The student definitely could have submitted a much better piece of work.

So, what grades do you give? Do you give the grades that they deserve? Well, yes, but what grades do they deserve? Should you grade according to some absolute standard, according to a relative scale, according to effort, according to improvement, according to fidelity to the texts, according to creative spark? What grade is the fair grade to give?

4. *Hospital Janitors and Patients.* A final illustration, much more prosaic, concerns some vignettes from the lives of hospital janitors. In hospital settings, which tend to be quite hierarchical, at the very bottom of the

---

[5] See Barry Schwartz and Kenneth Sharpe, "Practical Wisdom: Aristotle Meets Positive Psychology," *Journal of Happiness Studies* 7 (2006): 377–78.

hierarchy are the custodial staff, the people who clean up. A colleague of ours studied them and wrote some wonderfully detailed case histories.[6] Here are a few quotes from various hospital janitors: "Sometimes I might start waxing and a patient comes out and he wants to walk up and down the hall. He wants to get the exercise. As soon as I get ready, he'll start. I don't bother him. I'll just wait 'cause I know I can't tell them to go sit down. They need to build themselves up and that's what I have to tell my supervisor: 'Couldn't do it, 'cause the patients.'" Another one:

> I treat them with respect. I know that, you know, why they're here and, you know, like a lot of times when I go into the visitors lounge, you know, to clean, uh, I have to ask them, too. Sometimes I don't bother because a lot of times when I go in to clean, they'd be asleep. So, uh, but, you know, supervisors, my supervisor has told me that I'm supposed to do this and I'm supposed to do that, but I, I prefer not to, so sometimes I have to bite the bullet for that. But, uh, I try to work with them because I know, you know, some of the things that they're going through with their relative.

One last example—Luke:

> And there was this other guy who snapped at me. I kind of knew the situation about his son. His son had been here for a long time and…from what I hear, his son had got into a fight and he was paralyzed. That's why he got there,… and he was in a coma and he wasn't coming out of the coma and I heard how he got that way. He had got into a fight with a black guy and the black guy really, well, you know, because he was here. Well, I guess his father felt a little angry toward blacks and I went and cleaned his room. His father would stay here every day, all day, but he smoked cigarettes. So, he had went out to smoke a cigarette and after I cleaned the room, he came back up to the room. I ran into him in the hall, and he just freaked out…telling me I didn't do it. I didn't clean the room

---

[6] The research on hospital custodians was done by Amy Wrzesniewski and her collaborators. See A. Wrzesniewski and J.E. Dutton, "Caring Moves: Seeing the Competence in Interpersonal Citizenship Behavior," working paper on file with authors (2010); A. Wrzesniewski , J. E. Dutton, and G. Debebe, "Caring in Constrained Contexts," working paper on file with authors (2009); A. Wrzesniewski and J. E. Dutton, "Crafting a Job: Revisioning Employees as Active Crafters of Their Work," *Academy of Management Review* 26 (2001): 179–201; A. Wrzesniewski, J. E. Dutton, and G. Debebe, "Interpersonal Sensemaking and the Meaning of Work," *Research in Organizational Behavior* 25 (2003): 93–135.

and all this stuff. And at first, I got on the defensive, and I was going to argue with him. But I don't know. Something caught me and I said, "I'm sorry, I'll go clean the room."

The interviewer asked, "And you cleaned it again?" Luke said: "Yeah, I cleaned it so he could see me clean it...I can understand how he could be. It was like six months that his son was here. He'd be a little frustrated, and so I cleaned it again. But I wasn't angry with him. I guess I could understand."

So, these are three examples from many of the janitors describing the work they do every day. And what is salient about these examples, *all* of them, is that in the three-page job description for a "Custodian II"—wet mop floors and stairways, unplug commodes, collect and dispose of soiled linen—not a single task mentions another human being. None of this is part of their job as defined by the people who employ them and supervise them.

B. The Nature of Practical Wisdom

What are we to make of these choices by Groopman, by Simon, by teachers, by the custodians? They are not the "knock-your-socks-off" moral choices that we often teach in ethics classes—the ones about abortion or euthanasia or plagiarism. They are examples of small, common choices that are embedded in everyday practices. But they are deeply ethical choices: about when to be honest and how honest to be; about who should decide for a patient or a client (the patient's autonomy versus the professional's benevolence or, some would say, paternalism); about how to handle an unjust and maybe racially motivated accusation; about what's fair treatment for students; and about how to treat patients and their families who are dealing with adversity. So, how do we make these everyday ethical choices?

1. *The Insufficiency of Rules and Principles.* One thing we do is turn to rules and principles. They provide us with anchors, with guidelines. Examples include: be patient, be honest, be kind, respect a patient's autonomy, give the patient choices. However, such rules or principles are almost never enough.

Philosophers from Aristotle to Dewey and Wallace have reminded us that rules by themselves fail us.[7] There are several reasons for this. First,

---

[7] *Nicomachean Ethics: Aristotle*, trans. Martin Ostwald (New York: Library of Liberal Arts, 1962); John Dewey, *Human Nature and Conduct* (New York: Modern Library, 1930);

there is no rule or principle that tells us which rule or principle is relevant in a particular case. Is this a case that calls for honesty? Or is this a case that calls for kindness? No rule tells us. Second, principles often conflict with each other. How do we choose between letting the patient decide and paternalistically nudging the patient to pick the treatment we think is best? Or how does a parent choose between letting children make their own choices so they can learn to be independent, and making decisions for them to keep them safe? There is often no rule that decides between conflicting principles. Third, how does one apply a rule in any particular case? There is no rule to tell us how to be honest even if we know we need to be honest. There is no rule to tell us how to grade fairly even if we are disposed to grade fairly. We don't need to labor this; all of us know the problem with simply following rules because we all find ourselves saying from time to time, "Oh, there is an exception to every rule."

Aristotle captured both the problem and the solution with his famous metaphor of the lesbian rule, using that term somewhat differently than we would use it today.[8] Aristotle was particularly fascinated by how the masons on the Isle of Lesbos used a ruler. A normal straightedge wooden ruler allows one to measure the length of the stone that has to be cut. But what does one do when one needs to measure the circumference of a round column being carved from a slab of stone? The masons on Lesbos figured out a way to bend the rule by fashioning a flexible ruler out of lead, which of course is a forerunner of today's tape measure. And so, too, for moral rules: to get the measurement right, you have to know how and when to bend them.

2. *The Insufficiency of Character Virtues*. If rules fail as a guide, perhaps virtues might do the trick. Well, yes and no. In the last thirty years, there has been a great revival of Aristotelian ethics—a challenge to the rule and procedure-based ethics we encounter in Kant or utilitarianism. The primary concern in virtue ethics is with a person's character: enduring traits or virtues that guide a good life. Doing the right thing is first and foremost a question of being a certain kind of person, of being habitually disposed to be brave or caring or loyal or generous. On this view, virtues are learned

---

James D. Wallace, *Moral Relevance and Moral Conflict* (Ithaca New York: Cornell University Press, 1988).

[8] Unless otherwise noted, all references to Aristotle are from *Nicomachean Ethics: Aristotle*, trans. Martin Ostwald (New York: Library of Liberal Arts, 1962).

dispositions to act in certain ways—and they are guides, not rules. Moreover, they are anchored in emotion, not juxtaposed to emotions as rules are in modern ethical theories. They point us to the right thing. They point us to be loyal, to be fair, to be kind, and—this is where the emotion comes in—we desire to do the right thing because it is the right thing, because it is the aim of the practice. As Aristotle says, we learn to do the right thing, and for the right reasons.

It is such virtues that guide Dr. Groopman in wanting to give Maxine hope and trying to be honest with her, as well as kind.[9] It is because lawyer William Simon embodies fairness in his character that he is outraged at the injustice done to Mrs. Jones. It is because he is respectful of her autonomy that he wants her to choose whether to accept the plea bargain.[10]

So, the classical alternative to rules is character. But these virtues of good character are not enough either, even as a supplement to rules. They aim us in the right direction, they make us well intentioned, but they, too, are only guides. Without something else, they do not tell us when and how to balance kindness with honesty, or when loyalty deteriorates into blind loyalty, or how to be fair. That is why Aristotle was so insistent that we also know how to find what he called the "mean." Courage, he famously said, was not just fearlessness in the face of death, and retreating from the battlefield was not always cowardice. When he said that courage was the mean, or the balance point between recklessness and too much fear, he was telling us that we need the knowledge to find the balance in the context of the particular circumstance. Sometimes we need to stand firm, but it would be recklessness, not courage, to risk our lives in vain, so sometimes we need to flee to fight another day.

3. *Practical Wisdom and the Moral Abilities of the Wise Person.* Virtues, like rules, fail as a solution to ethical choices, absent something else—and that something else, not surprisingly given the topic of our lecture, is practical wisdom. Aristotle called it *phronesis.* It was for him a kind of master virtue: one that gave order, coherence, and direction to all the other virtues, that transformed them from unruly children into steady adults or that turned a cacophony into a symphony. This practical wisdom demanded more than just moral will, more than just the disposition, the wanting to do something;

---

[9] See *supra,* subsection I.A.1.
[10] See *supra,* subsection I.A.2.

it demanded a kind of expertise or moral skill. So, we cannot be virtuous, benevolent, brave, fair, or honest without practical wisdom, and the same holds true for the application of even good rules. We don't know what rule to apply, or what to do when two rules or principles conflict, without practical wisdom.

So, what, then, is practical wisdom? Admittedly, it is somewhat elusive. And simple definitions do not tell us much, although we can learn much from looking at individual cases. We could say, very abstractly, that it is the capacity to know the right thing to do in a particular circumstance and the motivation and courage actually to do it. We could say, rightly, that it is good judgment or horse sense or ethical intelligence. Our grandmothers would have listened to our philosophical jabber and said, "Ah, I know what you mean. It's being a mensch." Elusive as it is, we can say something about the moral abilities possessed by a wise person or a mensch.

First, a wise person knows that no two patients, no two students, no two clients are alike. So rules and standard procedures must always be crafted to the circumstances. For example, a wise person knows when and how to make an exception to every rule. A wise person knows when and how to be honest, and when and how to be kind.

Second, a wise person knows how to balance conflicting virtues and conflicting rules, how to find the mean—not just between cowardice and recklessness, but between empathy and detachment, or between fairness, treating all students alike, and giving this unique individual what he or she deserves.

Third, a wise person knows how to improvise, like a good jazz musician. Real-world problems are often ambiguous and ill-defined, and the context is always changing, so that circumstances demand ethical improvisation.

Fourth, a wise person can take the perspective of another to see the situation as he or she does, to understand how he or she feels. This perspective-taking is what enables wise people to feel empathy for others.

Fifth, a wise person aims at the right things, at the purpose of the activity in which he or she is engaged. These aims turn out to be crucial guides in figuring out the right thing to do in a particular circumstance. In fact, it is these practical aims that often motivate the wise person not only to do the right thing, but to do it for the right reason. And notice something else here. This means that wisdom is not just about judging. It is about doing. More colloquially: it's not just about talking the talk; it's about walking the walk.

Finally, a wise person is an experienced person. People learn how to be brave, said Aristotle, not by studying but by doing brave things. They learn it just as musicians learn improvisation in jazz through the experience of improvising. But it is not just any experience that teaches the skills of moral improvisation. Developing wisdom requires that people be able to take initiative, to make mistakes, to learn from mistakes.

To summarize, practical wisdom is ethical intelligence and ethical motivation. It is the moral skill and the moral will we all need to make ethical choices. Aiming at the right thing and desiring it is critical: that's the moral will. Knowing how to hit the mark is also essential: that's the moral expertise, the moral skill.[11]

II. The Threat to Practical Wisdom:
The Dangerous Allure of Carrots and Sticks

With this understanding of the nature of wisdom, let us now ask why we are engaged in a war on wisdom, something that is hard to understand since it would seem that this is how we want every doctor, lawyer, and teacher we ever encounter to be, and we want to be like this ourselves. So, why make war on wisdom? Well, no one is deliberately making war on wisdom. There is, rather, a stealth war on wisdom. It is largely the unintended consequence of the dangerous allure of carrots and sticks.

Practical wisdom is rooted in experience, but experience can have a dark side. The kinds of experiences professionals face in their daily work often threaten to corrode the very wisdom they need to do the work well. We think one of the major reasons for this is that managers, administrators,

---

[11] One might say that practical wisdom combines moral "know-how" with moral "know-why." Our understanding of practical wisdom, then, is different from that of William May, who does not seem to build the element of the *telos* or purpose of an activity into his understanding of practical wisdom itself but instead sees it as relevant to certain other virtues. See William May, "Forming Professionals and the Quest for Common Ground in the University," *supra* chapter 7, at 125-26. It is crucial to attend to the *telos* or purpose of the activity because moral skills or technique alone may enable a person to use them for great evil—for example, skills of empathy may enable a person to manipulate others, as when Iago feigns friendship with and manipulates Othello.

and policymakers reach for the wrong tools when they try to solve problems. They reach for carrots and sticks, incentives and rules, in an effort to change the behavior of professionals. But the more professionals rely on rules and external incentives, the more the wisdom they need is endangered. Let us consider some examples: first, some examples of the war on moral skill and then some examples of the war on moral will.

A. The War on Moral Skill: Rules and Procedures

The first example is titled "lemonade" and was featured on the NPR radio show "Morning Edition."[12] One day, early in spring 2008, a father, a professor of archeology at the University of Michigan, took his seven-year-old son to a Detroit Tigers game. A few innings into the game, his son asked for a glass of lemonade. The father dutifully went to a concession stand. "Mike's Hard Lemonade," which is 5 percent alcohol, was all they had; and the father, never having heard of it, bought some and brought it to his son.

While they were cheering on the Tigers, a security guard happened to notice the child sipping lemonade from the bottle. He called the police, who in turn called an ambulance. The ambulance came to the ballpark and rushed the child to the hospital. Fortunately, he had no trace of alcohol in him, and the doctors were ready to discharge him. But no, not so fast! The police put the child in a Wayne County Child Protective Services foster home. They hated to do it, but they "had to follow procedure." County officials kept him there for three days. They also hated to do it, but they also "had to follow procedure." Next, a judge ruled that the child could go home to his mother, finally, but only if his father left the house and checked into a hotel. The judge hated to do it, but he "had to follow procedure." After two weeks, the family finally was reunited. In telling this story on "Morning Edition," Scott Simon observed that "[p]rocedures may be dumb, but they spare you from thinking...And to be fair, procedures are often imposed because previous officials have been lax and let a child go back to an abusive household."

The second example concerns Judge Lois Forer, who was a judge in the Philadelphia Court of Common Pleas Criminal Division when she

---

[12] Scott Simon, "Music Cue: The Case of Mistaken Lemonade," *Weekend Edition*, National Public Radio, 3 May 2008.

encountered the case of Michael.[13] The case appeared to be quite typical, involving an accused who was young, black, and male, a high-school dropout without a job. The charge was an insignificant hold-up that had occurred the year before, occasioning no comment in the press. And, in the busy life of a judge, the trial itself was a very run-of-the-mill event.

Brandishing a toy gun, Michael held up a taxi and took fifty dollars from the driver and the passenger, harming neither. This was Michael's first offense, Forer explains:

> Although he had dropped out of school to marry his pregnant girlfriend, Michael later obtained a high school equivalency diploma. He had been steadily employed, earning enough to send his daughter to parochial school—a considerable sacrifice for him and his wife. Shortly before the holdup, Michael had lost his job. Despondent because he could not support his family, he went out on a Saturday night, had more than a few drinks, and then robbed the taxi.

"There was no doubt that Michael was guilty," said Judge Forer. But the penalty posed problems. The prosecutor wanted a five-year sentence. So Forer turned to the Pennsylvania sentencing guidelines, a state statute designed to give a similar sentence to offenders who commit similar crimes. The minimum sentence prescribed by the guidelines was twenty-four months. "I decided to deviate from the guidelines," she explained, sentencing Michael to eleven and a half months in the county jail and permitting him to work outside the prison during the day to support his family:

> I also imposed a sentence of two years probation following his imprisonment conditioned upon repayment of the $50. My rationale for the lesser penalty, outlined in my lengthy opinion, was that this was a first offense, no one was harmed, Michael acted under the pressures of unemployment and need, and he seemed truly contrite. He had never committed a violent act and posed no danger to the public. A sentence of close to a year seemed adequate to convince Michael of the seriousness of his crime.

Two years after Judge Lois Forer had sentenced Michael for the toy-gun hold up, Michael had fully complied with the sentence. He had successfully completed his term of imprisonment and probation. He had paid restitution

---

[13] This and other quotes from Lois Forer come from Forer's "Justice by Numbers," *Washington Monthly* 24/4 (April 1992): 12–18.

to the taxi driver. He had returned to his family and obtained steady employment. He had not been rearrested. But Forer's sentence had not sat well with the prosecutor. He appealed her decision, asking the Pennsylvania supreme court to require Forer to re-sentence Michael and to send him back to prison. Forer said:

> I was faced with a legal and moral dilemma. As a judge I had sworn to uphold the law, and I could find no legal grounds for violating an order of the supreme court. Yet...[t]he usual grounds for imprisonment are retribution, deterrence, and rehabilitation. Michael had paid his retribution by a short term of imprisonment and by making restitution to the victims. He had been effectively deterred from committing future crimes. And by any measurable standard he had been rehabilitated. There was no social or criminological justification for sending him back to prison. Given the choice between defying a court order or my conscience, I decided to leave the bench where I had sat for 16 years. That didn't help Michael, of course; he was resentenced by another judge...Faced with this prospect, he disappeared.

The third example is the story of Christine Jabbari, a kindergarten teacher in Chicago.[14] She began her fifty-third day teaching at Chicago's Joyce Kilmer Elementary School with a clear lesson plan. She opened a thick white binder on her desk to Day 53. Twenty-six thousand other Chicago teachers had identical binders crammed with goals, conversation starters, and step-by-step questions. What Ms. Jabbari saw was this:

> Script for Day: 053
> TITLE: Reading and enjoying literature/words with "b"
> TEXT: *The Bath*
> LECTURE: Assemble students on the rug or reading area. ...Give students a warning about the dangers of hot water. ...Say, "Listen very quietly as I read the story." ...Say, "Think of other pictures that make the same sound as the sound bath begins with."

Her students sat cross-legged on a corner rug. The children's book *The Bath* was not available, so Ms. Jabbari chose *Jesse Bear, What Will You Wear?* But no matter. She still began with the script, reminding them: "It's always

---

[14] Jacques Steinberg, "Teachers in Chicago Schools Follow Script From Day 001," *New York Times*, 26 November 1999.

safe to have an adult around when you take your bath." We could read you all of the script. Unfortunately, there are seventy-five items after the ones I just read for teaching five-year-olds the letter "b."

So, these are three examples of people who are following rules. The rules are well intentioned, to be sure: we follow procedures so that parents will not abuse their children again; we have sentencing guidelines to eliminate any apparent inequities in criminal sentencing; we have rule-driven, lock-step curricula in the classroom because we do not trust teachers to be able to use their judgment to form lesson plans on their own.

Now imagine that a similar set of rules governed the behavior of the custodians described previously. The custodians would no longer engage in any of the activities we discussed, because none of those activities is a part of their job. Wisdom is learned, but it cannot be taught. To become wise, people must try, fail, learn from their failures, and try again. Rules are designed to prevent mistakes, and rightly so. Some mistakes are just too serious and must be prevented. But the price that is paid for too many rules is that they deprive people of the opportunity to learn from their mistakes, which in turn undermines their ability to improvise, to find solutions to problems that rules cover imperfectly or not at all. And if one accepts, as previously discussed, that virtually all situations are situations that rules cover imperfectly or not at all, anything that impedes the ability to improvise is likely to produce disastrous results.

The reliance on rules is a war against mistakes, a war against trial and error, a war against discretion, a war against judgment—all of it well intentioned. Furthermore, it is self-reinforcing, not self-correcting. The more we take moral skill out of practices, the less wise practitioners will become. And the less wise practitioners become, the more rules we will need to create to make sure they do the right thing.

B. The War on Moral Will: Incentives

Instead of rules, then, perhaps we can come up with clever incentives that will *induce* people to do the right thing. We know, of course, that it is easy to give people incentives to do the wrong thing. When we see such things, our response tends to be, "Well, some dummy set up these bad incentives. Just let me in, roll up my sleeves, and I'll change the incentives so that instead of getting paid off for doing bad things, people get paid off for doing good things." The problem is that even good incentives fail. Let us consider two examples among many.

The first example concerns a daycare center in Israel.[15] Parents were coming late to pick up their children. The daycare center closed at 6:00 in the evening, but they were coming at 6:10, even 6:15. It was discourteous; the teachers could not very well lock the door and leave the children sitting on the stoop; and appeals to the parents to show up on time seemed to have no effect. So, the director of the daycare center had a very clever idea—a fine: If you come late, you pay a fine. Guess what happened? Lateness did not decrease; it *increased*. And it did so because the fine—which was meant to convey a message that the parents were misbehaving, that they were transgressing—was interpreted by them not as a fine, but as a *price*; and it was a price worth paying. No doubt the fine could be set high enough so that it would not be a price worth paying, but the important point is that by giving the fines to parents, the daycare center essentially legitimized their coming late. In effect, the parents said to themselves, "I know the rules. If I am willing to pay the fine, I will pick up my child whenever I can get there; and paying fifteen bucks for an extra half an hour in the office is well worth it to me."

So, very clever incentives can end up actually having an effect opposite to what is intended, and indeed can actually make matters worse. And here is another interesting thing. Since the fines did not work, the daycare center stopped imposing them. But lateness *continued* to be worse than it was before. What happened was that the incentive—the fine—had *de-moralized* lateness, and having de-moralized it, one could not *re-moralize* it simply by taking a financial incentive away. The daycare center had altered the moral status of this behavior in the minds of parents, and for at least six months after this regimen of fines, the lateness problem persisted.

A second example that we all know about is teaching to the test: "No Child Left Behind"—standards, standards, standards; accountability, accountability, accountability. This may all be well intentioned but the results are often not good education or good teaching. Teachers end up aiming at what is being measured and incentivized—high test scores, for example. But teachers, in some dramatic cases, have found ways to get their test scores up by cheating in ways that ensure their students do well. Or in less dramatic cases, they simply teach what will be on the test without concern for whether

---

[15] For a discussion of the daycare case, see Uri Gneezy and Aldo Rustichini, "A Fine Is a Price," *Journal of Legal Studies* 29 (2000): 1–17.

or not this is what their students actually need to learn. Be careful what you measure, because what you measure is what you'll get.

We recently encountered a striking instance during which teachers were advised, in dealing with individual students, to pay attention to students who are "on the bubble"—that is to say, those students who are not going to pass the test without special attention, but who are close enough to passing the test that giving them special attention will nudge them over the right side of the line. In other words, the teachers are told not to waste their time with students who are far from the "bubble" because they are still not going to make it; the critical objective is to get the school's test scores up by focusing only on those students who are on the "bubble" and nudging them in the right direction. Low-performing students with little chance of doing well are ignored.

What often happens, then, when behavior is incentivized is something called "moral crowding out." Take someone who is acting for moral reasons, because it is the right thing to do. Incentivizing the behavior, however, implicitly sanctions thinking about it in different terms. The question of right or wrong stops being relevant, and the question instead becomes: Is this in my interest or not? In this way, even good incentives can have a bad effect.

C. Assessment

The responses we have seen so far from public officials to the collapse of our financial system are a perfect example of what we are talking about. Many people have many ideas about how to fix the problem in the short run, and many people have ideas about how to fix the problem in the long run. Every single idea seems to fall into one of two categories: We need better regulations, or we need smarter incentives. If we could just adopt better rules or provide smarter incentives, bankers would be bankers instead of being whatever it is they have been for the last ten years. There is no mention at all that we might be able to solve or mitigate this problem by re-moralizing the activities in which the bankers have been engaged.

Each set of rules and incentives is a response to past failures of previous rules and incentives. But the problem is that water will find any crack. There *is* no set of rules or set of incentives clever enough and subtle enough to prevent people from subverting them if people are not inclined to do the right thing because it is the right thing. And so, there is a downward spiral. It is very similar to addiction. If you are an alcoholic and you wake up hung over at seven o'clock in the morning, you treat the hangover by taking another drink. This is an effective way to eliminate the hangover in the short run. But, as we all know, in the long run it makes the problem worse. Rules and incentives may be effective ways to treat problems in the short run, but our view is that, in the long run, like taking another drink, they make worse the problem they are designed to correct.

III. Fighting the War on Wisdom

If we are convinced about the importance of wisdom, and that there is a war against it, certain questions arise: What can we do about it? How can we defend wisdom in our professions? Is the best defense a good offense? What is the role of professional education in cultivating wisdom? In this section we will explore some tentative answers to these questions.[16]

A. Waging the War in the Professions

The institutions that professional practices inhabit—the HMOs, the construction firms, the law firms, and even many universities—may share some of the intrinsic aims of the professions, but they also need to stay afloat. They need to worry about external goods: like gain, and like glory, status, and power. So there is a built-in tension between the practices of the professions and the institutions these practices inhabit. The professions can only survive inside of those organizations, but those organizations often aim at different, very contradictory things. The last three decades have shown how hard it is to manage these tensions. We have witnessed how the twin forces of mammoth size (mega medical institutions, mega law firms, and mega universities) and market competition create a logic to control the behavior of professionals with exactly the carrots and sticks we think have been so dangerous.

We do have some concrete illustrations demonstrating how large, hierarchical organizations can reform to nurture character and wisdom—for example, a law firm in Buffalo, a big city veterans' court, a medical training

---

[16] In section III the editors have reorganized the material presented in the keynote address for the purposes of publication. In particular, in the keynote address the material that is now the opening paragraph of section A and the material in subsection A.1–4, presented by Barry Schwartz, was delivered after the material in the first two paragraphs of subsection A and the material in subsection B, presented by Kenneth Sharpe.

program in Cambridge, Massachusetts, and a school system in Vermont.[17] The present discussion, however, will focus on some general principles for managing the tensions, and for encouraging virtue and wisdom, in our professions.

1. *Appreciating and Defending Practical Wisdom.* First, we must appreciate the importance of practical wisdom and be able to defend it in words and argument. It is an understatement to say that encouraging wisdom has not been a central aim of most academic and professional institutions. We must be able to show what practical wisdom is and why it is critical to being a professional. Practical wisdom is not an add-on, something that is nice to have along with technical expertise. Rather, it is essential—we cannot serve others unless we know what service is; unless we know what to aim at; unless we have the moral expertise to act on these aims with this particular person, in this particular context; and unless we have the will, the moral will, the motivation to do it. During the last few years at Mercer, in your conversations about the values and virtues of professionalism, you have made very important strides in this direction.

2. *The Role of Management and Administration in Nurturing Wisdom.* Second, we need to engage management and administration and help them figure out ways to nurture wisdom instead of undermining it. As discussed above, the institutions in which we practice our professions are always in tension with these professions. The institutions need gain, they need glory, and they need power to survive. Our professions aim at caring for the human body and spirit, at protecting safety and promoting health, at promoting happiness and minimizing suffering and pain, and at educating minds and hearts. But we cannot practice these professions outside of the institutions that support them; and these institutions will implode, just like the market has imploded, if they undermine the virtues and the wisdom that are part of our practice. We must take the lead in managing this ongoing tension, and that demands not only commitment, but also organization and struggle.

A good first step would be to understand what de-motivates and de-skills us as teachers. What are the structures in our own colleges and universities and professional schools that are undermining or diverting us

---

[17] See Barry Schwartz and Kenneth Sharpe, *Practical Wisdom: The Right Way to Do the Right Thing* (New York: Riverhead, 2010) ch. 12.

from the goods of teaching, getting us to aim at the wrong things or corroding our motivation? What are the structures that are undermining our moral skills? Is it class-size? Is it lack of contact with students? Is it a system of rules and incentives that prioritizes research and makes students seem a threat to advancement? If we are to be the kind of reflective practitioners that Donald Schön[18] and William Sullivan have written about,[19] that reflection has to begin at home with the practice of teaching and the policies and structures that shape it.

3. *De-Emphasizing Rules and Incentives.* Third, we need to resist the temptation to confront every problem by reaching into our toolkit and pulling out another carrot or another stick. Incentives and rules can change behavior, but they risk corrupting our ethical expertise and will. We need first to ask: What will this carrot or stick do to the moral will and the moral skill that people need to do the right thing? And we also need to ask: Can training, counseling, mentoring, or modeling solve the problem better? The golden rule for using rules or incentives is this: rules and incentives should be tools of last resort; try character and wisdom first.[20]

4. *Re-moralizing the Professions.* The final thing we need to do, and this is implicit in everything else, is to pay attention to re-moralizing the professions.[21] We need to think about what we teach, and the kinds of

---

[18] See Donald Schön, *Educating the Reflective Practitioner: Toward a New Design for Teaching and Learning in the Professions* (San Francisco: Jossey-Bass, 1987).

[19] See William M. Sullivan, *Work and Integrity: The Crisis and Promise of Professionalism in America,* 2nd ed. (San Francisco: Jossey-Bass, 2005); and Sullivan's "Professionalism and Vocation Across the Professions," *supra* chapter 6.

[20] It is not that rules and incentives do not have their place, but they have to be kept *in* their place. Rules and incentives are among those things that simplify complexity. Ideology is something else that simplifies complexity, by interpreting everything that happens in the world through one particular lens. Rules and incentives alone, like ideology alone, make it impossible to come up with wise solutions to complicated problems. They may be important, and provide an initial moral orientation, but one must often go beyond them to achieve a wise outcome in a particular case.

[21] Re-moralizing has two related meanings. Because we think professionals have lost morale due to the way they are forced to practice, the first meaning of re-moralizing is re-motivating or re-dedicating. The second meaning is reintroducing the moral dimension. And we think that if you re-moralize in the second sense, you will re-moralize in the first sense. Using cold, rational, technical expertise just to make money demoralizes. People are happy when they have close connections with other people and do meaningful work. And,

experiences we encourage. That means that we need to do more than hash out the common ideals of service and vocation to which we want to commit ourselves. That's important, but we also need to reflect on how to become wiser teachers if we are serious about having our professional students learn wisdom from us. And they *are* going to learn *something* from us. We want that something to be wisdom. To do this, we need to take heed of the words of that famous—if under-recognized and, until recently, under-appreciated—neo-Aristotelian Karl Marx: "The educators themselves must be educated."[22]

B. Waging the War in Professional Education

Let us explore this last point in some more detail. What can professional schools like those here at Mercer do? How can they develop practitioners who are dedicated and wise enough to practice well, but also wise enough to resist some of the corrosive forces that threaten to undermine moral will and moral skill? How can we encourage dedication and wisdom in our students, whom we are sending out into a rather cruel world?

1. *Structuring Experiences to Teach Elements of Practical Wisdom*. To begin with, recall the paradox, an important one for teachers or educational planners: wisdom can be learned, but wisdom cannot be taught. The rules and ethical principles and moral decision-making procedures and algorithms we can teach in an ethics class may point students in the right direction, but this is not how they learn the moral skills and moral will to be wise. What is important in the real world of practice is having the ethical

---

if our story is right, practical wisdom is necessary for both of those. And so, practical wisdom is necessary for happiness, which is, of course, what Aristotle thought. Think of George Bailey, the local banker played by Jimmy Stewart in the movie *It's A Wonderful Life*. (F. Capra, Director [1946] Liberty Films). George Bailey is not in banking as a charity. He, and his bank, must make money to survive. But the purpose of banking is not simply the making of money. Banking aims to organize capital in a community so that borrowers can build homes and businesses and educate their children, so that lenders can make interest on their deposits, and so that the community can develop. And doing that work well allows George Bailey to flourish. He can have a wonderful life serving others—giving loans to those who need them and taking care of and being responsible for their money. In that practice, then, he can do well while doing good.

[22] Karl Marx, *Theses on Feuerbach* (1845) http://www.marxists.org/archive/marx/works/1845/theses/index.htm (accessed August 11, 2012).

expertise or know-how to handle situations that are almost always difficult and ambiguous. Teachers cannot teach moral know-how with a lecture, with a book, or a test. So, practical wisdom can be learned but it cannot be "taught." But there is a second paradox here that most of you know from your own teaching and learning: wisdom cannot be taught, yet we are teaching it in almost every encounter we have with our students. We do this by the examples we set, by the ways we mentor, by how we counsel. So, the fact that we cannot teach practical wisdom in any simple or straightforward way does not mean we should give up and that nothing can be done in the classroom. Teachers *can* structure experiences in ways that encourage students to learn wisdom.

There are many good examples of such experiences. There is a pilot project at Harvard, which Dr. Jerome Groopman helped devise, that assigns first-year students to faculty members who serve as mentors and that matches the students with a patient they are tasked to follow for a year. They write a casebook about the patient and his or her disease, not only about the genetics of the disease and the treatment options, but also about the patient's emotions, suffering, financial difficulties, and family situation.[23] Many law schools organize hands-on law clinics that mentor students in practical wisdom by exposing them to real-life, ill-structured, ambiguous cases. The students are not just role-playing the plaintiff or the defendant or the judge, but taking responsibility for real people, not names in a casebook.[24] Various professional schools use narratives and stories to teach wisdom. In her highly readable little book called *Poetic Justice,* Martha Nussbaum discusses her experience using novels at the University of Chicago Law School to help lawyers-to-be understand other people "from the inside" in order to appreciate what a situation and the people in it require.[25] Dr. Rita Charon at the Columbia University Medical School has her medical students keep a parallel chart, a notebook in which they write their feelings about a patient with whom they are working. These notebooks then become an integral part

---

[23] See Melanie Thernstrom, "The Writing Cure," *New York Times Magazine* (18 April 2004): 42.

[24] See, for example, William M. Sullivan, Anne Colby, Judith Welch Wegner, Lloyd Bond, and Lee Shulman, *Educating Lawyers: Preparation for the Practice of Law* (San Francisco: Jossey-Bass, 2007).

[25] Martha Nussbaum, *Poetic Justice: The Literary Imagination and Public Life* (Boston: Beacon Press, 1995).

of teaching perceptiveness and empathy to doctors-to-be who take her literary narratives course.[26]

Stories can serve another function, too. Whether fictional or real, they can provide moral exemplars, prototypes that motivate and guide us. They put in our minds an image of what work well done looks like, an image of what a good professional looks like. It could be an exemplary figure from a book or a movie: the lawyer Atticus Finch in *To Kill a Mockingbird* comes to mind.[27] It could be an exemplary figure from history: for John F. Kennedy, for example, it was the great senators like Daniel Webster and Robert Taft he wrote about in his book *Profiles in Courage*.[28] When we just train our students in the massive, ever-growing body of technical detail, there is always a risk of inadvertently demoralizing young professionals. Finding ways to keep aspirational exemplars at the center, even while we do the technical training, can sustain the commitment many students start with and help re-moralize the professions.

2. *Characteristics of Wisdom-Inducing Experiences.* There is already much local knowledge right here at Mercer about how to structure experiences that teach and encourage practical wisdom; indeed, that is what the workshop tomorrow is all about. Simply talking at a university across programs and across disciplines about what is already being done can trigger all sorts of ideas. To frame some of these discussions, we will conclude by mentioning and illustrating three characteristics we have observed about what might be called "wisdom-inducing experiences" that can take place at universities.

First, wisdom-inducing experiences give students practice reflecting upon their experiences, and provide opportunities to engage in such reflection with each other and with teachers. You can ask: How did you make that tough call? Why did you shade the truth in this way with that patient? Why didn't you tell that client about plea bargaining after you explained the risks of going to trial and losing? Notice that such reflection takes place together. It is not just teachers critiquing and suggesting, and it is not just teachers lecturing. So, we need to find ways to help teachers teach judgment without being judgmental, which itself takes more than a modicum of wisdom.

---

[26] See Thernstrom, *supra*, note 23.
[27] Harper Lee, *To Kill a Mockingbird* (New York: HarperCollins, 1960).
[28] John F. Kennedy, *Profiles in Courage* (New York: Harper & Brothers, 1955).

Second, wisdom-inducing experiences are ones in which the possibility for trial and error is built in. Dr. Groopman tells the following story about learning to deliver bad news:

> Claire Allen was a small, straw-haired librarian in her forties with breast cancer; she was married, with two young children. ...We met in my clinic office, and she looked at me expectantly.
> "Claire, with this disease, a remission would ordinarily last three to six months," I told her bluntly. "A person could expect to survive between one to two years."
> She appeared to take the news stalwartly, but I later learned from her husband that she had left the appointment deeply shaken. She told her children that she had only one Christmas left. Her face was full of despair whenever I saw her. And yet Claire lived for nearly four years. She was able to travel, work part time, and take care of her children, but was unable to stop thinking that she could die at any moment.
> Chastened, I tried a different approach. Henry Gold, a short-order cook in his sixties, had acute leukemia that had resisted all treatment. At one point, he asked me what else could be done. I reassured him that there were drugs that had not yet been tried, even though I knew they were unlikely to help. When Henry started to bleed around his lungs, I had the interns drain the hemorrhage with test tubes; I insisted he be intubated, supported on the respirator in the I.C.U., and given numerous blood transfusions. His heart developed a dangerous arrhythmia, so I gave orders for cardiac medications and electroshock. I never asked Henry what he wanted. He stayed alive for more than a week on the respirator, a catheter in his heart, tubes in his throat, unable to speak to family and friends who had come to his bed-side.[29]

Groopman characterizes these decisions as "early blunders."[30] They are not surprising, however. It is difficult, he says, for doctors to deliver bad news. Some doctors do not want to acknowledge their patient is going to die; there is always the possibility of one more test, one more procedure.[31] Moreover, until recently it was the conventional wisdom that doctors should

---

[29] Groopman, *supra*, note 2, at 64–65.
[30] Ibid., 70.
[31] Ibid., 68.

spare patients the anguish of knowing they were going to die and should keep them optimistic.[32]

It takes some wisdom to build such experiences into our teaching. Think of the delicate balance: we don't want professionals to make mistakes, but the only way they will learn practical wisdom is by learning from their mistakes. We need to structure experiences where students are both trained and motivated to get it right—and where they feel safe to exercise discretion and make mistakes. A number of interesting programs that are now being tried in medical schools actually bring in professional actors trained to be patients, have the students work with those actors, and let them make their mistakes.[33] More comprehensive efforts at medical school reform have introduced problem-based and case-based learning models. Perhaps most interesting are the "longitudinal integrated clerkship" programs for third-year students. In these hands-on models, students are assigned to a group of faculty for six months to a year, and they are assigned a group of patients whom they intensively follow for the whole time.[34] But having programs like these demands an organizational structure that actually builds trust between faculty and students, where everyone takes at least some responsibility for their mistakes, and where fear of punishment does not give the student an incentive to hide or cover up or dissemble.[35]

The third characteristic is this: As teachers, we need to be modeling proper motivations and moral skills ourselves. Groopman reflects on his own experiences as an intern and resident:

> [D]uring my nine years of medical school and professional training in the nineteen-seventies, I was never instructed in how to speak about dying to a gravely ill patient and the patient's family. It was presumed that, as medical students, we learned how to deliver bad news through careful observation of our mentors, just as we learned how to lance a deep

---

[32] Ibid., 64.

[33] See, for example, Howard Barrows, "An Overview of the Uses of Standardized Patients for Teaching and Evaluating Clinical Skills," *Academic Medicine* 68/6 (1993): 443–53.

[34] See, for example, Molly Cooke, David M. Irby, and Bridget C. O'Brien, *Educating Physicians: A Call for Reform of Medical School and Residency* (San Francisco: Jossey-Bass, 2010), especially 80–89.

[35] For a case example at Harvard Medical School, see Schwartz and Sharpe, *Practical Wisdom*, ch. 12, *supra*, note 17.

abscess by watching doctors and trying it ourselves. But most physicians preferred to speak to their patients in private. And the subject was never raised in our classrooms.[36]

The Groopman story highlights the second paradox mentioned earlier. Although wisdom cannot be taught, as teachers we are actually teaching it all the time. When we go in front of a class, when we advise students in our offices, when we grade their papers, we are role models, whether we want to be or not. When we choose whom to call on in class, or whose answers to criticize, and what tone to use, we are modeling fairness. When we listen to students, when we choose whether to ask or to tell, we are demonstrating how to balance empathy and detachment. When we choose whom to interrupt and how to interrupt them, we are demonstrating when patience or impatience is justified. When a student challenges our conclusions or points to our mistakes, our response will be a model for how people deal with error, with uncertainty, with criticism. And, when we blow it, as we inevitably do, we can take comfort in Will Rogers's famous aphorism that the only way to learn good judgment is through experience, and most of that experience is the exercise of bad judgment.

---

[36] Groopman, *supra*, note 2, at 64.

13

Practical Wisdom and Vocation in Professional Formation: A Schematic Account

Mark Jones[*]

This brief essay offers a schematic account of practical wisdom and vocation in professional formation. I first develop a generic schematic model for practical wisdom that can be applied to many decision-making domains—personal, political, and professional. The model is intended to accommodate the development and articulation of varying detailed substantive accounts of what, more precisely, may be involved in acting with practical wisdom and/or of how to help cultivate the capacity to do so.[1] Such accounts may vary, presumably, depending on the decision-making domain in question. In the following section of this essay, for example, I apply the model to professional practice. I then conclude with an account that considers the implications of the model thus applied for a proper understanding and discernment of professional vocation or calling, although again this account is intended to be expansive enough to accommodate the development and articulation of varying detailed substantive accounts of what, more precisely, may be involved in having and/or in cultivating a sense of vocation or calling.[2]

---

[*] I would like to thank Peter Brown, Paul Lewis, David Ritchie, and Jack Sammons for sharing their wisdom during the drafting of this schematic account. Even though I take sole responsibility for its contents, and even though they may perhaps not agree with every detail of the account, much of it has originated with them rather than with me.

[1] See, for example, the accounts given by Barry Schwartz and Kenneth Sharpe, David Ritchie, and Jack Sammons in the present part III of this volume. See also the accounts of moral expertise given by Darcia Narvaez and Thomas Lickona in part I. Of course, this does not imply that the originators of these accounts would necessarily agree with all aspects of the analytical framework or "scaffolding" set out here.

[2] See, for example, the accounts given by William Sullivan, William May, John Dunaway, Timothy Floyd, and Jack Sammons in part II of this volume. Once again, of

Practical Wisdom in General

Practical wisdom is relevant and desirable across the entire range of matters requiring practical judgment and action. Practical wisdom *in general* may be defined as the master virtue that enables a practically wise person (a *phronimos*) to act well in context, to do "the right thing in the right way at the right time," and thus flourish as an authentic human being in community. More specifically, it enables the *phronimos* to engage in good practical reasoning about ends (to aim at "the right thing") and about means (to determine how to achieve the aim "in the right way at the right time"), as well as to translate thinking into action—and to do so, moreover, as a matter of "second nature" in the way that a *phronimos* would.

Even more specifically, in doing so, a *phronimos* calls into play relevant attributes from an ensemble of deeply ingrained and seamlessly integrated attributes comprising theoretical knowledge (knowledge of the head), practical skills (knowledge of the hand), and guiding affective dispositions or values or attitudes or orientations or virtues (i.e., qualities of character or knowledge of the heart) in a manner that is appropriately responsive to context (a context that is frequently complex and/or ambiguous). It is the *phronimos's* master virtue of practical wisdom, then, that enables the *phronimos* to call into play the relevant attributes from the ensemble of attributes and to conduct the entire ensemble appropriately.

In some situations, the practical reasoning involved when making a practically wise judgment (and calling into play relevant attributes to do so) may appear "intuitive" and instantaneous; in other situations, especially those that are complex and ambiguous, the practical reasoning involved requires careful deliberation. When a situation involves others, as is usually the case, practical wisdom necessarily involves an ethical dimension and, therefore, requires good ethical judgment. Sometimes the context for the exercise of practical wisdom is complex and/or ambiguous because it is dilemmatic due to conflicting demands from different roles one may inhabit. For example, the demands of one's role as a family member or as a friend may conflict with the demands of one's role as a neighbor or as a member of the broader community. Although study alone may be sufficient for the

---

course, this does not imply that the originators of these accounts would necessarily agree with all aspects of the analytical framework or "scaffolding" set out here.

acquisition of much requisite theoretical knowledge, habitual practice and experience are necessary for the cultivation of requisite practical skills and qualities of character in the ensemble of attributes.

Practical Wisdom in Professional Practice

A "good practitioner" in a professional field is a practically wise practitioner, a *phronimos* in the practice. In light of the preceding generic account of practical wisdom, professional practical wisdom may be defined as the ability to act well in a professional context, to do "the right thing in the right way at the right time," and thus flourish as an authentic practitioner in the practice. An account of professional practical wisdom has the same structure as the generic account, but the practical reasoning involved is about professional ends and means, the attributes are professional attributes (professional knowledge, professional practical skills, and qualities of professional character), and the conflicting demands that make the professional context complex and/or ambiguous may include the demands of professional role morality or professional ethics.

Professional practical wisdom may call into play professional theoretical knowledge, professional practical skills, and qualities of professional character that incorporate, build upon, and extend or modify theoretical knowledge, practical skills, and qualities of character deriving from outside the profession (which are thereby appropriately "refracted" or "inflected" or "modulated" into a profession-specific form within the practice of the profession) as well as professional theoretical knowledge, professional practical skills, and qualities of professional character originating solely within the profession itself. In addition, in any given situation, professional practical wisdom may also call for the application of theoretical knowledge, practical skills, and qualities of character deriving from outside the profession that have not been refracted or inflected or modulated into a profession-specific form.

For example, profession-specific theoretical knowledge may incorporate, build upon, and extend/modify general theoretical knowledge (e.g., general knowledge about the human body, in the medical field); profession-specific reasoning skills (including profession-specific ethical decision-making skills) may incorporate, build upon, and extend/modify general reasoning skills (including general ethical reasoning skills); profession-specific communication skills may incorporate, build upon, and extend/modify general communication skills (including listening skills);

professional courage may incorporate, build upon, and extend/modify courage in general; professional honesty may incorporate, build upon, and extend/modify honesty in general; and professional civility may incorporate, build upon, and extend/modify general civility.

This account of the nature of the relevant theoretical knowledge, practical skills, and qualities of character suggests that professional practical wisdom likely will be at least partly unique to the profession in question. Crucial in determining the distinctive character of the good practitioner and the distinctive nature of that practitioner's practical wisdom in any particular professional field (i.e., how "thinking like a lawyer," "thinking like a physician," or "thinking like an engineer," etc. differ from each other) will be the role of professional dispositions or values or attitudes or orientations or virtues within the above account. The central guiding role of qualities or excellences of professional character suggests that, in order to cultivate professional practical wisdom, proper attention must be given not only to the "to know" and "to do," but also to the "to be" of professional education, and especially that the "to be" must be properly integrated with the "to know" and "to do."

Professional Vocation and Practical Wisdom

The related sense of professional vocation or "calling" is concerned not so much with the "what" of professional practice as with the "why." More precisely, it is concerned with the motivations or reasons for entering the profession that have to do with achieving a sense of fulfillment or meaning and a sense of identity in one's professional work. Those motivations or reasons can, of course, change over time.

For some practitioners, such motivations or reasons may be focused on the attainment of goods internal to the professional practice and regarded as having intrinsic value, such as a particular responsive desire to serve the profession and those whom it serves in those unique ways that are determined by the profession itself, and/or a particular responsive desire to develop and realize one's capacities in ways that can be achieved only through that type of professional practice and, thus, to become a *phronimos* in the practice. Such a calling to the goods of the practice may perhaps be discovered only once the practitioner is well within the practice.

For other practitioners, those motivations or reasons may be focused, also or instead, on the attainment of certain types of goods external to the practice through the instrumentality of one's work—such as a general responsive desire to serve one's God and neighbor, or to serve one's community, or to serve a "cause," without regard to whether such goods may have been appropriately refracted or inflected or modulated into a profession-specific form within the practice of the profession and, thus, may have become internal goods of the professional practice itself. Such a calling to external goods may even be discovered well before the practitioner enters the practice. The desire to attain other types of goods external to the practice, such as money, power, or status, would not normally be considered in connection with a sense of vocation or calling. This is presumably because a vocation or calling tends to be viewed as engaging "higher" motivations to do with one's "spiritual" or non-material interests rather than "lower" motivations to do with one's material or non-spiritual interests, and/or with answering a "call to service" to something outside of oneself.

One serious problem with a focus on goods external to the practice, however, is that, because it may tempt the professional practitioner to "cheat," even the "higher" type of motivation may have the undesirable result of effectively disabling the practitioner from attaining the internal goods of the practice, including acquiring the practical wisdom of the practice and/or exercising such practical wisdom in any given case or in general depending on the extent, duration, and intensity of such motivation.[3] Moreover, to the extent that the practitioner views the profession as an instrument for achieving such external good, however worthy, the practitioner is arguably called to that external good and not to the profession itself. This suggests that having the appropriate vocational disposition or sense of calling is one of the necessary qualities of character required by the good practitioner

---

[3] For an excellent and illuminating discussion of the notion of "cheating" as applied to a professional practice, see Jack L. Sammons, "'Cheater!': The Central Moral Admonition of Legal Ethics, Games, Lusory Attitudes, Internal Perspectives, and Justice," *Idaho Law Review* 39 (2003): 273. Sammons applies a much expanded version of Bernard Suit's definition of a "game," with its four components of "prelusory goal," "lusory means," "constitutive rules," and "lusory attitude." In an excess of zeal to achieve the prelusory goal, cheaters are willing to violate the constitutive rules restricting them to the use of lusory means because they lack the lusory attitude. Thus, a cheater "does not view the game from the internal perspective in which the game itself is an end, as Suit's players do, but externally and instrumentally as a means toward some external end." Ibid., 281.

as part of the ensemble of professional attributes. It also suggests the need for practical wisdom in the process of vocational discernment itself.

14

Being Pragmatic about Practical Wisdom

David Ritchie[1]

I have been involved in the Professionalism and Vocation Across the Professions Project (later to be merged with the Phronesis Project) at Mercer University since I joined the faculty in 2005. I have greatly appreciated being able to attend workshops, lectures, and other sessions related to this project. Throughout all of these activities, one thing has struck me over and over: the continued relevance of philosophical pragmatism in the context of professional competency and identity. In one of the very early meetings of the project, I had the good fortune to meet William Sullivan, who was then a senior scholar at the Carnegie Foundation for the Advancement of Teaching. It became apparent in this short meeting that Bill and I shared an interest in the work of the American pragmatist John Dewey. In fact, both Bill and I have devoted some of our academic work to Dewey's pragmatism.[2]

What became exceedingly apparent to me during the numerous discussions and workshops hosted by this project is that a mark of competency in all professions is the ability to think through problems pragmatically. As a result, I will suggest in what follows that practical wisdom is defined by this ability. In order to make this case, I will briefly set out the basic epistemology behind Dewey's pragmatism. Then I will link what Dewey calls the "common pattern or structure of human reasoning"[3] to the sorts of problems this project has utilized to illustrate professional decision-making by people from an array of professional backgrounds. It is my hope that by explicitly (re)introducing pragmatism here, practical

---

[1] The author would like to thank Lisa A. Mazzie for her comments on an earlier draft of this essay.

[2] See, for example, David T. Ritchie, *Mastering Legal Analysis and Communication* (Chapel Hill NC: Carolina Academic Press, 2008); and William M. Sullivan, *Reconstructing Public Philosophy* (Berkeley: University of California Press, 1986).

[3] John Dewey, *Logic: The Theory of Inquiry* (Champaign IL: Southern Illinois University Press, 1938) 105.

wisdom will not be seen as some difficult-to-attain ideal but recognized as the mark of experts operating competently within their professional domains. Practical wisdom is, not to put too fine a point on it, a trait that flows from competency, not a virtue that must (or can) be taught independently.

The American pragmatist John Dewey is perhaps most well known for his work on education and democracy. In my view, his most important work, however, was on epistemology, his theory of human knowledge.[4] Dewey was, of course, responding to the grand European philosophical tradition of universalizing theories of knowledge like those offered by Rene Descartes, Baruch Spinoza, Gottfried Leibniz, and Immanuel Kant. For Dewey, such universalizing theories were problematic because they attempted to make human knowledge static and mechanical. The development and teaching of formal logic typifies this perspective. In Dewey's view, our minds are much more dynamic and practically oriented. In his epistemological writings, Dewey set out to explain a more consequentialist theory of how we think, one that depends more on intellectual trial and error than on abstract universals.[5] He called this "experimental logic."[6]

Traditional philosophical theories of knowledge were geared toward finding universally correct answers to questions. Dewey (and other pragmatists), however, abandoned this quest. Instead of searching for universal truths, Dewey suggested that we search instead for the best answers we can find to the problems we face. This is both an epistemological and a metaphysical shift.[7] Our task as thinkers should not be focused on abstract ideals, but instead should be concentrated on "methods which experience up to the present time shows to be the best methods available for achieving certain results...."[8] Pragmatic reasoning is applicable to any sort of human endeavor, but is employed contextually by domain according to the needs of

---

[4] Dewey's most important epistemological works were *Logic: The Theory of Inquiry* (NY: Holt, Rinehart, and Winston, 1938); *How We Think* (Minneola, NY: Dover Publications Inc., 1997); and *The Quest for Certainty* (Champaigne IL: Southern Illinois University Press, 1929).

[5] John Dewey, "Logical Method and the Law," *Cornell Law Quarterly* 10 (1924): 17.

[6] See John Dewey, *Essays in Experimental Logic* (Charleston SC: Nabu Press, 2010).

[7] See John Stuhr, *Pragmatism, Postmodernism, and the Future of Philosophy* (London: Routledge, 2002) 154–63.

[8] Dewey, *Logic*, 108.

the problems faced by those operating within that domain.⁹ According to Dewey, then, educators, lawyers, physicians, and psychologists all employ the method of thinking pragmatically; they simply do so within their own spheres of knowledge.

The process we utilize as we think through problems to find the best solutions, which Dewey calls "inquiry," is the same regardless of the domain. The "distinct steps" of inquiry are: "(1) a felt difficulty; (2) its location and definition; (3) suggestion of [a] possible solution; (4) development by reasoning of the bearings of the suggestion; and (5) further observation and experiment leading to its acceptance or rejection...."¹⁰ The interesting thing about this process is that Dewey is not trying to teach us a new and improved way of thinking through problems; he maintains that we already do think in this way.¹¹ There is a logic at work here. It is not a fixed and formal logic, however, but one of pragmatic fluidity. As Dewey puts it, this is "a logic of prediction of probabilities rather than one of deduction of certainties."¹² This process of inquiry, then, is designed not to lead us to universally true or certain answers to problems, but to practical answers to these problems that are the best solutions we can arrive at given the information we have at the time the decision needs to be made.

Let us examine these steps in slightly more detail to understand what Dewey means when he says that this method is "a single way of treating cases for certain purposes or consequences in spite of their diversity."¹³ The first step in this process of inquiry is "a felt difficulty," or, as he described it elsewhere, "recognizing [an] indeterminate situation."¹⁴ This seems simple enough, but if we look closer, we will see that sometimes recognizing there is a problem that needs to be addressed is harder than it may seem. Often, it takes others to point out to us that there is a problem that needs to be addressed. And once we do recognize, or have been informed, that a problem exists, we must categorize exactly what type of a problem it might be.

---

⁹ Ibid., 105.
¹⁰ Dewey, *How We Think*, 72.
¹¹ Dewey, *Logic*, 105–22.
¹² Dewey, "Logical Method and the Law," 26.
¹³ Ibid., 22.
¹⁴ Dewey, *Logic*, 108–20.

Let us consider the process of inquiry a school superintendent might employ in the sort of problem that is listed in the case study in appendix D of this volume. She might be unaware of the placement of a particular child with developmental issues into the school district until alerted by her teachers and staff, or until the parents bring it to her attention. When she does become aware of the issues presented by such a placement, she will immediately turn this "indeterminate situation" into a set of possible (or highly probable) questions that need to be addressed: What is the nature of this student's developmental difficulties? Are they medically related? Are they psychological? Are they a mixture of both? Whom should she get involved in this situation in order to most fairly and comprehensively deal with the issues raised (teachers? the school psychologist? the parents? legal counsel for the school district?)? Given her expertise in the domain, these questions will help her hone in on the "felt difficulty" in order to define more discretely what the issues are and how to approach them.

In fact, asking these questions will commence the second step in the process of inquiry—the location of the "problem" within the domain and the definition of that problem in terms that fit within the lexicon of that domain. By answering the set of questions listed above, and very likely a host more, the superintendent will categorize the issue or issues implicated in this situation into a set of identifiable and addressable concerns that she and her team can work on. It is important to note here that, in locating the problem into a definable and addressable category, we are drawing from past experiences to determine how to think through this problem. The superintendent isn't making things up as she goes along. She is relying on her considerable experience, and the experience of those around her who will assist in the inquiry, in defining and categorizing this student's needs. Others involved in the process—including the parents, for example—may suggest other questions that will provoke different definitions and categorizations. Taken together, these refined definitions and categorizations will (or should) give everyone involved in the inquiry a better picture of what the issues are. This realization will, in turn, lead us to the third step in the process of inquiry—the suggestion of a possible solution.

Once the issue or problem of an inquiry becomes clear and has been categorized into an understandable concern that can be addressed within the domain, the decision-maker will almost instantly light upon a probable solution to the problem. As Dewey puts it, "[W]e generally begin with some vague anticipation of a conclusion (or at least of alternative conclusions), and then we look around for principles and data which will substantiate it or which will enable us to choose between rival conclusions."[15] This is a predetermination of sorts. According to Dewey, decision-makers do not deduce a solution (or solutions). Instead, they snap to a judgment that—based on their prior experiences—is likely to be a successful resolution.

Our school superintendent, then, will very likely arrive at (probable or likely) solutions to the issues raised by the placement of the developmentally challenged child within the district. This predisposition may seem illegitimate to some (especially the parents), but in reality it is a necessary part of the process of inquiry. Without probable solutions being proffered, the inquiry will stall. Our superintendent will predetermine likely solutions that will balance all the interests involved (given her understanding of the situation). Often these predeterminations are based on similar cases she has dealt with in the past, but the "experiences" drawn upon need not be so specific. Given her training and expertise, the superintendent will still be able to address unique situations and can develop predetermined solutions. These solutions can then be presented and debated by her team and the parents.

The interesting thing about these first three steps in the process of inquiry is that they happen very rapidly cognitively—one might almost say, simultaneously. Once one becomes aware of a problem or "felt difficulty," the categorization and predetermination of a possible problem solution happen in rapid succession. As Dewey describes it, the "way in which a problem is conceived decides what specific suggestions are entertained and which are dismissed...."[16] So, decision-makers often, in colloquial terms, jump to a conclusion once they realize there is a problem that needs to be addressed, particularly if they are experts within a domain. This rapid process of identification, categorization, and predetermination becomes a problem only if the decision-maker freezes the inquiry right there. If so, then the categorization and predetermination are static and perhaps even dogmatic. Short-circuiting the process of inquiry in this way is the antithesis of practical wisdom. The process of inquiry must continue its course.

This, then, leads us to the fourth step in the process of inquiry—reasoning about the proposed solution in the context of the particular

---

[15] Dewey, "Logical Method and the Law," 23.
[16] Dewey, *Logic*, 112.

problem being addressed. Once this rapid process of identification, categorization, and predetermination takes place, Dewey suggests we need to check our predetermination against the perceived problem to ensure that the solution proposed is indeed effective.[17] If the predetermined solution—which, remember, was linked conceptually almost immediately to the recognition of the problem in the first instance—does solve the problem, then the inquiry was successful. If not, however, then further inquiry is required. Indeed, the acknowledgement that the predetermined solution does not solve the problem restarts the inquiry or, perhaps more properly, starts a new iteration of the inquiry. This last point is important in that Dewey's pragmatic epistemology should not be seen as linear; it is instead reiterative, like a sort of looping spiral to a workable conclusion.

So, once our hypothetical school superintendent arrives at a predetermination of a set of solutions to the issues raised by the placement of the developmentally challenged child in the school district, she will almost inevitably check these solutions to ensure that they really do address the issues. It will very likely be the case that she will have to make some adjustments and rethink some aspects of her predeterminations. She will do this "on the fly" as she and her team work through the issues, continually adjusting and readjusting the inquiry as she goes.

Once these readjustments are refined and the determination of the problem solution(s) is/are tailored as closely as possible to any issues raised by the "felt difficulty," the decision-maker will then continue to observe the situation to ensure that the solution(s) remain(s) responsive to the problem(s). This is the last step in the inquiry but, as you might notice, it does not dispense with the problem; the difficulty may re-emerge as circumstances change or as the original solution(s) no longer address(es) the problem(s) adequately. One might view this as "tending to" the results of our inquiries. This is perhaps the best illustration of the fluid and practical nature of Dewey's experimental logic. The process of inquiry is constantly re-evaluated and adjusted to accommodate any new information, changed circumstances, or ineffective solutions.

Where does this leave our superintendent? Exactly where one might expect: monitoring the progress of the solutions that she and her team

---

[17] Ibid., 108–20.

crafted to address the issues raised by the placement of the developmentally challenged student in the district. All those involved will periodically report—either formally or informally—on the status of the situation. Adjustments can be, and undoubtedly will be, made based on this new information. What was deemed to be the best solution at the outset will likely change given any new data. The fluidity of the process allows for these adjustments. In fact, it encourages adjustments to be factored in to ensure that the best solution is maintained given whatever changed circumstances may occur.

The situated character of this sort of process is vital to understanding the usefulness of experimental logic to making practical decisions. The reason professional education crafts our faculties of inquiry within the domain of our professions is so we do not start afresh with each new inquiry. "[T]he search for the pattern of inquiry is…not one instituted in the dark or at large. It is checked and controlled by knowledge of the kinds of inquiry that have and have not worked; methods which…can be so compared as to yield reasoned or rational conclusions."[18] Indeed, professional education is designed to equip us with this knowledge of what has and has not worked.[19] It is, in fact, the mark (or at least one mark) of professionalism to be able to utilize this process of inquiry in uncertain situations to arrive at thoughtful and useful conclusions.[20] My education as a lawyer has given me the professional and vocational background to think through problems that have legal implications in well-reasoned and constructive ways. The same can be said of one who has been educated as an educator, a nurse, or a pharmacist; their training in these domains gives them context for using the process of inquiry to arrive at professionally competent and practical solutions to problems they face within their domains of expertise.

The work of the Professionalism and Vocation Across the Professions Project repeatedly brought this home to me. The project events brought together professionals from many of the domains I mentioned above. In my role as an observer for the practical wisdom workshop, for example, it was both intriguing and encouraging to see the results of discussions concerning

---

[18] Dewey, *Logic,* 108.

[19] William M. Sullivan et al., *Educating Lawyers: Preparation for the Profession of Law* (San Francisco: Jossey-Bass, 2007) 8.

[20] Ibid., 9.

the case study in appendix D of this volume (to which I have made reference throughout this essay). Each professional utilized the process of inquiry within his or her domain of expertise. Education professionals brought their professional and vocational expertise to bear on the problem, as did lawyers, physicians, psychologists, and so on. Each used his or her professional lens to focus the process of inquiry. Having them all in the same room, discussing the same problem from their various professional perspectives, was a rich and rewarding exercise. It also showed just how relevant pragmatism is to addressing complex interdisciplinary problems, especially if we desire practical and wise decisions. Professionals do not need to be taught how to engage in practically sound and competent decision-making. Practical wisdom is not an independent virtue. It is a sign of competency within the context of professional or vocational action. By using the "common pattern or structure" of human reasoning within their expertise, professionals from any domain can arrive at the best solutions to the problems they face. There is no real secret to practical wisdom; it is simply competent and thoughtful action by people making the best decisions they can, given their expertise and experience.

15

Guidelines for Observing Practical Wisdom at Work

Jack Sammons

Although practical wisdom is a concept that makes the most sense when applied to a single mind at work, it is very difficult to observe a single mind at work in an exercise of practical wisdom for a variety of obvious reasons: the thoughts expressed are not the only ones considered; often the choice of the thought expressed is a matter of intuition beyond explanation by the individual; the speaking of the thought changes it, as does the audience's perception; and so forth. This problem for the observer of practical wisdom is nicely captured in E. M. Forster's line, "How do I know what I think until I hear what I have to say?"[1]

Groups, however, *when thought of as a single mind at work*, have the distinct advantage of allowing us to hear these thoughts and to observe the processes of reaching a decision that manifest practical wisdom. Now, of course, groups also can introduce what we might call, borrowing from economics, externalities that can interfere with practical wisdom arising from deliberation, as anyone who has ever served on a committee knows, and this must be a concern for the observer. Nevertheless, in our exercise today,[2] we are hoping that you will think of the group deliberations as those

---

[1] E.M. Forster, *Aspects of the Novel* (New York: Harcourt, Brace, and Company, 1927) 152.

[2] As discussed in the introduction to this volume (see p. 12, note 4), the author developed these guidelines to assist the observers in the two parallel case study discussion groups at the Practical Wisdom Workshop that was part of the symposium on Practical Wisdom held by the Professionalism and Vocation Across the Professions Project in October 2008, and repeated for a new group of participants in November 2009, and at both of which he also served as one of those observers. Although the substantive discussion of practical wisdom in these guidelines warrants including them as an independent contribution in part III, they also serve as the "Guidelines for Observers" in the materials for the case study exercise in appendix D.

of a single mind at work and look at those deliberations as an exercise of practical wisdom.

In commenting on the group deliberations, observers should not offer their judgment about the group's decision. (There is no agreed-upon outcome by which practical wisdom could or should be measured.) Nor should they base their comments on some assumed model of a good problem-solving process. (Practical wisdom does not follow any particular analytical model, and often those with practical wisdom will appear to simply jump to conclusions.) Instead, they should think of themselves as commenting only on the specific virtue of practical wisdom, although admittedly, according to Aristotle, this is a virtue that requires and is required by all the others.

Commenting on a virtue in this context means commenting on the character of the deliberation. There are numerous factors external to this character that can affect the particular decision in one way or another. These should not be of immediate concern to observers. So, for example, it would not be useful for these purposes for the observer to note those matters that were not considered in the group deliberation unless the observer can discern a flaw in the character of the deliberation that might have prevented these matters from being considered.

* * *

Since, when you are looking for practical wisdom, you are looking for a specific virtue, it will be best to focus your observations and to organize your comments around this virtue's central components. What these components are—a matter that has been greatly debated over the centuries—is something about which the observer will have to reach his or her own conclusion. As a starting point, however, and for present purposes only, we suggest the following components with the caveat that no description of practical wisdom reaches its essence, for our inability to do this is part of what makes it "practical" wisdom:

1. Deliberation involving *means and ends* within the realm of the *ethical*[3] and consistent with its characteristics.

---

[3] "Ethical," as used here, is Aristotle's description of those areas of human activity in which no generalities can be applied well; all norms must be adjusted to the particular; each case, each agent, and each speaker must in some measure be considered unique; all

2. Deliberation driven by the *actual particularities* of a particular context.
3. Deliberation relying heavily upon *internalized past experiences*.
4. Deliberation that is *sufficiently aware of itself* to consider *honestly* its own limitations and potential limitations and to attempt to correct these in an ongoing manner.
5. Deliberation that considers the *character of the action* to be taken in addition to its consequences.

Now, all five of these will require elaboration before they can be usefully applied for observation and comments. Such elaboration should be able to account for much, if not all, of what might occur to you as the various skills, knowledge, and other virtues required for practical wisdom. Here, then, are some examples of how such an elaboration would go:

1. "Deliberation involving *means and ends* within the realm of the ethical and consistent with its characteristics" is the way in which practical wisdom is distinguished from other modes of thought not appropriate to the task at hand. Deliberation involving only "means" is the form taken by cleverness, as opposed to practical wisdom. Deliberation about "ends" is also the way in which practical wisdom can be distinguished from simply good problem-solving. Attempts to be too precise (seeking a clarity not permitted by the subject matter, as Aristotle put it), to be too driven by rules, principles, theories, biases, or convictions, would all be examples of a failure of the improvisational nuance that practical wisdom demands, or, rather, an observation that something other than practical wisdom best characterized the deliberation.

2. "Deliberation driven by the *actual particularities* of a particular context" requires strong abilities of perception, good listening, empathy with others (for the purposes of understanding) combined with the detachment honesty requires, moral and factual imagination, determinations of

---

matters are thought to be variable and subject to change; *ethos* is important to understanding, and the world is seen as in some measure indeterminate and to be measured, when it must, only by the relative mean, the fitting, and the opportune. See Kathy Eden, *Poetic and Legal Fiction in the Aristotelian Tradition* (Princeton: Princeton University Press, 1983).

relevance, and determinations of importance, including an insistence upon the relevance and importance of the emotions to deliberation, and so forth.

3. "Deliberation that relies heavily upon *internalized past experiences*" requires, in part, having intuitions[4] that can be applied to the task at hand and, in other part, an acquired practical knowledge about humanity—for example, how people are likely to react to various events tempered with an acute awareness of the human potential for unpredictability. Internalized experiences are often personal ones, but they can be derived from the experience of others, fictional or historical, if the experience is adequately internalized. So, for example, there is practical wisdom in the common law, which can become personal for those who relive the experience of common law through the narrative it provides. There is practical wisdom in history for those for whom the same is true. In fact, the way in which one internalizes the experiences of others is primarily through experiencing them as narratives. The application of this form of learning to the task at hand in the deliberation may well require that the task at hand be thought of as the creation of a narrative. Typically, practical wisdom will be manifested in a way that at least implies a certain future narrative of events.

4. "Deliberation that is *sufficiently aware of itself* to consider honestly its own limitations and potential limitations and to attempt to correct these in an ongoing manner" requires, in a group setting, a concern for the conversation itself—that is to say, that all voices are being heard, that the language of deliberation is being used with care, that there is sufficient openness in the deliberation for other thoughts and the thoughts of others to emerge, and, in all this, an acknowledgment of mutual dependence, and so forth. This may seem to be a reason for concern only in group deliberations,

---

[4] "Intuitions," as used here, are not something mysterious. They are the product of prior experiences and reflections upon these experiences. When they occur, they are experienced as matters requiring no further justification—that is, as non-inferentially justified, but that can be inferentially justified to others to make them persuasive. When someone has an insight into a difficult problem, the insight is experienced as an intuition. If the character of the person with the insight is sufficiently persuasive, nothing else needs to be said—that is to say, there are people whose judgments based on their experiences we just trust. Often, however, the person with the insight will then need to offer a justification of its value in the situation to make the insight persuasive. Offering the justification, however, does not change the intuitive nature of the insight.

but individual deliberations—Hannah Arendt's "two-in-one"[5]—really raise quite the same concerns. In this component, observers are looking at the character of the group and asking, as Aristotle says you would ask of a person, about its character for truth. This character for truth within the realm of the ethical will require a self-reflective ability to shift the style of the deliberation in response to changing demands. Such an ability is dependent upon the deliberation maintaining a certain distance from itself—not a radical distance, but "a little to one side, but not outside."[6]

5. "Deliberation that considers the *character of the action* to be taken in addition to its consequences" means that the deliberation is not driven solely by consequences, even broadly considered, for the concerns of practical wisdom necessarily are broader than these. Consideration of the character of the action, like consideration of the character of a person, is a narrative inquiry with an implicit teleology such that the products of practical wisdom produce their own motivations. In this, each exercise of practical wisdom is inescapably connected in some fashion to an offered way of life, one among many potential ways of life. It is, then, and must be, a multi-dimensional normative inquiry with no criteria of success or failure that can be previously determined.

* * *

These elaborations, you can readily see, require further elaboration themselves. Rather than continuing to these here, however, it would be best if observers would use these components, as elaborated here, to develop a check list of vices—that is to say, those things that would move a group's deliberations away from practical wisdom, that could serve to focus the observer's observations and comments. For example, in the first component, some of the vices might be described as a failure sufficiently to consider ends (which might be manifested as an excessive concern with cleverness); deliberations that were too rule-, principle-, theory-, bias-, or conviction-dependent (in which these serve as ending points rather than points of further inquiry); relatedly, deliberation that lacked the nuance required for

---

[5] See the chapter "The Two-in-One" in Hannah Arendt, *The Life of the Mind* (New York: Harvest Books, Harcourt Publishing, 1978) 179ff.

[6] Michael Walzer, *Interpretation and Social Criticism* (Cambridge: Harvard University Press, 1987) 61.

the task at hand; and so forth. If observers do this for each of the components, we believe they will be well prepared to observe and to comment upon exercises.

Conclusion

Mark Jones, Paul Lewis, Kelly Reffitt

We have set forth a trajectory of inquiry in this volume, most explicitly in the introduction, chapter 1, and appendices A and B. We have called for educators to join together across disciplines and the institutional boundaries that divide different levels of education, from pre-K to professional schools. Such alliances are crucial if we are to come to fuller understandings of moral development across the lifespan and develop better ways to promote that development in age-appropriate ways. Such an effort will require us to revisit both pedagogy and how we structure our lives as teachers and learners in our various formal roles, whether that of teacher, student, or administrator. We hope this book can serve as a catalyst for these endeavors by drawing together people with similar and complementary interests and insights for the sake of the shared goal of fostering practical wisdom.

Indeed, one of the convictions that has emerged for us out of the research, conversations, and events that gave rise to this work is that practical wisdom serves as the *summum bonum* of moral development. We may not always use the term "practical wisdom." We might instead speak of mature moral functioning (Narvaez), the responsible agent (Lickona), tell stories of professionals struggling to make sense of their lives (Sherman), discuss various apprenticeships (Sullivan), or talk about the inherent quailties of being a professional (May). Nevertheless, we all point in the same direction: toward the integration of the knowledge, skills, and dispositions needed to achieve the most possible of what is authentically good in a given situation in community with others. That this trajectory is shared by a variety of people from a variety of backgrounds gives us reason for hope, as does the enthusiasm they have expressed for this work. Such shared direction and enthusiasm do not preclude ongoing debate, however—as is evident in the critiques of Sullivan leveled by Sammons and May in this volume—but the shared trajectory at least makes debate meaningful and productive.

Of course, we know that this book has, at best, only plowed some ground. There are many different kinds of seeds that still must be planted and nurtured, even as we nurture the plants beginning to surface here. Future work necessarily means addressing the complex and contested notion of whether we can identify a consensus about what constitutes an authentically human existence that has intellectual rigor and credibility across disciplines. We need to develop, or engage and refine, existing thick descriptions of our pluralistic society and come to identify more fully the virtues—as well as the practices necessary for nurturing those virtues—that are needed for democracy to survive in this pluralistic, relativistic age. Sustaining a spirit of liberal education throughout the range of educational institutions also will require delving into curricular reform so that our whole curriculum provides ample opportunities to integrate content knowledge and process skills in the service of the good of liberal education (whether for elementary students, undergraduates, or professionals). Taking on that task requires asking the kinds of questions about institutional life raised herein by Schwartz and Sharpe so that institutional reform will enable our institutional cultures both to model and promote the development of practical wisdom.

Doing so will itself entail wrestling with the profound challenge made by many critics that we no longer live in a democratic republic and that such a project as we envision here is irrelevant.[1] Wrestling with those criticisms will require that we do more to engage and come to terms with the larger cultural forces, mentioned by Brown in this volume, that make liberal education difficult—if not impossible—to sustain. These forces include the lazy relativism that characterizes popular moral thought (or, to be more accurate, the popular evasion of moral thought) and the ongoing colonization of all of life by economic values that reflect positivistic assumptions about what is true and valuable, thereby reducing all measures of the good, the true, and the beautiful to crass metrics.

We are not naïve enough to think that practical wisdom will be attained easily or by everyone. Aristotle himself taught that human flourishing,

---

[1] Or that, even if necessary, is doomed to fail. Such seems to be Alasdair MacIntyre's assessment of our situation throughout his writings. See, for example, his "The Idea of an Educated Public," in *Education and Values: The Richard Peters Lectures*, ed. Graham Haydon (London: The Institute of Education, 1987) 15–36. Therein, MacIntyre offers a history of the Scottish Enlightenment as a case study of the factors that make an educated public impossible in the modern age. These include size, economic growth, shifts of power away from the educated classes, and increasing specialization, not only at the intellectual level, but in manufacturing as well. All of these factors, for MacIntyre, shift one's allegiance away from society as a whole, thereby making it impossible to produce the educated public that educational institutions say is their *raison de être*.

Guidelines for Observing Practical Wisdom at Work

marked by the acquisition of the virtues, took a lifetime and was, moreover, contingent on many factors, including background, level of material comfort, and luck, as well as good formative education. Nevertheless, we see the quest as both noble and necessary, for we live in an age of pluralism, cheap relativism, and apathy masquerading as tolerance. We live in an age of deep and growing inequities between rich and poor, along with a host of other serious challenges.

We therefore need to develop wisdom in finding ways to hold to our convictions with integrity while respecting the convictions of others. We need to develop the wisdom that will allow us to find ways to reach agreements with others who may hold to radically different convictions, but with whom we nonetheless can make common cause in the quest for justice. We need wisdom so as to know both how much of the good of liberal education can be sustained under present social circumstances and how to go about achieving it. And we need wisdom to know how to help champion and cultivate wisdom in a way that responds appropriately to our contemporary context. It is our earnest and heartfelt hope that the present volume and the continuing work of the Phronesis Project, as outlined in appendix B, together with further exploration and research of the issues related to professionalism and vocation identified in appendices A and C, will serve to support, to complement, and to supplement the work of others who pursue this same goal.

Appendix A:
Building Bridges and Discovering Commonality: The Story of Mercer University's Professionalism and Vocation Across the Professions Project

Mark Jones

Mercer University's Professionalism and Vocation Across the Professions Project, of which I have been privileged to serve as coordinator since its inception, was launched in 2005. For the reasons given in the introduction to this volume, we consider that the story of the project is one worth telling. Doing so also will provide context for the materials in parts II and III and, indeed, for the materials in part I.

The project is an exciting and innovative initiative that, to date, has brought together over 100 participants from across the entire university (most especially team members representing Mercer's various colleges, schools, and other relevant educational units). Many of the same participants have participated in several of the five major events we have held in the project so far:

1. A symposium on "Professionalism and Vocation Across the Professions" held in November 2005, with William M. Sullivan as keynote speaker;
2. A follow-up roundtable discussion meeting held in May 2006;
3. A second symposium on "Cultivating Professionalism and Vocation Across the Professions: Challenges for Higher Education" held in November 2006 with William F. May as keynote speaker;
4. A third symposium on "Practical Wisdom: The Character of the Professions" held in October 2008, with Barry Schwartz and Kenneth Sharpe as keynote speakers, and including a case-study workshop; and
5. A second case-study workshop in November 2009 designed to replicate the experience of the October 2008 Practical Wisdom Symposium for a new group of participants.

By the time of this last event, the Professionalism and Vocation Across the Professions Project had been incorporated into the broader Phronesis Project for the Exploration of Character, Practical Wisdom, and Professional Formation, established earlier in 2009. Several of those who participated in the preceding events also participated in the Phronesis Project Conference on "Character Across the Disciplines" held in April 2010.

Origins and Development of the Project

In hindsight, Mercer University's Professionalism and Vocation Across the Professions Project can be seen as a response to the sense of crisis in the professions discussed in the introduction to this volume. Indeed, many of the participants in the project have been aware of some such sense of crisis in their individual professional fields from the very beginning of the project in 2005, and probably well before. It would be accurate, however, to characterize our experience in the project as a voyage of collective discovery, both of a sense of crisis and of promise, to use William Sullivan's terminology again,[1] that is more widely shared across the professions than we may have realized before we joined together in the project. It also would be accurate to interpret the launching of the project in 2005 as a response to an intuition, a calling, if you will, that undertaking a collective effort to promote conversation across Mercer's wide range of colleges and schools[2] offered the potential not only for collective discovery, but also for mutual enrichment. And while many of the participants may have been motivated to participate in the project by a sense of crisis in their individual professional fields, other motivations included the general desire of professional educators to learn from each other and the very particular attraction of an unprecedented opportunity to interact with colleagues from across the university in so many different professional fields and disciplines.

More specifically, the plan to hold a university-wide symposium on Professionalism and Vocation Across the Professions in November 2005—an event that, again in hindsight, can now be seen as having launched the project—had a dual inspiration. To begin with, during her presentation to the law school faculty when interviewing for the position of Dean of Mercer

---

[1] See William M. Sullivan, *Work and Integrity: The Crisis and Promise of Professionalism in America*, 2nd ed. (San Francisco: Jossey-Bass, 2005).

[2] Mercer University has eleven colleges and schools. Some of them are based in Macon, about eighty miles south of Atlanta (Liberal Arts, Law, Medicine, Engineering, and Music, established as a separate school in 2006); some are based in Atlanta (Pharmacy and Health Sciences, Nursing, and Theology); and some are based in both Macon and Atlanta (Education, Continuing and Professional Studies, and Business and Economics). Since 1999, the medical school also has had a significant presence in Savannah.

Appendix A

Law School (which she assumed in 2004), Daisy Floyd told us about her work as a Carnegie Scholar with the Carnegie Foundation for the Advancement of Teaching. She also told us about the Foundation's Preparation for the Professions Project, which was in the process of undertaking several profession-specific studies addressing clergy, lawyers, engineers, physicians, and nurses, as well as a related study on teachers, under the direction of William Sullivan. In addition, and more immediately, during spring semester 2005, I audited Pat Longan's required first-year Legal Profession course in order to deepen my understanding of lawyer professionalism both as a matter of general interest and also from a more particular need to inform my work as a Mercer Commons Fellow.[3] Early on in the course, Pat had us study and compare three different statements on professionalism—for physicians, for clergy, and for lawyers—in order to identify important commonalities and differences.[4] Once articulated, the suggestion that we extend this idea by holding an interdisciplinary university-wide event to examine and compare issues of professionalism and vocation across the many different professions and professionalism-related programs represented at Mercer's various colleges and schools received immediate and enthusiastic support from Pat, Daisy, and John Dunaway, Director of the Mercer Commons. The idea also was taken up by another university entity, the Quality Enhancement Plan (QEP), overseen by Peter Brown, which the university had established as part of its preparation

---

[3] The mission of the Mercer Commons has been to promote the exploration of faith, learning, and vocation. One of its regular activities has been to appoint a group of fellows from various colleges and schools for two-year renewable terms to undertake joint study of various issues and to pursue individual projects of common interest. I was appointed a fellow in fall semester 2004, with the support and encouragement of Dean Daisy Floyd, to pursue an individual project focused on a particular component of a long-term project concerned with the re-liberalization of legal education, which I see as implicating lawyer professionalism.

[4] For a description of this innovative and ABA award-winning course in 2009, see Patrick E. Longan, "Teaching Professionalism," *Mercer Law Review* 60 (2009): 659–99. For a shorter description of the course in its current form after significant restructuring, inspired in part by experience in the Professionalism and Vocation Across the Professions Project, see Patrick Longan and Timothy Floyd, "Mercer Law School's Focus on Professionalism," *Bloomberg Law Reports—Student Edition* 2/1 (2011) (also describing the law school's public interest program).

for the SACS re-accreditation visit in 2004 and part of whose remit was to promote and enhance the study of ethics in the professional schools. In this way, the November 2005 symposium featuring William Sullivan came to be co-sponsored and jointly funded by the Law School, the Mercer Commons, and the QEP.

With this support from key individuals and university administrative centers in place, a planning committee consisting of nine members representing the three co-sponsors, plus myself, was formed to plan and prepare for the November 2005 symposium. This same committee also under-took the planning for the follow-up roundtable discussion held in May 2006. After that event, the planning committee was expanded to include a representative from each of the university's colleges, schools, and other relevant educational units based solely or partly in Macon. The expanded planning committee of seventeen members then undertook the planning and preparation for the November 2006 symposium. Following a meeting in May 2007, this expanded planning committee effectively ceded authority for the planning of the November 2008 symposium and the drafting of the case study for the associated workshop to a much smaller planning committee comprising seven members. Whatever its composition, and acting on suggestions generated by its members, the planning committee decided on the nature, structure, and content of each event.[5] These planning committee mandates were then implemented by me as the project coordinator, with logistical support provided by various entities within the university administration.

The QEP was the sole sponsor and source of funding for the May 2006 roundtable discussion and the November 2006 symposium, and jointly sponsored the October 2008 symposium with the Law School and the Mercer Commons. The November 2009 repeat case-study workshop was sponsored by the Phronesis Project, which was funded during academic year 2009–2010 by the university's Academic Initiatives Monetary (AIM) Fund.

Details regarding the structure and content of each event, as well as what was done to plan, organize, and prepare for it, can be found on the Phronesis Project website at http://www2.mercer.edu/phronesis. All of the events share certain important features in common, however:

---

[5] Please see the acknowledgements for the names of those colleagues who have served on the planning committee in its various configurations.

Appendix A

1. All, or almost all, of Mercer's colleges and schools have been represented by team members at each event.
2. The teams, which have sometimes included students as well as faculty, were nominated by their respective deans.[6]
3. The participants in each event were expected to prepare for the event by reading certain preparatory materials.
4. Each event was structured to ensure extensive interdisciplinary interaction among the participants.[7]

---

[6] The project events also have involved the participation of some outside full-time practitioners.

[7] Each of the three symposia was structured to provide a keynote address by an invited speaker or speakers, and several opportunities for interdisciplinary interaction by the team members. At the first symposium in November 2005, that interdisciplinary interaction consisted of table discussion at the evening banquet as well as Q&A with the speaker, followed the next day by several presentations (with Q&A), including one on the topic of vocation in general and a presentation by each of the teams on the understanding of professionalism and vocation in their particular fields, three parallel interdisciplinary group discussions during lunch, and a summing-up by two observers who attended the lunchtime group discussions.

At the second symposium in November 2006, a day of interdisciplinary interaction following the keynote address consisted of presentations on emerging model practices by several teams (with Q&A) as well as four parallel interdisciplinary group discussions during lunch. This symposium also involved a second day of meetings between the keynote speaker and three interdisciplinary groups of faculty.

At the third symposium in November 2008, the interdisciplinary interaction consisted of table discussion at the dinner before the keynote address (with Q&A), followed the next day by two parallel interdisciplinary group discussions of the Practical Wisdom Case Study Exercise, lunch discussion in the two groups, and a plenary concluding evaluation session with discussion led by the observers in each group. The 2009 case-study workshop sought to replicate the structure of the 2008 symposium (including having the participants view a video recording of the 2008 keynote address on a university website as part of their preparation for the workshop). The 2006 roundtable discussion also involved two parallel interdisciplinary group discussions together with some plenary group discussion.

The interdisciplinary interaction at these various events was maximized through a strategy of assigned membership in discussion groups and assigned table seating at meals. The structure and approach followed at the Phronesis Project Conference on Character Across the Disciplines in April 2010, organized by Paul Lewis, also were designed to maximize interdisciplinary interaction among the participants, with evening keynote

5. Each event was relatively inexpensive. Indeed, the total combined cost for all five events did not exceed $25,000.

This history of the project underscores three central truths. First, it demonstrates the inadvertent, and serendipitous, origins of the project and its essentially grassroots character as an initiative driven forward by the enthusiasm and commitment of a small group of committed colleagues operating outside of any formal university committee structure. Second, even before the broader Phronesis Project was conceived, the Professionalism and Vocation Across the Professions Project had come to be regarded as an important part of a more general university strategy focusing on issues of professionalism, ethics, and vocation, and as complementary to certain other university initiatives in the area of ethics.[8] Thus, the history of the project's development demonstrates how much a small group of enthusiastic and committed colleagues can achieve, even when not acting within a formal university committee structure, if they receive the encouragement, support, and cooperation of colleagues in positions of administrative authority and the cooperation of other colleagues critical to the success of such an endeavor: the team members representing the various colleges and schools and other educational units who prepared for and participated in various project events; the deans who nominated the team members and, in some cases, were regular participants in project events themselves; and the many others in administrative positions who provided the logistical support necessary to ensure the effective execution of plans for project events. The third truth, then, is a humbling one about our interdependence, but also an inspiring one about the collective discovery of mutual talent and institutional friendship, and a hopeful one about the potential for successful outcomes across an entire university when all those concerned work together in pursuit of a common purpose. These truths have been verified through our experience in the broader Phronesis Project as well.

---

addresses (with Q&A), followed the next day by three parallel interdisciplinary workshop groups and a concluding plenary (with Q&A).

[8] Another QEP project, with a planning committee that included representatives of Mercer's colleges, schools, and other educational units based in Atlanta, focused specifically on ethics, while our own project focused on broader questions of professionalism and vocation (including certain aspects of professional ethics). The expanded planning committee formed after the 2006 roundtable discussion also included a liaison from the Atlanta QEP planning committee.

Appendix A

Goals, Scope, and Focus of the Project

The original planning committee articulated two central goals for our first event, the November 2005 symposium featuring William Sullivan. The first goal was to raise collective awareness across Mercer University's colleges, schools, and other educational units and across the professional practice communities regarding (a) how the concepts of professionalism and vocation are understood in the various professional fields; and (b) how professionalism and vocation are promoted during the educational process and, in particular, within the university's various colleges, schools, and other educational units.

The second goal was to facilitate comparisons (the discovery of similarities and differences) across the professional fields regarding these two matters and thereby (a) to create mutual insights and enhance the professionalism efforts (including cross-professional collaboration) in the university's colleges, schools, and other educational units, and in the professional practitioner communities; and (b) to permit the drawing of systemic conclusions regarding professionalism and vocation issues across the various professional fields and across professional (and pre-professional) education.

The planning committee also determined that the November 2005 symposium would seek to achieve these goals by focusing on two main types of questions along two different axes (five questions along each axis), reflecting the division between the first and second set of goals. Along a vertical (profession-specific) axis, the five questions were:

1. How is professionalism defined in your professional field?
2. What values and virtues is professionalism in your professional field understood to include?
3. How is professionalism in your professional field promoted and cultivated during professional education in general and in your professional school/program in particular?
4. How is the concept of vocation understood in your professional field?
5. What is the relationship between the concept of vocation, and its promotion and cultivation during professional education in your professional field, and the first three questions?

Along a horizontal (cross-professional) axis, the five questions were:
1. Is there a general conception of professionalism (for example, one based on William Sullivan's "three apprenticeships" framework) and a general

conception of vocation, identifying common features of professionalism and vocation across many different professional fields, that can illuminate each other, and that can illuminate and be illuminated by our understanding of the questions (and answers) along the vertical axis?

2. What is the relationship between our understanding and promotion of professionalism and vocation on the one hand, and pre-professional education, in particular a general college education, on the other?

3. What mutual insights can we gain from each other that may help us enhance our understanding, and promotion and cultivation, of professionalism and vocation in our various professional fields and educational endeavors?

4. What are the opportunities and imperatives for collaboration: (a) among practitioners in the different specialized professional fields and among educators in the different colleges and schools (for example, collaborative medicine involving medicine, nursing, pharmacy, and psychotherapy, and multidisciplinary legal practice involving lawyers and finance professionals or collaborative lawyering involving lawyers and psychotherapists); and (b) between such practitioners and educators on the one hand, and professionals in fields providing general support for professional practices (such as library science and information technology), or specific support for the individual practitioner (such as psychotherapists offering stress management techniques), on the other?

5. Is there a general conception of professional education that can illuminate and be illuminated by our understanding of all the preceding questions (and answers) along both the vertical and horizontal axes?

The teams representing Mercer's various colleges, schools, and other educational units (i.e., the university's libraries) were asked to prepare a presentation addressing, in particular, the five "vertical" questions (especially the first three questions) and/or (as appropriate) certain of the "horizontal" questions set out above. The presenters had been asked to provide an outline ahead of time. They also had been asked to use William Sullivan's "three apprenticeships" framework in preparing their presentations. It was made clear, however, that the dual focus and the two sets of questions were intended as a *guide* for our exploration, not as a *rigid constraint* on that exploration.

Although we have continued to be guided by the above framework of goals and inquiries in developing the project, our experiences and conversations within the project also have resulted in an evolving understanding of

Appendix A

relevant issues and an evolution in emphasis (including some expansion of focus) as certain matters have come more clearly into view. Thus, many in the project have come to think of our collective endeavors as being concerned with "professional formation"—with the formation of professional character and professional identity, and with the virtues and ideals that are central to such professional character and identity.

Second, we have recognized the need to ask additional questions such as: (a) To what extent have changes in the institutional and social context in which the professions are practiced resulted in changing expectations regarding professional practice and professional formation and in the creation of impediments to attaining the virtues and ideals that are central to professional character and professional identity? and (b) How can our conversations within the project be translated appropriately and effectively into specific, concrete, and practical measures designed to cultivate these virtues and ideals in our students?

Third, two notions that have become increasingly central in our evolving understanding and in the evolution of project emphasis are the notions of practical wisdom and a vocation for the common good.

Fourth, as we learned more about the Carnegie Foundation's Preparation for the Professions Project[9] and about the foundation's later Life of the Mind for Practice Project (which focuses on the cultivation of practical reason and explores the synergies between undergraduate liberal education and professional education in this regard)[10]—especially from Daisy Floyd, who was a member of the Life of the Mind for Practice Seminar, and of course from Bill Sullivan—we also came to see the strong resonances, and parallels, between the work in our own Professionalism and Vocation Across the Professions Project and these two Carnegie Foundation initiatives.

Finally, taking inspiration from the sorts of inquiries undertaken in Pat Longan's Legal Profession course, we expanded the list of focus questions along the vertical (profession-specific) axis into a much more detailed set of focus questions that could serve as the basis for ongoing exploration and

---

[9] For references to the profession-specific publications resulting from the Carnegie Foundation's Preparation for the Professions Project in 2006 (clergy), 2007 (lawyers), 2009 (engineers), and 2010 (physicians and nurses), see William M. Sullivan, "Professionalism and Vocation Across the Professions" in part II.

[10] William M. Sullivan and Matthew S. Rosin, *A New Agenda for Higher Education: Shaping a Life of the Mind for Practice* (San Francisco: Jossey-Bass, 2008).

research regarding the history, current state, and future of professionalism and professional vocation in the various professions. This expanded list of focus questions is contained in appendix C in this volume.

The evolution in our understanding and in the emphasis of our project, of course, helps to explain the origin of the Phronesis Project in early 2009 and the incorporation of the Professionalism and Vocation Across the Professions Project within an even broader framework, one in which we combined the work from our project with the work of Paul Lewis in the area of moral development and Kelly Reffitt in the area of character education, and, since 2010, also with the work of Daisy Floyd in the area of ethical formation and Tanya Sharon in the area of psychology. As stated in the introduction, it seems to make good sense that colleagues interested in the development of character, moral capacity, and practical wisdom at any stage of the educational continuum should collaborate in a broader endeavor that promises to maximize the prospects for mutual enrichment and synergistic effect.

Our evolving understanding of relevant issues and the resulting evolution in emphasis within the project can be traced in the materials in part II on professional character and professional formation and in part III on practical wisdom in practical context. We invite readers to share our experience of discovery as they proceed through these materials, and then to revisit (or visit) the materials in part I on character development and moral formation.

* * *

Regarding the future development of the Professionalism and Vocation Across the Professions component of the Phronesis Project, we plan to hold further practical wisdom workshops involving both faculty and students and also to develop additional case studies for use in these workshops as well as in classroom teaching. We also intend to be guided by the focus questions we have identified, both those along a vertical profession-specific axis set out in appendix C and those along a horizontal, cross-professional axis set out above, in planning other kinds of events and in undertaking further research.

Appendix B: Moral Development Across Disciplines, Schools, and Life Span: The Phronesis Project

Paul Lewis

Genesis of the Phronesis Project

As indicated in the introduction to this volume, the Phronesis Project began in 2009 with funding from Mercer University's Academic Initiatives Monetary Fund.[1] The project represents both the continuation of the Professionalism and Vocation Across the Professions Project, begun under the leadership of Mark Jones in 2005, and its expansion in light of the interests of Paul Lewis, Associate Professor of Christianity in Mercer's College of Liberal Arts. Professors Jones and Lewis met while serving together as fellows in the Mercer Commons during the 2006–2007 academic year.[2] Lewis, whose training is in theological ethics, was laying the groundwork for a sabbatical project on moral development by exploring ways that Michael Polanyi's ideas about personal knowing, commitment, responsibility, and calling could inform moral education.

Exposure to Jones's work led Lewis to consider how trends in professional education could be adapted to teaching undergraduate liberal arts students. That line of inquiry dovetailed nicely with the question Lewis had been contemplating for his sabbatical: "If the primary task of teaching ethics is that of helping people become good, how do we accomplish that in our teaching?" After Lewis had spent his fall 2008 sabbatical reading psychological and philosophical literature on moral development, Jones and Lewis decided to pursue AIM funding for a joint project. In keeping with the intent of the funding source that projects should foster collaboration between multiple units of the university—and in recognition that it would be

---

[1] The AIM fund is a university initiative that supports interdisciplinary teaching, learning, and scholarship at the highest levels of excellence. It provides initial funding to develop innovative, interdisciplinary, and cross-institutional academic initiatives that have the potential to become national centers of excellence for the university. Projects are thereafter intended to become self-supporting.

[2] See appendix A for more on the Commons and the Professionalism and Vocation Across the Professions Project.

important to include a representative from Mercer's Tift College of Education in a project of this nature—Jones and Lewis enlisted Kelly Reffitt, whose specialization is character education in effective schools. She quickly agreed to join, and so the project began with lead faculty from Mercer's Walter F. George School of Law, College of Liberal Arts, and Tift College of Education. In addition, nine other faculty and administrators from across the university were enlisted as collaborating or advisory faculty, making this project the most broadly based of any AIM-funded initiative before or since. In 2010 Jones, Lewis, and Reffitt were joined as lead faculty by Tanya Sharon, a developmental psychologist in the College of Liberal Arts, and Daisy Floyd, former Dean of the Law School, who assumed her duties as university Professor of Law and Ethical Formation in fall 2011 after a year's post-decanal sabbatical.

Goals, Objectives, and Guiding Principles

The Phronesis Project incorporates the particular goals and objectives of the Professionalism and Vocation Across the Professions Project. Much more broadly, however, the Phronesis Project responds to the need for collaboration and cooperation among educators who are concerned with some dimension of moral development across the entire educational span (Lewis's essay in this volume charts the lack of connection in the field). In particular, it seeks to foster a conversation between different constituencies, both nationally and locally at Mercer, with a view to producing both a more coherent understanding of moral development and ways of fostering such development among students at all educational levels. The project thus promotes comprehensive and interdisciplinary investigation into the nature and stage-appropriate development of "good character" and practical wisdom. It is comprehensive in its focus on life's various contexts and stages and in its efforts to draw upon and integrate a range of theories of moral development, pedagogical practices, and insights from the neurosciences. It is interdisciplinary in its reach across all relevant disciplines and all professional fields with their corresponding departments and colleges/schools at Mercer. In this way, the Phronesis Project seeks to undertake and facilitate comprehensive, comparative, and collaborative work on character, practical wisdom, and professional formation that is difficult, if not impossible, to accomplish when done in isolation from other efforts.

Appendix B

The overarching goal is therefore not just to achieve a greater understanding of the nature of "good character" and practical wisdom, but also to determine the most effective stage-appropriate pedagogies for developing these qualities across the educational continuum in general, and at Mercer University in particular. These pedagogies include those that are explicit in the curriculum as well as those that are implicit in the social environment and ethos of the educational institution.

More specifically, to achieve its various goals, the project seeks to:

- foster cross-disciplinary conversation and learning about character, practical wisdom, and professional formation;
- develop or identify methods and resources for teaching that promote character development from preK–graduate school;
- develop or identify resources for assessing such development;
- promote conversation and collaboration about the Mercer environment and ethos across the lines of academic, administrative, and student life offices;
- promote the development and implementation of new academic courses involving students from different departments/schools; and
- promote student and faculty research on character, practical wisdom, and professional formation.

The principles that guide us in pursuing these goals and objectives are set out in the introduction to this volume.

Project Activities

During 2009–2010, the project engaged in several activities that involved 305 students, as well as faculty, staff, and administrators from nine of Mercer's eleven colleges and schools. We repeated the case-study workshop, first held as part of the symposium on practical wisdom in 2008, for a new group of participants, again drawn from faculty across the university community in Macon and Atlanta. One of those new participants, collaborating faculty member David Gushee, who is also University Professor of Ethics, repeated the workshop on Mercer's Atlanta campus with a group of more than thirty students.

In addition, the project sponsored two roundtable discussions on Mercer's "moral climate" that included students, faculty, and administration. The rationale for this discussion was the realization that institutional culture or climate is one of the most significant factors in student moral development. Students in an honors service learning course developed and administered an instrument for determining Mercer's moral climate to 238 undergraduate students. One of the statistically significant findings is that students who reported participation in community service said that their Mercer education made them more morally discerning, a finding that Tanya Sharon has continued to research with students.

The "main event" in 2009–2010 was a multi-disciplinary conference on character for Mercer faculty, students, and administrators. As noted elsewhere in this volume, this conference brought to campus Darcia Narvaez, Thomas Lickona, and Nancy Sherman as keynote speakers, each to address some dimension of character from the perspective of their disciplinary expertise. The event was designed to allow for public presentations on a Friday evening and Saturday-morning workshops for fifty participants led by each of the speakers, followed by a concluding plenary and meal for participants. The topics of the workshops were "Creating Smart & Good Schools" (Lickona), "An Integrative Approach to Educating Virtue" (Narvaez), and "The Guilt They Carry" (Sherman).

Less publicly, the project generated ideas for several curricular enhancements. Faculty in the College of Liberal Arts' Senior Capstone program participated in a faculty-development workshop on teaching for practical wisdom led by Daisy Floyd. In addition, Paul Lewis and Tanya Sharon worked with administration and the College of Liberal Arts' General Education Committee to make practical wisdom central to the new general education curriculum. The College of Liberal Arts has since approved a new general education curriculum that went into effect at the start of the 2012–2013 academic year. The signature part of the curriculum is the requirement that students take an integrative seminar in each of their first three years of college. Those seminars will be designed to encourage students to synthesize knowledge from all domains and will be structured so as to promote, in developmentally appropriate ways, the moral maturation of Mercer students. In the law school, Mark Jones helped initiate the proposal for the semester-long course on teamwork skills that was originated by our editorial assistant Jon Simpson, then a 2L student, and offered as the interdisciplinary service learning course in spring 2011, as well as a proposal for a one-week intersession course on practical wisdom that remains pending.

In 2010–2011, Phronesis went underground, so to speak, to review and evaluate, but it also continues at work. Key project participants were part of the planning group for a spring 2011 initiative, Local Engagement Against Poverty (LEAP), that has set in motion structures for giving 10,000 hours of service to poverty-alleviation efforts in Macon, Georgia. In addition, the project co-sponsored and helped plan the Mercer Law Review symposium on "Citizenship and Civility in a Divided Democracy: Political, Religious, and Legal Concerns" for fall 2011. Mark Jones, who is coordinating the Law Review symposium, is also working on developing additional case-study exercises for use in future practical wisdom workshops involving both faculty and students as well as in-classroom teaching. Tanya Sharon continues to work with senior psychology majors to understand better the relationship between service learning and moral discernment. Kelly Reffitt is working with preK–grade 12 school personnel to enhance their character education efforts. Paul Lewis continues to explore the role in moral formation played by institutional climate/corporate culture and will follow up the earlier roundtable discussions on Mercer's moral climate by assessing how well institutional practices and polices promote wisdom. This investigation is inspired by the observation of Barry Schwarz and Ken Sharpe, who argue that too many institutions put in place policies and procedures that prevent people from developing practical wisdom.[3]

The Phronesis Project and Transformative Education

Whether working overtly or covertly, the Phronesis Project, with its emphasis on shaping student lives, is another powerful expression of Mercer University's longstanding commitment to transformative education. That commitment grows out of Mercer's religious heritage. Founded by Baptists, initially for the education of Baptist clergy, Mercer has for most of its existence been affiliated with the Georgia Baptist Convention. One historic Baptist distinctive has been that one must present evidence of transformation (the traditional term is "conversion") in order to be allowed into church membership. While Mercer no longer has formal ties to any Baptist entity, that insistence on transformation remains.

This commitment to transformative education has been forged by several key events in Mercer's past. These include a heresy trial conducted in 1939, when thirteen students, led by John Birch, accused professors in

---

[3] See chapter 12 in this volume.

Christianity and other departments of teaching ideas that contradicted Baptist beliefs in the Bible and creation. Although all professors were cleared of charges, this event has come to be a key part of Mercer's lore and self-identity as an institution that is not afraid of intellectual inquiry and a mutually critical conversation between multiple modes of inquiry.[4] Another event, or series of events, out of which Mercer's commitment to transformative education and "the Mercer ethic" was forged can be found in Mercer's experiences during the Civil Rights era and the integration of the Macon campus (one of the first college campuses in Georgia to do so).[5]

Mercer has a history of curricular experimentation as well. These experiments are described in the unpublished documents "Three Great Mercer Ideas," by retired Professor of English Mike Cass, and "The Legacy of Transformative Education at Mercer," by Peter Brown, of Mercer's Department of Philosophy.[6] This heritage is currently embodied in programs in the College of Liberal Arts' Integrative seminars, as well as several programs in community engagement, including service learning and Mercer on Mission. Seen in this historical context, then, the Phronesis Project is a natural and authentic expression of the character of Mercer University.

---

[4] The trial is chronicled today in the second edition of *The Mercer Reader* (Acton MA: Copley Custom Textbooks, 2009) 587–98. It also has been dramatized by Mercer Professor Andy Silver in an unpublished play from 2007, *The Disciples*.

[5] This story can be found in *The Mercer Reader* (Acton MA: Copley Custom Textbooks, 2009) 605–30; Will Campbell's account of the 1960s at Mercer, *The Stem of Jesse: The Cost of Community at a 1960s Southern School* (Macon GA: Mercer University Press, 1995); and Andy Silver's play, *Combustible/Burn* (Macon GA: Mercer University Press, 2002).

[6] Much of that material can be found in chapter 10 of this volume.

Appendix C: Focus Questions on Professionalism and Vocation in the Professions

Mark Jones

This appendix sets out a detailed list of focus questions along a vertical (profession-specific) axis addressing the history, current state, and future of professionalism and vocation in the United States. Taking inspiration from the sorts of inquiries undertaken in Pat Longan's Legal Profession course at Mercer Law School, these questions expand upon the original five questions along the vertical axis that, together with five questions along a horizontal (cross-professional) axis, were formulated to focus our inquiries at the first symposium held by the Professionalism and Vocation Across the Professions Project in 2005.This expanded list of questions along the vertical axis, as well as the original five questions along the horizontal axis, is designed to help guide ongoing exploration and research on issues of professionalism and vocation. Both sets of original questions and this expanded list of questions are discussed further in the narrative in appendix A.

Focus Questions on Professionalism

1. What is the history of the concept or moral ideal of professionalism within your profession?
    a. What is the current state of professionalism within your profession?
    b. How does the current state of professionalism in your profession compare with the state of professionalism during earlier periods in the history of your profession?
    c. Has there been a perceived lack or deficiency or decline in professionalism within your profession in recent years—perceived by the public, and/or perceived by clients/patients, and/or per-ceived by the profession itself?
    d. What are the perceived causes and/or manifestations of any such lack or deficiency or decline (e.g., growing commercialization of the profession)?
2. How is professionalism defined in your profession?

a. What values and virtues is professionalism within your profession understood to include?

b. What values and virtues *should* professionalism within your profession be understood to include, if different from your previous answer?

3. How are the values and virtues of professionalism promoted, and how are those values and virtues challenged in your profession in the context of:

   a. Professional education (admissions process, programs, institutional ethos)?

   b. The professional licensing process?

   c. Various practice environments (e.g., large, medium, small, and solo private practice; corporate practice; public sector practice; etc.)?

4. What coercive mechanisms exist for enforcing compliance with the values and virtues of professionalism in your profession (e.g., malpractice litigation, disciplinary regulation, market forces, etc.)? How, and how effectively, do these mechanisms operate?

5. What non-coercive mechanisms and/or incentives exist for encouraging compliance with the values and virtues of professionalism in your profession (e.g., continuing professional education, guidance and exhortation from professional bodies, etc.)? How, and how effectively, do these mechanisms and/or incentives operate?

6. To what extent are any of the above reflected in news reporting or fictional media portrayals?

7. What solutions are being considered, and/or should be considered, to address any perceived lack or deficiency or decline in professionalism, and to ensure the realization and instantiation of professionalism among members of your profession?

Focus Questions on Vocation

1. What is the history of the concept or sense of vocation or calling in your profession?

   a. How strong is the current sense of vocation or calling in your profession?

Appendix C

      b. How does the current sense of vocation or calling in your profession compare with the sense of vocation or calling during earlier periods in the history of your profession?
      c. Has there been a perceived lack or deficiency or decline in the sense of vocation or calling within your profession in recent years?
      d. What are the perceived causes and/or manifestations of any such lack or deficiency or decline?
2. How is the concept or sense of vocation or calling understood within your profession? How *should* it be understood?
3. How is a sense of vocation or calling promoted, and how is such sense challenged in your profession in the context of:
      a. Professional education (admissions process, programs, institutional ethos)?
      b. The professional licensing process?
      c. Various practice environments (e.g., large, medium, small, and solo private practice; corporate practice; public sector practice; etc.)?
4. What non-coercive mechanisms and/or incentives exist for developing and maintaining a sense of vocation or calling in your profession (e.g., continuing professional education, guidance and exhortation from professional bodies, etc.)? How, and how effectively, do these mechanisms and/or incentives operate?
5. The same questions as 1–4 above as applied to a sense of personal fulfillment or satisfaction.
6. Has there been a noticeable increase in the incidence of dysfunction, substance abuse, and/or psychological problems among members of your profession in recent years?
7. To what extent are any of the above reflected in news reporting or fictional media portrayals?
8. How much emphasis is placed in your profession upon treating the practitioner and/or the client or patient as complete persons and on integrating the many different aspects of their lives (including the "spiritual" aspects) within the context of professional activities?
9. What solutions are being considered, and/or should be considered, to address any perceived lack or deficiency or decline in the sense of vocation or calling and/or sense of personal fulfillment or satisfaction,

and to ensure the realization and instantiation of such sense, among members of your profession, including:
   a. Practical measures for reducing stress and work-related pressures?
   b. Encouragement of a holistic and integrative approach towards practice (so as to treat both the practitioner and the client or patient as a complete and multidimensional person with many different relevant interests and concerns, including spiritual interests and concerns)?
10. How are these focus questions related to the preceding focus questions on professionalism in your profession?

Appendix D: Case-Study Exercise

Introduction

Mark Jones

As explained in the introduction and in appendix A, we held the third symposium in the Professionalism and Vocation Across the Professions Project in October 2008 on the subject of practical wisdom. Early in the planning process, the planning committee decided to hold a case-study workshop as part of the symposium. This decision was inspired by the success of the QEP Ethics Group based in Atlanta in using case studies during their annual ethics event on the Atlanta campus.[1]

The planning committee decided to draft a difficult hypothetical case study focused on disability law and the challenges in providing adequate educational, medical, and social services for an autistic child. The committee drafted the following documents:

(1) Case Study Part I: Whose Decision Is It Really?
(2) Case Study Part II: Best for Whom?
(3) Case Study Supporting Materials
(4) Guidelines for Observers
(5) Teaching Note: "Difference, Disability, and Professional Judgment"

These materials are reproduced in this appendix, except for the "Guidelines for Observers," which are reproduced in chapter 15 in part III with an appropriately expanded title.[2]

The workshop was repeated for a new group of participants in October 2009. However, the basic approach was the same for both workshops. We

---

[1] See appendix A, note 8, for discussion of this group.
[2] See Jack Sammons's "Guidelines for Observing Practical Wisdom at Work." Each part of the case study notes that it was drafted as a basis for discussion rather than to illustrate either effective or ineffective handling of the situation, that it is a composite of several situations, and that none of the names used represent real persons. Readers who use case study part II in real time will need to change the dates on the letters accordingly. The errors in the third letter are deliberate.

are providing this introduction in case those readers who would like to use such a case-study exercise themselves may find our own experience helpful. Our particular purpose in holding the case-study workshops was to enable the participants to learn more about the nature of practical wisdom, especially the similarities and differences among the practical wisdoms of our different professions as these were manifested in the group deliberations, as well as to field test a promising interdisciplinary pedagogy. However, such a case-study workshop also could be usefully conducted for participants from the same discipline or professional field. Moreover, although the participants in the 2008 and 2009 workshops were mostly faculty, the same case study also has been used successfully, both at the undergraduate level and at the graduate professional school level, with various interdisciplinary groups composed exclusively of students.

* * *

The following will give some further information regarding how we organized, structured, and conducted the workshops and how we asked the participants to prepare for them.

(1) *Organization of Workshop.* We wanted to be able to conduct two parallel interdisciplinary discussion groups with maximum representation from across the university. We therefore asked the deans of each college and school, as well as the dean of the university libraries, to nominate two team members from their respective units. We then assigned each member of each team to a different group. We also thought it important to involve outside experts who had to deal with such issues on a regular basis in practice. We therefore invited representatives from the Bibb County and Monroe County school systems to attend the event and participate as discussants. At the first workshop in 2008, we had five outside experts—a school psychologist, a special education coordinator (and former school psychologist), a special education director, a principal, and an assistant superintendent. At the 2009 workshop, we had three outside experts—the same special education director, a different principal, and a different school psychologist. We asked members of the planning committee and some of those who had participated in earlier project events to act as discussion facilitators and observers. (At the 2008 workshop, Barry Schwartz and Kenneth Sharpe also acted as observers.)

(2) *Invitation to Participate.* In contacting the deans requesting nominations, we included an announcement giving some advance details about

Appendix D

the event. In addition to setting out the tentative schedule and indicating that participants would be asked to read some materials before the event itself, we described the nature of the workshop in the following terms:

> The workshop is part of our ongoing exploration of the question how best to educate professionals "to do the right thing in the right way at the right time." "Practical wisdom" is a key virtue across the professions, part of what makes a *good* lawyer, *good* doctor, *good* teacher, *good* engineer, *good* pastor, and so on. It transcends knowledge of the head (*episteme* or science) or of the hand (*techne* or skills)—it is knowledge of the heart (*phronesis* or practical wisdom). Practical wisdom guides the professional to aim at true human flourishing in any specific context of practice ("to do the right thing") and to apply the professional's knowledge and skills to hit that mark ("in the right way at the right time"). Rules and principles can mislead and knowledge and skills can be misused—without the judgment that comes from practical wisdom. What and how should we teach to develop our students' capacity for practical wisdom?
>
> Teams of two from each of the academic units of the university will be invited to participate in the workshop, as nominated by their deans. Several practitioners from outside the university will also be invited to join the discussion. A key component of the workshop will be the use of a difficult hypothetical case study focused on disability law and the challenges in providing adequate medical, social, and educational services for an autistic child. The case study is designed to illuminate the nature of practical wisdom from the perspective of several different professions. The participants will attempt to discover what virtues are necessary for the professionals involved to succeed in identifying the crucial interests in the case, including serving the well-being of the child and his family.

In the announcement for the 2009 repeat of the workshop, we indicated that we would try something new by asking the participants to prepare a reflection paper following the workshop (we also offered a small stipend in recognition of the extra work involved):

> In addition, this year we will ask the participants to do something new in the days following the workshop. Specifically, we will ask them to send us a short "reflection paper" (one page or so), addressing ways in which they might be able to make use of the workshop materials and their workshop experience in their teaching. Our purpose here is simply to stimulate thinking and to help us gauge the potential impact of this kind

of workshop experience on student learning. Although some may choose to follow through by implementing these ideas in the classroom, the participants will not be understood as making any kind of *commitment* to do so.

(3) *Preparation for the Case-Study Workshop.* We asked the participants in the 2008 symposium to prepare for the symposium and workshop by reading the following materials that we distributed to them by e-mail about two weeks before the event:
- An article by Barry Schwartz and Kenneth Sharpe, "Practical Wisdom: Aristotle Meets Positive Psychology," *Journal of Happiness Studies* 7 (2006): 377–95;
- An article by Jerome Groopman, "Dying Words: How Should Doctors Deliver Bad News?" *The New Yorker* (22 October 2002): 62–70;
- Case Study Part I: Whose Decision Is It Really?; and
- Case Study Supporting Materials (providing an overview of the relevant legal framework and procedures).

In addition to reading these materials, the workshop participants were required to attend the public lecture given by Barry Schwartz and Kenneth Sharpe the evening before the workshop.

The only difference with the 2009 repeat of the workshop is that, because Barry and Ken were not with us in person again, we required the participants to view the video recording of their lecture before they attended the workshop, accessible at http://www.youtube.com/mercerlawschool#p/a/EAA6E278F5F6F483/0/LUlSABvpYi4.[3]

The edited, revised, and updated text of the public lecture is included in chapter 12 of this volume. In addition, we note that the authors have since published their book on practical wisdom, which is therefore another resource that is now available for consultation or assignment.[4]

(4) *Structure and Conduct of the Workshop.* On the morning of the workshop, the participants received a folder of materials including a list of

---

[3] Barry Schwartz & Kenneth Sharpe, "The War on Wisdom and How to Fight It." Symposium on "Practical Wisdom: The Character of the Professions" sponsored by the Mercer University Professionalism and Vocation Across the Professions Project. Mercer University, Macon, Georgia. 30 October, 2008.

[4] See Barry Schwartz and Kenneth Sharpe, *Practical Wisdom: The Right Way to Do the Right Thing* (New York: Riverhead Books, 2010).

Appendix D

participants; a list of discussants, discussion facilitators, and observers in each breakout discussion group; a schedule of events; and additional copies of the materials they had been asked to read before the workshop as set out above. The basic structure of the workshop in 2008 was as follows:

8:30 A.M.	Continental breakfast
9:00 A.M.	Orientation (welcome and logistics; introduction to project and to case study)
9:30 A.M.	Breakout groups to discuss Case Study Part I
10:45 A.M.	Break
11:15 A.M.	Breakout groups to discuss Case Study Part II
12:30 P.M.	Lunch
1:15 P.M.	Plenary meeting
2:45 P.M.	Adjourn

Since the case study was not intended as a theoretical exercise, but as a realistic simulation requiring important decisions to be made (in both Parts I and II), the task of the discussion facilitators was to impress this fact upon the discussants, to keep the discussions on track by making the occasional intervention, if that seemed necessary, and to ensure that the discussants evaluated decisions already made and moved towards making those still to be made.

It is important to emphasize that the discussion facilitators distributed Case Study Part II only at the end of the discussion of Case Study Part I and asked the discussants to read it during the thirty-minute break. We postponed distribution of Case Study Part II until then because we wanted to preserve the conditions of ambiguity and uncertainty that called for the exercise of practical wisdom in making decisions at the earlier point in time in Case Study Part I.

Each discussion group was attended by two observers who used the "Guidelines for Observers" to help guide their judgment regarding the extent to which practical wisdom was (or was not) being manifested in the group deliberations. The observers shared their conclusions with all the participants in the plenary meeting after lunch and then helped lead a discussion among the participants regarding their experience at the workshop, including what the participants had learned from it and how they thought it might help them in their teaching. At the 2009 workshop, we decided to experiment and vary this structure slightly. Thus, the observers shared their conclusions regarding the discussion of Case Study Part I in a thirty-minute plenary meeting immediately following that discussion, followed by a fifteen-minute break before the discussion of Case Study Part II.

Although we decided to use only the "guidelines" at the workshops, we also have included the "Teaching Note: 'Difference, Disability, and Professional Judgment'" for those who would like to use the same case study, but want to give the observers more structured guidance either instead of, or in addition to, the guidelines. The guidelines are much more generic and could be used for any case-study exercise. The teaching note is tailored specifically to the facts of the case study reproduced here, although its basic structure and methodology are adaptable to other fact patterns as well. At the beginning of the plenary meeting after lunch, we distributed both the "Guidelines for Observers" and the "Teaching Note" to all the participants to include with the rest of the materials in their folders.

One additional option for those wishing to conduct such a case-study exercise is to videotape the proceedings for later consultation and analysis. We did this on both occasions without any apparent chilling effect upon the discussions.

Case Study Part I: Whose Decision Is It Really?[1]

Peter Brown

The car hadn't gone two blocks before Monica Jackson swung around to face her husband, Jimmy, and burst out, "What kind of man are you? You won't even fight for your son!" From the moment they had walked out of the meeting with the assistant superintendent, she had been torn between tears and rage. Rage won out. She continued, "He's your flesh and blood. Don't you love him like I do?" Jimmy swung the car to the curb and slammed on the brakes. "Godammit, Monica! You embarrassed the hell out of me in there. Those people are just trying to do their jobs. It's not their fault Carl is like he is." "And whose fault is it, then?" she shot back. Jimmy had just looked at her then and sighed and reached over and hugged her. Then the tears came. By a kind of unspoken agreement, she and Jimmy didn't mention it again that night. Now—the next morning—she was trying to get a handle on it, telling her best friend and neighbor, Pearlie, about the blow-up. Pearlie had always had a heart for Carl. What would she have done without her backup these last few years? Talking to Pearlie always helped her get her thoughts together.

Monica finished laying the options out as she saw them and turned to face her friend. "Pearlie, what are we going to do?"

What's Wrong, Doctor?

When Carl was two, Monica had noted a few oddities in his behavior that, in retrospect, were clearly part of his autism. He would repeat some actions over and over, waving his hand in front of his eyes, or bouncing and bouncing on his rocking horse. On walks, he was fascinated with turning window fans. He was not speaking yet, but at the time, Monica just thought he was late in developing. He had always avoided certain kinds of eye contact and didn't like to be cuddled. Monica thought a lot of it was shyness.

Just before his third birthday, the manager of their church's daycare suggested to Monica that they might want to have Carl evaluated. He wasn't

---

[1] This case study was prepared as a basis for discussion rather than to illustrate either effective or ineffective handling of the situation. The case is a composite of several situations; none of the names represent real persons.

potty-trained and still wasn't speaking. After Monica brought her concerns to their pediatrician, he referred them to a neurological pediatrician, who observed Carl several times over a three-week period. When they met with him to hear his report, they were both very nervous. After all, Carl didn't seem sick or unhappy. What could be wrong with him?

The neurologist was very clear. Carl had "classic" autism, a developmental disorder. Autism was something that wasn't very well understood, but children did not grow out of it. They were socially isolated and developed socially unacceptable behaviors. There could be other complications, including epilepsy or depression. Carl would not develop normally. He would need speech therapy and occupational therapy. It was too soon to tell how far he might be trainable or might be able to progress in school. Usually, in moderately severe cases like Carl's, progress could be made. But don't expect any miracles. He had concluded, "Just love him like he is. You have certain rights under the law to care and education. We understand this better every day, and I'm sure when he is school age, there will be well-trained people to care for him." Monica knew that this very educated young man was trying to be sympathetic. She believed him. But everything in her was revolting. She thought to herself, "Not *my* baby. Not if *I* can help it. Not *my* baby."

When Monica finally admitted that Carl wasn't "normal," she had gone to see her pastor, Reverend Simmons. Was this something she had done? If she had quit smoking, like all the ads said, would Carl be alright? Reverend Simmons assured her that this, too, was God's will. She and her husband were being tested. They would rise to the challenge. One thing he had said had really stuck with her: "Perhaps baby Carl has a special destiny to draw out the love and care of those who will deal with him in life? He could be a special source of joy to you and Jimmy and an inspiration to the whole church. God loves all his children, especially the special children." As usual, Reverend Simmons made her feel better and worse at the same time. Her Carl was special, but it was up to her to be sure he was loved enough to bring joy to Jimmy and her—and the whole church. Not for the last time, she had wondered if she was up to the task.

Creating a Future

Within months, Monica had met many other parents of autistic children. They all had theories, advice, and ideas about how to manage the bad episodes, how to stimulate attention and interaction. Most importantly,

Appendix D

they seemed to know all the best places and best people to work with these special kids. She had heard the horror stories, too. A constant theme was how important one-on-one interaction was. Some of these mothers seemed truly heroic to Monica in their devotion to their children. With the guidance of these other parents, Monica plunged into day-long interventions with Carl—getting him used to touching and being touched, blowing bubbles, repeating sounds to him, rolling balls: for hours at a time.

Monica vowed that she would never fail Carl—she would do whatever was necessary for him to get better, to grow up and have a life. Somewhere along the way, she and Jimmy sort of came to an understanding that they wouldn't try to have another child. Carl took up so much time and energy, sometimes it seemed that she didn't have much left for Jimmy. But Jimmy had been a rock. He rarely complained about the unmade beds and takeout meals. He helped with Carl on the weekends. At any rate, when Monica went on the pill, Jimmy didn't object, just mumbled, "Maybe it's for the best." She hoped, someday, Jimmy would be proud of Carl.

When he was three, the school district was notified of Carl's disability, and he was enrolled in the district's morning preschool program. By this time, he was daytime potty-trained. He said his first word, "Momma," on Christmas Day. However, on Valentine's Day at a school pageant, Carl crawled under a table and began screaming, covering his ears with his hands. He screamed for fifteen minutes. After re-evaluation by a school team of a psychologist and speech therapist and consultation with Jimmy and Monica, Carl was transferred to a private institute, the Children with Disabilities Institute of Achievement (CDIA). The school system paid the tuition. Carl received ninety minutes of speech language pathology a week and ninety minutes of occupational therapy a week.

In his fourth year, Carl began receiving music therapy at CDIA. It became his favorite time. And the occupational therapist seemed to Monica to be a genius at finding ways for Carl to experience his own body in space—swinging him, working with balance balls, improving his coordination. To Monica's delight, Carl began demonstrating developmental progress in several areas. He was communicating in phrases and then short sentences. When given choices, he was able to choose an option rather than have a behavior spell. By the end of the year, Carl's "Summary of Progress," prepared by his lead teacher at CDIA, indicated that he had mastered 80 percent of the curriculum and was kindergarten ready.

Monica loved the fact that Jimmy was spending more time playing with Carl, reading to him, playing catch with him, matching and lining up long lines of LEGO® bricks, one of Carl's favorite pastimes. She felt more and more comfortable letting Pearlie look after Carl while she did errands and got her hair done. Simple things. And she and Jimmy seemed closer too. Monica vowed to herself more than once, "I mustn't neglect Jimmy. He needs my love, too."

Hard Choices

When Sarah Upshaw, the director of CDIA, had invited Monica and Jimmy to a conference in March, Monica hadn't expected that they would eventually be faced with some hard choices. Ms. Upshaw had praised Carl's progress and said how delightful it was to have parents like them to work with, how lucky Carl was to have them as his parents. But then she had told them the real reason for the meeting. Carl was ready for kindergarten. The local school system was obligated to provide an education for Carl, just as it did for all the other school-age children in the county. As Ms. Upshaw explained the options, "We would love to have Carl with us another year or two. He has made great progress and become part of our family, too. If the school system agrees, they will continue to pay for our services. Our center has fully qualified instructors who will work with Carl and other kindergarteners to move them forward and prepare them for full inclusion by second grade." She continued, "However, the system may feel that Carl is better served within a school setting. They have to provide educational services for Carl, but they get to decide what they think is best for him."

Ms. Upshaw said she would arrange for a time for all of them to meet with the assistant superintendent for educational services to discuss Carl's needs and readiness. There might be some other testing they would want to do. And she was sure that Jimmy and Monica would have questions. She concluded, "If you have a friend or an attorney that you would feel comfortable bringing to this meeting, you should feel free to invite them." Monica was a little surprised at this, but it was Jimmy who said, "Why would we want an attorney? Are we being sued?" He laughed like that was a joke, but afterward, he said to Monica, "I don't like this. It should be our decision what's best for our son. Is this going to be a hassle?"

The Jacksons learned that the school would develop an individualized educational plan ("IEP") for Carl. Dr. Martha Carson, the assistant superintendent, told them that they would be included on the IEP team,

Appendix D

along with one of the kindergarten teachers at Bonaire Elementary School, the school psychologist, the special education teacher, and a speech therapist. Bonaire was the school that the Jacksons were zoned for. The IEP that was developed mainstreamed Carl as much as possible. He would spend half the day in special education classes in a small group setting and the other half in a regular classroom. The Jacksons liked the idea of inclusion. Jimmy was particularly pleased that Carl would "be in with normal kids." After all, Ms. Upshaw had said he was ready for kindergarten. They enrolled Carl in Bonaire with high hopes.

To the Jacksons' dismay, however, Carl didn't seem to make any progress at all in language, math, or social skills. His behavior spells became more frequent. Monica was terrified that he was regressing. Halfway through the school year, they petitioned the district to transfer Carl back to CDIA. The Jacksons were invited to meet with the IEP team to revise the IEP. They did not attend the meeting and repeated their request to transfer Carl back to the CDIA. The team recommended transferring Carl to Scott Elementary School, which had a special program for autistic children.

In response to this decision, the Jacksons requested another meeting with the assistant superintendent. When they got to the meeting, they found it included the principal of Scott Elementary School, the system psychologist, and the attorney who represented the school system. Dr. Carson introduced everyone to the Jacksons and asked the principal to talk about the special program for autistic children at Scott Elementary. As she explained, each day Carl would receive sixty minutes of individualized speech therapy; sixty minutes of individualized academics focused on language arts and social studies; social recess group (six or seven children in a group); small lunch group with one other child; thirty minutes of music therapy; thirty minutes of occupational therapy; and sixty minutes of individualized academics focused on math.

When she finished, Jimmy had said, "This sounds pretty good to me. He does well with occupational therapy and music therapy." Monica couldn't believe her ears; she thought they had agreed to insist on the transfer back to CDIA. She cut in, "It may sound good, but these people don't know Carl. He's gotten worse. How do we know this will work, just transferring him from one place to another? We want him back at the institute. These people don't really care about him anyway." Dr. Carson looked over at Jimmy. Staring at the floor, he said, "I don't know, babe. Maybe we should think it over." In the silence that followed, Dr. Carson finally cleared her throat and said that she appreciated the Jacksons' coming in. If they still disagreed with the IEP recommendation, they could request mediation or a due process hearing. She concluded, "We would like to transfer Carl to Scott as soon as possible. Please let me know your decision as soon as possible, so we can begin getting ready for him at Scott." Without another word, Monica got up and stalked out. Jimmy jumped up and followed her to the car.

What's Best?

After the blowup in the car, Monica wished she could take back what she had said to Jimmy. She meekly fixed spaghetti for dinner. Carl loved drawing the strands up through his lips one by one. They always put a big bib on him, and she didn't mind the mess. Jimmy went to bed early. He worked ten-hour days laying carpet. He usually slept like a log. After she put Carl to bed, she stood looking at him fall asleep. She always rocked and sang to him until he was drowsy. Sometimes she thought that those were her and Carl's happiest times. He loved being sung to—it was the only time she could really hold him.

The next morning, she fixed Jimmy his usual quick breakfast; his workday started at 7:30 and it was a thirty-minute drive into work. As she served it to him, she couldn't get the scene with the school officials out of her head. But she and Jimmy didn't say anything to each other about the meeting or the decisions that had been made. Monica got Carl up and on the van to Bonaire. Then she made herself wait until 9:30, when she was sure Pearlie was up, and called her friend: "I need so bad to talk with someone. Jimmy and I had a big fight, but it wasn't really him...it was them... I don't know, maybe it's just me." Pearlie calmed her down a bit and said she'd be over at eleven. They could fix lunch together and talk it out. Pearlie also offered to keep Carl that evening, "if you and Jimmy want to go out for dinner or a movie, or anything."

After getting her frustrations out and lambasting the school system for refusing to do what they knew was best for Carl, Monica laid out the options for Pearlie as she saw them: "We can go along with their decision. We can fight them, get a lawyer if we have to. Or I could ask my parents for a loan to help pay for the institute for the rest of the year." Looking across the table at her friend, she calmly asked, "Pearlie, what are we going to do? Jimmy is ready to go along with their decision. I know that I don't know all the stuff they do, but I know my son. He did real well at the institute. He was making

Appendix D

real progress. For the first time in years, I thought maybe he can have a normal life—a *shot* at a normal life. Am I just being hysterical? He's my baby. I can't take a chance we'll mess this up. What are we going to do?"

At that moment, Monica heard Jimmy come through the front door. He never came home for lunch. She had gotten through to him. Now what?

Case Study Part II: Best for Whom?[1]

Tom Glennon, Anne Hathaway, and Stephen Wills

Carl Jackson, at the request of his mother, was placed in the sixth grade at Crestview Middle School, in opposition to the recommendation of the principal, Allen Anderson. Carl's schooling experience included the private institute, the Children with Disabilities Institute of Achievement (CDIA), public elementary school without a program for autistic children, public elementary school with a program for autistic children, and hospital homebound. Crestview Middle School, while providing for special needs, did not provide a special program for autistic children. The school used an inclusion model that provided assistance to special-needs children through the use of paraprofessionals and co-teachers.

At the beginning of the fall semester, an IEP team was appointed to review and assess Carl's record to ascertain the best placement and course of study. Mrs. Williams, a sixth-grade teacher and an instructional team leader at Crestview Middle School, was requested to attend the IEP meeting. After the meeting ended, Mrs. Williams could not believe the IEP meeting she had just attended. While she is in favor of inclusion, in the IEP meeting she found out that an autistic boy was being assigned to her instructional team and would be in her homeroom and first-period English class. In addition to that information, the boy, Carl, was in the meeting, rocking back and forth and making grunting sounds.

Carl's reading level had been determined to have reached a mid-second-grade level, with 50 percent comprehension. His understanding of basic mathematical concepts was at beginning-first-grade level. Socially, he was able to attend to familiar activities with minimal distraction, but was disturbed by sensory inputs such as movements and noise. He also was able to take conversational turns and responded to positive behavioral supports and redirection. He needed prompts and one-on-one assistance to complete most tasks and daily living routines. Of course, the system promised

---

[1] This case study was prepared as a basis for discussion rather than to illustrate either effective or ineffective handling of the situation. The case is a composite of several situations; none of the names represent real persons. The errors in Pearlie Moncrief's letter in Carl Jackson File Document 3 are deliberate.

appropriate technology and support from inclusion teachers, behavior specialists, paraprofessionals, and such, but Mrs. Williams knew how all that really worked.

After Mrs. Williams left the meeting, she discussed the issue with her friend and colleague, Mrs. Henderson. Mrs. Williams was very concerned about how her teammate, Mr. Barnes, would handle Carl in his science class. She knew Mr. Barnes already had trouble with learning-disabled children in his classes and was concerned that having an autistic child in the science class would drive Mr. Barnes insane. Mrs. Williams and Mrs. Henderson both agreed that Mr. Barnes would probably cope with the situation by putting Carl in a corner and ignoring him.

Mrs. Williams, on the other hand, expressed to Mrs. Henderson that, while she would complain, she would try to do her best with the situation and with Carl. Mrs. Williams was very impressed with Carl's mother and how she had stood up for her child. Mr. Anderson had done all he could do as principal to keep Carl from being enrolled. However, the mother was adamant, and as soon as she suggested a lawsuit, all the administrators gave in to the mother's request. Actually, Mrs. Williams admired the mother for such tenacity.

When Carl arrived for his first day of school at Crestview, Mrs. Williams's fears were actualized. Carl rocked and made noises constantly. He also threw a huge tantrum, during which he got out of his seat, started flailing his arms, and made semi-yelling, semi-crying sounds, right in the middle of Mrs. Williams's English class. The other students did not know what to think of Carl. They were overall pretty terrified, so they stayed away from Carl, but called him a "freak" behind his back.

Later in the day, Carl went to the class of another of Mrs. Williams's teammates, Mr. Maddox. That situation apparently was not much better. When Carl's paraprofessional, Mrs. Tasker, walked Carl into Mr. Maddox's room, Mr. Maddox told her he had put some crayons on his desk in the corner and asked her just to keep him quiet so the rest of the students could have class. Neither Mrs. Tasker nor Mr. Maddox knew what to do when Carl began throwing crayons.

The situations in the team's classrooms were bad enough, but then Mrs. Williams, the team leader, found out that the PTA president, an influential parent who was helping with registration, had become aware of the situation and was extremely upset. This woman went to the principal and told him to do something. As a result, Carl was removed from the team and spent the rest of the day in the inclusion teacher's room with the paraprofessional in order to allow Carl to be "broken in slowly" to his new surroundings.

It was evident to Mrs. Williams that, as time went on, Carl's behavior worsened. The students became no longer afraid of Carl. In fact, a few of the boys, while a teacher wasn't looking, would often go up to Carl and wave their hands in front of his face just to set Carl off on another tantrum. The boys figured this was a good way of getting out of doing work.

To Mrs. Williams's dismay, the PTA president and several other parents heard about the disruption from their children and met with the principal and told him that their children were unable to learn in this environment. Rather than meet with the instructional team, they requested that the principal either remove Carl or place their children in another sixth-grade team. The principal told the parents to give the situation a little bit more time and that he would work on it. Then he asked the special education inclusion teacher if there was any medication that could be given to Carl to calm him down.

As the year progressed toward mid-October, Carl's behavior did not improve. Mrs. Tasker was frequently absent, and when she was there, she would give Carl treats and toys when he acted up to calm him down. The inclusion teacher and Mrs. Williams told the paraprofessional that this only increased the inappropriate behavior because he was getting rewarded for misbehaving. The paraprofessional responded that it was the only thing that worked and basically told the teachers to deal with the student themselves. Carl increasingly started spending more time out of the classroom with the paraprofessional, the speech pathologist, or the inclusion teacher so that the instructional team classrooms could keep some form of normalcy.

As Mrs. Williams would expect, Carl's parents often checked in with the teacher by visiting the school. However, they did notice that Carl was spending less and less time in regular classrooms. As a result, Carl's mother accused Mrs. Williams and the principal of not following the IEP and threatened a lawsuit against the school system.

Mrs. Williams became very upset and sought the advice of other teachers. Word of the lawsuit spread to the PTA president and other parents. In a countermeasure, these parents got together and hired an attorney of their own, claiming the school system had failed to create a proper educational environment for their children and demanding that either Carl leave or their children be placed in other classrooms. Now there was the possibility of *two* lawsuits. To make matters worse, Mrs. Williams had

Appendix D

received a call from the principal asking for her recommendation regarding the action to be taken concerning Carl. The IEP team was meeting again tomorrow; how was she going to handle this?

Carl Jackson File, Document 1:

August 1, 2008

Dr. Janet Smith
Special Education Director
Simmons County School System

Dr. Smith,
After a careful review of files, a personal observation of the student in question, and multiple interviews with present and past teachers and administrators, it is my professional opinion that it is neither in the student's best interest nor in the best interest of the school for Carl Jackson to be enrolled at Crestview Middle School.

In middle school, Carl would need to be successful in at least six different learning environments because he would be expected to change classes every period of the day. If the creation of one successful learning environment proved difficult for Carl in a self-contained setting at Scott Elementary, the creation of six successful environments would be impossible in a more difficult middle-school setting. If Carl did not change classes, he would still have to adjust to six different classes of students each day as they entered the classroom. Carl's records indicate that he does not handle change well and that we are still discovering the objects and events that set off his tantrums. The daily change of a middle-school environment would set Carl and the classrooms up for certain failure.

Also, in middle school, finding students who would be supportive of Carl despite his disabilities would be difficult. As you are aware, in middle school, fitting in is essential. Any characteristic a student may have that seems "different" would likely become a source of embarrassment and ridicule for that student. Given this common attitude among middle-school students, a student as "different" as Carl would stand little chance of being accepted by his peers and would likely endure constant ridicule.

Finally, I am concerned that the academic demands of middle-grades courses would be impossible to modify to Carl's present academic functioning without totally abandoning the constructs of the courses. In my opinion, if Carl would be doing something totally different from the rest of the class, I see little reason for him to be in the regular classroom environment.

No one wants to see Carl set up for failure. A failure of this sort not only could erase any social gains he may have made over the school year, it may in fact cause permanent damage to Carl's self-esteem and self-identity. My recommendation for Carl would be for him to be enrolled in one of the self-contained classrooms at Gibson Middle for students with severe disabilities. He may also be able to be included in some regular non-academic classrooms such as music, physical education, and lunch to maintain socialization.

Sincerely,

Allen Anderson, Principal
Crestview Middle School

Carl Jackson File, Document 2:

8/3/08

Dr. Janet Smith
Special Education Director
Simmons County School System

Dear Dr. Smith:
I am requesting that my son Carl be allowed to attend Crestview Middle School next year. For all of Carl's life, we have been told what he can't do. Now, without even being given a chance, we are again told that Carl will fail and will not be able to attend his zoned middle school.

I know realistically that Carl will always be different, but it is my goal for him to be in a school situation where he fits in and is included with the other children from the community. I had my doubts about transferring Carl out of CDIA and including him in a regular kindergarten. It took me until he reached second grade to realize that I can't protect Carl from the harsh realities of the world. I came to realize that it is best that he learn to get along with regular children than to protect him through isolation. It is important for Carl to establish these other children as behavioral role models. Only then will Carl have a chance of functioning in the real world. He certainly will not be able to function if the only other people he is ever around also have autism.

Carl proved a lot of people wrong when we made the situation at Scott Elementary work. Keep in mind that after being on hospital homebound his entire third and fourth grade years with tuberous sclerosis, people then were also afraid of Carl being in the regular classroom. However, after a few rough patches and adjustments, the situation was made positive. Please give Carl the chance to prove these "experts" wrong again. Do not limit Carl's potential, especially after he has made such positive strides.

I look forward to the IEP meeting with you and the rest of the IEP team and ironing out the specifics of Carl's educational plan.

Sincerely,

Monica Jackson

Carl Jackson File, Document 3:

To the Special-Education Director

Dear Mrs. Smith,

I want to begin by admitting that I am not a professional. I have no special degrees or credentials. I am a friend and neighbor of Carl and his family. Our families attend the same church. Carl's mother and father asked me to attend his IEP and to say a few words on behalf of Carl.

I have known Carl since he was a baby, and a beautiful baby he was. My husband, George, and I recognized, almost from the start, that he was different. I mean, different from our own three children. He was sick a lot. His parents worried about him and were often stressed. You could often see it in their faces. Their relationship was in trouble. Each wanted to know if the other was responsible for Carl [sic] condition, and I believe that they blamed each other. I can't fault them for their feelings. When your children are born, you hope they will grow up, finish school, enjoy life, get married. It must be terrible to live with the prospect that your children will not have this kind of future.

They were afraid to leave Carl even for a little while. Fortunately, they trusted us. We were one of the few people who they would allow in their home to baby-sit. We did this about once a month. I believe it helped. They needed time alone to reconnect with each other. Carl did not seem to mind and he did well with us.

It is very true that Carl does not make eye contact, but you get use [sic] to this after awhile. That is just the way he is. It is also true that he does not like to have his routines interrupted. If you do, he will surely have one of his "spells." He may even strike out and hit you, but it's not personal.

There is nothing malicious in him. In fact, he is a very gentle young man. He loves animals and country music...he loves to work on his computer...and he loves baseball. I think he loves the shape of the diamond and the organ playing "Take Me Out to the Ball Game." He mouths the words and rocks back and forth. Once you get to know him, however, it's easy to make him feel comfortable. My rambunctious teenaged children are found [sic] of Carl, and they have, in fact, found some very interesting ways to make him happy.

I read the diagnostic evaluations of Carl. I can understand the pictures that the professionals and teachers took of him, but I also understand that what they reported were just "snapshots." They do not represent him completely. Yes, he hits out sometime [sic] but that is not violence. It's his way of protecting his privacy and the world he creates from [sic] himself. We would probably do the same thing if our worlds were threatened or if our safe places were suddenly taken away. I was surprised that he was measured and summarized by what he did or did not do on tests or in classrooms. You and I are more than our school performances and so is Carl. I am personally glad that I was not judged solely by what I did in classrooms or on tests.

Schools are very familiar places for most of us. They are full of sights and sounds and smells. Students sit in rooms full of other children. Bells ring, kids walk down hallways with their backpacks, teachers balk [sic] out commands and pass out papers. There is a structure and an architecture to it all, and both are almost impossible to change. Shoemakers know that making just one shoe will not fit all feet. I don't think schools have many shoemakers.

When I was in college, I took a humanities seminar that asked us to define the purposes of an education. Some of what I read suggested that school was a place where one learns how to be useful and productive and

Appendix D

how to be a good person. Forgive me if I am missing something here, but I don't understand how the things that are currently being done for Carl have anything to do with making him a useful and productive person in this society. What is being done for him does make sense, however, but only if I assume that Carl is not expected to be productive, not ever. I hope this is not the case. I hope that school does not turn out to be an outrageous waist [sic] of Carl's time.

I often think about Carl. I wonder what the future holds for him. I wonder what will happen to him after school is over, assuming he makes it through school. Where will he go? Will he be ready to live on his own or will he need some kind of program? What will happen to him if his parents divorce? What is to become of him when they die? Is there no place on earth for him? I do not know the answer to these questions. I am a bit perplexed and outraged, however, that these questions were not answered before he entered the educational system. And I am disturbed that they are not being addressed in this planning process.

Very truly yours,

Mrs. Pearlie Moncrief
August 15, 2008

Case Study Supporting Materials[1]

Alice Baker

Statutes Affecting a Disabled Child's Right to Primary or Secondary Education

Individuals with Disabilities Education Act (IDEA)

Requires school districts to provide disabled children with a Free and Appropriate Public Education (FAPE).

Protected Child: Child aged 3-21 with any of several listed physical and mental impairments (mental retardation, hearing impairments, visual impairments, orthopedic impairments, autism, specific learning disabilities, etc) who needs special education and related services as a result of the impairment.

A child aged 3-9 may also be covered, at the discretion of the state, if s/he is developmentally delayed and needs special education and related services as a result.

What's required:

School must provide a Free and Appropriate Public Education (FAPE).

School creates an Individualized Education Plan (IEP).
    The IEP is a formal, written statement that specifies the student's education goals, objectives, curriculum, and related services. It is created by a team that includes educational professionals, the child's parents, and other professionals (psychologist, audiologist, doctor, etc., as needed in individual cases). The IEP is updated annually.

Student must be educated in the Least Restrictive Environment (LRE), which is presumptively a placement in a regular classroom. The child is removed from the regular classroom only if s/he cannot be mainstreamed.

---

[1] These materials were developed solely for the purpose of the present Case Study Exercise and are not intended to provide legal advice. The flow chart on pages 264-66 is reproduced from a document that is identified as "Handout 2-A" and that bears the following notation: "This flow chart is adapted from *Communicating with Your Child's School Through Letter Writing: A Parent's Guide*, a 2002 publication of the National Dissemination Center for Children with Disabilities (NICHCY), 1.800.695-0285, nichcy@aed.org, www.nichcy.org." That document also bears the running footer "Handouts for Theme A: Modules 1-2." The NICHCY website home page includes the following statement: "[F]eel free to share our materials with others. Everything we offer on our site is copyright-free and intended to be shared far and wide."

> Example: Amy is a single-leg amputee and uses a wheelchair. She functions at grade level in all academic subjects. Amy has the right to be educated in a regular classroom.
>
> Example: Brian is deaf and uses a Sign Language interpreter. Brian has the right to be educated in a regular classroom.
>
> Example: Carlos, age 9, has severe mental retardation and autism. He cannot benefit from placement in a regular fourth-grade classroom. Carlos should be educated in a special classroom.

School must provide "related services," such as speech therapy, audiology services, counseling, interpreters, and school nurse services, as needed.

> Example: D'Andrea has a cleft palate. D'Andrea is entitled to speech therapy as part of her educational program.

There is no cost defense.

> Example: Emily, who is deaf, requires a full-time Sign Language interpreter at a cost of $25,000 a year. The school must pay for Emily's interpreter.

Discipline:
If a student engages in serious misconduct, the school conducts a Manifestation Determination to determine whether the misconduct is a manifestation of the disability. If the misconduct was caused by the disability, the IEP must be adjusted. If the misconduct was not caused by the disability, the student can be disciplined, except that the school cannot expel the disabled student.

> Example: Felix has Tourette syndrome and occasionally produces outbursts of profanity. Since the misconduct is caused by Felix's disability, he cannot be disciplined.
>
> Example: George, who has cerebral palsy, spray-paints the school gym in the colors of a rival school. George can be suspended.

The school can immediately remove a child who brings a weapon to school or sells drugs, or where the current placement is substantially likely to result in injury to the child or others. If a student is dangerous and cannot be educated in a school environment, it must provide a FAPE through some other means.[2]

---

[2] The only exception is that a person incarcerated in a penal institution is sometimes not entitled to a FAPE. Since the IDEA applies to children until they graduate from high school or reach age 21, some otherwise IDEA-eligible people are in jail.

> Example: Hilda, who has cancer, sells drugs behind the school gym. Hilda can be removed from the school immediately. The school must provide her a FAPE through other means, such as by sending a teacher to her home.

What's not required:

School need not provide student an ideal education, or even the same level of education that is provided to non-disabled students. The standard is minimal: "some educational benefit."

> Example: Inez, age 12, has an I.Q. of about 70, ADHD, and obsessive compulsive disorder. She functions at the second-grade level in math and reading, and has extremely poor social skills. Inez can benefit from a day program in a regular school with a student-teacher ratio of 12:1. The "ideal" placement for Inez would be a residential school with a student-teacher ratio not in excess of 6:1. The "ideal" placement would cost about twice as much as a day program placement. The school need not provide the more expensive placement.

Children, even if they are disabled, are not covered by the IDEA if they don't require special education and related services as a result of the impairment.

> Example: Jamal has an artificial eye. He functions at grade level and requires no special services. Jamal is not covered by the IDEA.

Americans with Disabilities Act (ADA), Title II

Prohibits all state and local government entities from discriminating against individuals with disabilities.

Protected child: Anyone with a disability who is otherwise eligible for public education. "Disability is a "physical or mental impairment that substantially limits one or more of the major life activities of [the] individual."

What's required:

School district cannot:

- Exclude a disabled child from participating in its educational services.
    > Example: Keiko is HIV+. The school cannot exclude Keiko.

- Deny a disabled child the benefits of its educational services, programs, or activities.
    > Example: Lupe is severely mentally retarded and requires a great deal of individual attention to benefit from the school's educational program. The school cannot place Lupe in a regular classroom and let her sit staring at a wall all day, because the placement will not allow her to benefit educationally.

- Give a disabled child an opportunity to participate in or benefit from its educational services that is not equal to that afforded others.
    > Example: Mike is blind. The school cannot exclude Mike from AP and foreign language classes, if Mike is otherwise qualified for them.

Example: Nakesha has dyslexia and requires individual tutoring in order to learn to read. The school cannot place Nakesha in a regular class with 25 students during reading lessons, because that placement will not give her an equal opportunity to benefit from reading lessons.

- Give a disabled child different or separate education, unless the "different" education is necessary to provide the disabled child with an education that is as effective as that provided to nondisabled children.
Example: Continuing with Nakesha, the school can place Nakesha in a separate class for reading lessons, because giving her separate lessons is necessary to provide her with an education that is as effective as that provided to nondisabled children.

- Discriminate in any other way against a disabled child.

School district must:

- Make reasonable modifications to its policies, practices, and procedures.
Example: Omar has severe asthma and must carry an inhaler with him at all times. The school has a strict zero-tolerance policy for all drugs, including prescription pharmaceuticals. The school must waive this policy and allow Omar to carry his inhaler.

- Administer services, programs and activities in the most integrated setting appropriate to the needs of the disabled child.
Example: Peggy, age 16, is mentally retarded and functions below grade level in all academic subjects. Although the school can place her in separate academic classes, she should be mainstreamed for physical education and other nonacademic classes.

- Make appropriate modifications to its physical facilities, so they are accessible to the disabled child.
Example: Qushawn uses a wheelchair. The school must install wheelchair ramps so that he can get into his classrooms, the cafeteria, and other parts of the school.

- Provide appropriate communications accommodations, such as Braille or Sign Language interpreters.

- Provide accessible transportation.
Example: Rick uses a wheelchair. If the school provides transportation to its other students, the school must get a lift-equipped school bus or a van, so that Rick receives the same transportation services that other students receive.

These requirements are subject to the defense that a school is not required to engage in activities that would fundamentally alter the educational program or constitute an "undue burden."

Comparison: IDEA vs. ADA

Note that if the child wins under *either* statute, the child wins.

	IDEA	ADA
Definition of disability	**Impairment+ Need special education and related services**	**Impairment that substantially limits a major life activity**
Example: Susan has mild dyslexia and requires special education services in order to read.	She is disabled for purposes of the IDEA because she needs special ed services	She is not disabled for purposes of the ADA because her impairment is mild.
Example: Tyrone has a prosthetic arm, but requires no special services.	He is not disabled for purposes of the IDEA because he needs no special ed services.	He is disabled for purposes of the ADA because his impairment substantially limits his ability to grasp and lift.
Entitlement	**FAPE = "some" educational benefit**	**Equal access**
Example: Ursula is deaf and mentally gifted. She can function at grade level without a Sign Language interpreter, but will get straight A's in an advanced class with a Sign Language interpreter.	The IDEA does not require the school to provide her with a Sign Language interpreter, because she can get "some" educational benefit even without an interpreter.	The ADA does require the school to provide her with a Sign Language interpreter, because she needs the interpreter in order to get equal access to the educational program.
Example: Vonda, age 8, has cerebral palsy, and is severely mentally retarded. She will never learn to read or do math. A "good" educational program for her would be therapy designed to get her toilet trained, and to learn to feed herself.	The IDEA requires the school to provide an adapted curriculum in Vonda's case.	The ADA does not require the school to provide a fundamentally altered curriculum.
Cost defense?	**None**	**Not required to provide accommodations that would result in fundamental alteration or undue burden.**
William is ventilator-dependent and requires regular urinary catheterization. He requires a full-time aide, at a cost of $20,000/year	The IDEA requires the school to provide William with the aide, because it is a "related service" that will allow William to benefit from the educational program.	The ADA does not require the school to provide William with the aide, because it is so costly.

Other Statutes

Rehabilitation Act of 1973

Prohibits all entities that receive federal funding from discriminating against individuals with disabilities. Substantive provisions are essentially the same as ADA, Title II.

Americans with Disabilities Act (ADA), Title III

Prohibits all privately owned public accommodations – including private schools – from discriminating against individuals with disabilities. Substantive provisions that govern private schools are essentially the same as ADA, Title II.

Note that private schools are covered by ADA Title III, but not only by IDEA. Thus, a private school can raise a cost defense that would be unavailable to a public school, and is not required to provide accommodations that would fundamentally alter its program.

> Example: Ximena, who has dyslexia, is enrolled in the 10th grade at Shalom School. Shalom School requires all its students to study Hebrew. Ximena asks to be excused from the foreign language requirement, or at least allowed to take her Hebrew language exams using the Roman alphabet, because it is so difficult for her to learn a different writing system. The school is not required to excuse Ximena from Hebrew studies, if the accommodation would fundamentally alter the school's program.

State Constitutions

Most state constitutions create a right to an "adequate" education.

> Example: Georgia State Constitution, Article VIII, Section I, Paragraph 1
>
> "The provision of an adequate public education for the citizens shall be a primary obligation of the State of Georgia. . . ."

No Child Left Behind and Standards-Based Educational Reform

Standards-based educational reform, including No Child Left Behind, sets a minimum standard of academic achievement for all children. The focus shifts from process to expected outcomes. Disabled students are expected to meet the same standards, unless they are "significantly cognitively impaired."

The 2004 amendments to IDEA require states to establish performance standards for children with disabilities.

Handout A-2
Page 1

The Basic Special Education Process Under IDEA

Here's a brief look at how a child is identified as having a disability and needing special education and related services.

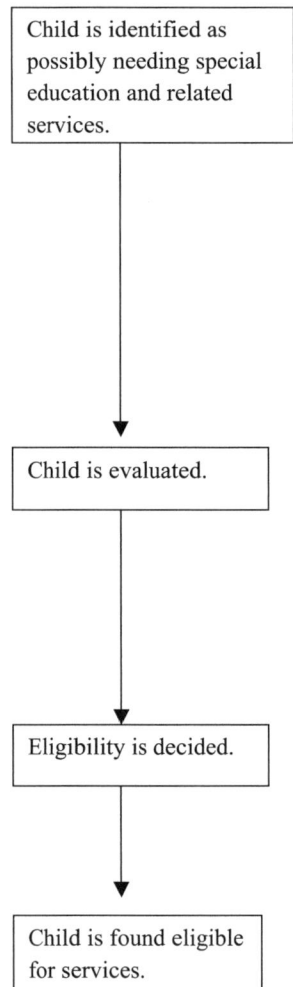

1 *Child Find."* The State must identify, locate, and evaluate all children with disabilities in the State who need special education and related services. To do so, States conduct "Child Find" activities. A child may be identified by "Child Find," and parents may be asked if the "Child Find" system can evaluate their child. Parents can also call the "Child Find" system and ask that their child be evaluated. Or—

Referral or request for evaluation. A school professional may ask that a child be evaluated to see if he or she has a disability. Parents may also contact the child's teacher or other school professional to ask that their child be evaluated. This request may be verbal or in writing. Parental consent is needed before the child may be evaluated. Evaluation needs to be completed 60 days after the parent gives consent (or, if the State has established a timeframe, within the *State's* timeframe).

2 The evaluation must assess the child in all areas related to the child's suspected disability. The evaluation results will be used to decide the child's eligibility for special education and related services and to make decisions about an appropriate educational program for the child. If the parents disagree with the evaluation, they have the right to take their child for an Independent Educational Evaluation (IEE). They may ask that the school system pay for this IEE. They may also request a due process hearing to challenge the school's evaluation.

3 A group of qualified professionals and the parents look at the child's evaluation results. Together, they decide if the child is a "child with a disability," as defined by IDEA. Parents may ask for a hearing to challenge the eligibility decision.

4 If the child is found to be a "child with a disability," as defined by IDEA, he or she is eligible for special education and related services. Within 30 calendar days after a child is determined eligible, the IEP Team must meet to write an IEP for the child.

Handout A-2
Page 2

The Basic Special Education Process Under IDEA

Once the student has been found eligible for services, the IEP must be written. The two steps below *summarize* what is involved in writing the IEP.

> IEP meeting is scheduled.

5 The school system schedules and conducts the IEP meeting. School staff must:

- contact the participants, including the parents;
- notify parents early enough to make sure they have an opportunity to attend;
- schedule the meeting at a time and place agreeable to parents and the school;
- tell the parents the purpose, time, and location of the meeting;
- tell the parents who will be attending; and
- tell the parents that they may invite people to the meeting who have knowledge or special expertise about the child.

> IEP meeting is held and the IEP is written

6 The IEP Team gathers to talk about the child's needs and write the student's IEP. Parents and the child (when appropriate) are part of the Team. If the child's placement is decided by a different group, the parents must be part of that group as well.

Before the school system may provide special education and related services to the child for the first time, the parents must give consent. The child begins to receive services as soon as possible after the meeting.

If the parents do not agree with the IEP and placement, they may discuss their concerns with other members of the IEP Team and try to work out an agreement. If they still disagree, parents can ask for mediation, or the school may offer mediation. Parents may file a complaint with the state education agency and may request a due process hearing, at which time a resolution session must be held and mediation must be available.

Handout A-2
Page 3

The Basic Special Education Process Under IDEA

Here is a brief summary of what happens *after* the IEP is written.

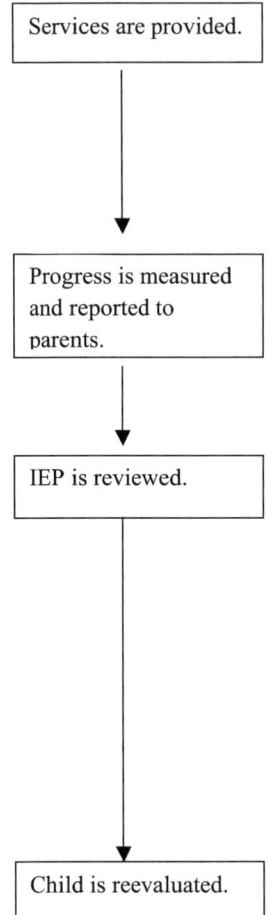

7 The school makes sure that the child's IEP is being carried out as it was written. Parents are given a copy of the IEP. Each of the child's teachers and service providers has access to the IEP and knows his or her specific responsibilities for carrying out the IEP. This includes the accommodations, modifications, and supports that must be provided to the child in keeping with the IEP.

8 The child's progress toward the annual goals is measured, as stated in the IEP. His or her parents are regularly informed of the child's progress and whether that progress is enough for the child to achieve the goals by the end of the year. Progress reports are provided to parents in keeping with the IEP.

9 The child's IEP is reviewed by the IEP Team at least once a year, or more often if the parents or school ask for a review. If necessary, the IEP is revised. Parents, as Team members, must be invited to attend these meetings. Parents can make suggestions for changes, can agree or disagree with the IEP goals, and agree or disagree with the placement.

If parents do not agree with the IEP and placement, they may discuss their concerns with other members of the IEP Team and try to work out an agreement. There are several options, including additional testing, an independent evaluation, or asking for mediation or a due process hearing. They may also file a complaint with the state education agency.

10 At least every three years the child must be reevaluated, unless the parents and school agree that a reevaluation is unnecessary. This evaluation is often called a "triennial." Its purpose is to find out if the child continues to be a "child with a disability," as defined by IDEA, and what the child's educational needs are. However, the child must be reevaluated more often if conditions warrant or if the child's parent or teacher asks for a new evaluation.

Teaching Note: Difference, Disability, and Professional Judgment

Peter Brown

A. Objectives:

1. To elicit the elements of practical wisdom in professional judgment.
2. To use the "expanded" case method as a means of professional development.

B. Characters:

1. Monica and Jimmy Jackson, parents of Carl
2. Carl Jackson, diagnosed as "classically" autistic as a toddler and, at age nine, with tuberous sclerosis
3. Pearlie Moncrief, the Jacksons' neighbor and friend, who has helped care for Carl through the years
4. Neurological pediatrician, who diagnosed Carl as autistic
5. Reverend Simmons, the Jacksons' pastor
6. Sarah Upshaw, Director of the Children with Disabilities Institute of Achievement (CDIA), where Carl was enrolled in morning preschool on recommendation of the school system after disrupting the system preschool program
7. Dr. Martha Carson, Assistant Superintendent of Simmons County School System
8. Principal of Scott Elementary, where Carl was transferred as a kindergartener (from Bonaire Elementary) and enrolled in a special program for autistic children
9. Allen Anderson, Principal of Crestview Middle School, where Carl was enrolled in sixth grade (over Anderson's objections)
10. Mrs. Williams, sixth-grade teacher and instructional team leader at Crestview Middle School, in whose homeroom and English class Carl is placed
11. Mrs. Henderson, Mrs. Williams's friend and colleague at Crestview
12. Mr. Barnes, science teacher on Mrs. Williams's instructional team who "ha[s] trouble with learning-disabled children in his classes"

13. Mr. Maddox, teacher on Mrs. Williams's instructional team, in whose class Carl acts out
14. Mrs. Tasker, the paraprofessional assigned to work with Carl and his teachers
15. PTA president at Crestview, an influential parent who objects to Carl's presence in class with her child and other parents' children and later threatens a lawsuit
16. Dr. Janet Smith, Special Education Director for Simmons County school system (recipient of letters in Carl's file)

C. Timeline:

PART I

age 2	ages 3–5	ages 5–8
First signs of autism	Diagnosed and enrolled in preschool	Enrolled in public school

PART II

ages 8–10	ages 10–11	ages 11–12
Hospital homebound services	5th-grade Scott Elem.	6th-grade Crestview Middle

D. Issues:

(Note: This is not an exhaustive list; participants may identify other issues):
1. The nature of and prognosis for autism, including degrees of severity
2. Parents' responsibilities to and for an autistic child
3. The rights and recourse of parents with respect to their children's treatment, education, and access to services and facilities
4. The strain of an autistic child on parents' relationship
5. Social attitudes toward autistic children and adults, including friends of the family and fellow church members
6. The status of autistic children as moral and spiritual agents, as friends, as neighbors, as citizens, as children of God
7. The social world of an autistic child
8. The desires and responsibilities of an autistic child
9. The legal rights to care, access, and education of an autistic child
10. School system responsibilities and liabilities for the education of an autistic child

Appendix D

11. School system responsibilities and liabilities to teachers, other parents, and other children
12. The responsibilities and liabilities of classroom teachers, instructional leaders, paraprofessionals, special education teachers, and administrators for the education and development of autistic children
13. Best educational and social developmental practices for autistic children
14. Cost-benefit of educational practices for autistic children
15. The rights and recourse of other parents when their children's education is affected by children with disabilities such as autism

E. Teaching Plan:

(Note: For a three-hour training session—two seventy-five-minute sessions, parts I and II, and a thirty-minute break between them):

1. PART I: "Whose Decision Is It Really?" (Read in advance.)
   1. Please introduce yourselves to the group (have first names on name badges). [ten minutes]
   2. Reflect for a moment on ways that learning disabilities have touched you personally or professionally. [two minutes]
   3. Will a few people share those connections? [three minutes]
   4. Let's begin by looking at the people in this case, who they are and what issues they face. We'll start with Carl Jackson. [fifteen minutes]
   (Flip Chart)
   NAME
      • Personal Characteristics   • Issues
   5. What is the key issue the case presents for us today? And why is it the key? [ten minutes]
      • Issue   • Rationale
   6. Which of these issues should we focus on at this point? (Get some consensus on one or two.) [five minutes]
   7. Let's dig deeper into "xyz" issue. What are the options for addressing this issue? (Break into five informal groups with markers and tear sheets to brainstorm responses—each group selects a reporter.) [ten minutes]
   8. Share the alternatives with the group. [ten minutes]
   9. Let's end this first session by trying to get at the basic considerations underlying these alternative options. Let's use a simplified schema, at least at first. There are a complex set of values and goals involved in this

case. There are also laws and regulations and procedures to be followed, under which different people have different responsibilities and rights. In addition, this case involves some very particular circumstances that might make its resolution quite different from a similar case. What matters most to our judgments in this case? Be as specific as possible. [fifteen minutes]
- Values and Goals
- Laws and Regulations
- Personal Responsibilities
- Particular Circumstances

10. Thank you; that was a great start. Now, we are going to follow Carl a few years farther into his and his parents' experience with his disability. Please read part II carefully, and we will reconvene in thirty minutes. (Hand out part II.)

2. PART II: "Best for Whom?"

1. A lot of water has gone under the bridge since we saw Carl and his parents in kindergarten; let's review his history to this point in the second part of our case. [five minutes]
(Rough timeline)

2. What additional people have been added to the situation? [ten minutes]
Names with brief identifiers

Note: Use either #3 or #4.

3.   a. What new issues, if any, have been introduced? [fifteen minutes]
- Issues

b. Whom is this case about professionally—really? And why? [fifteen minutes]
- Name   • Issue or Rationale

OR

4.   a. Let's put ourselves in the situation—a little role-play. We are going to be members of the IEP team, school administrators, and Monica Jackson. [twenty minutes]
(Ask for volunteers to play Monica Jackson, Mrs. Williams, Dr. Janet Smith, Mrs. Tasker, and Allen Anderson. Have stick-on identifiers for names and have the principal start the meeting. Thank participants at the end and relieve them of their roles.)

Appendix D

    b. Where were the participants true to their roles and where did they transcend those roles? Why did they transcend them? [ten minutes]

3. CONCLUDING CONSIDERATIONS
1. This is a rich, difficult set of issues and responsibilities. Let's spend the rest of the discussion reflecting some about how decisions get made and how they should be made in such settings.
   a. Where does personal experience come into the equation? How important is it? [ten minutes]
   b. What, if anything, in the discussion made you rethink or question your initial judgment? Explain why. [ten minutes]
   c. At the end of the day, what matters most to you about the character of the action taken? Explain why. [ten minutes]
2. Thank you for your openness to this process and willingness to contribute. These sorts of complex situations always will allow for divergent views and decisions. The challenge is to make the wisest choice—that is, to bring theory, experience, and a broad perspective to bear on the issues and responsibilities involved. I hope this discussion has made us all just a bit wiser than we were at the start.

Contributors

Alice Baker was a member of the Mercer University Law School faculty from 2001 until 2008. An assistant professor of law from 2001 until 2004, and then an associate professor of law until 2008, she taught courses in Alternative Dispute Resolution, Antitrust, Civil Procedure, Disability Law, Employment Law, Evidence, and Statutory Law and Analysis, and has written in the areas of employment law and immigration law. She is a graduate of the University of Virginia and a member of the Virginia Bar. Before joining Mercer, Alice held a judicial clerkship with a U.S. district court in Ohio and taught at the University of Toledo School of Law. Currently living near Sacramento, she plans to become a member of the California bar and to practice antitrust and/or employment law in California.

Peter Brown is Professor of Philosophy and, currently, Director of the Office of National Fellowships and Scholarships at Mercer University. His research interests are in postmodern ethics, case teaching, and community building. In 1998, Brown received the College of Liberal Arts' highest teaching honor, the Spencer B. King Distinguished Professor Award. From 1998 to 2006, Brown led a new initiative on the part of Mercer University to contribute to the improvement of neighborhoods around the university's main campus, receiving the Jimmy and Rosalynn Carter Partnership Award for Campus-Community Collaboration in 2002. In 2001, he was named a Knight Fellow in Community Building at the School of Architecture of the University of Miami, and in 2010, Brown was recognized as one of six national finalists for the Thomas Ehrlich Civically Engaged Faculty Member of the Year, given by Campus Compact. From 2006 to 2010, Brown served at Mercer as senior vice provost.

John Marson Dunaway is Professor of French and Interdisciplinary Studies in the College of Liberal Arts at Mercer, where he has taught since 1972. He was the director of the Mercer Commons (A Center for Faith, Learning, and Vocation) from 2004 to 2011. His research interests include primarily French religious writers. He is currently working on translations of Vladimir Volkoff's fiction and a book of essays by philosopher Jean-Louis Chrétien titled *Under the Gaze of the Bible*. He is also co-directing (with Bryan Whitfield, Assistant Professor of Christianity in the College of Liberal Arts at

Mercer) a mentoring program for new faculty that is supported by a grant from the Lilly Fellows Program.

Daisy Hurst Floyd is University Professor of Law and Ethical Formation at Mercer University Walter F. George School of Law, where she also served as dean from 2004 until 2010. Prior to coming to Mercer, she practiced law in Atlanta and served on the faculties of the University of Georgia School of Law and Texas Tech University School of Law. Her teaching and research interests include ethics, legal education, civil procedure, evidence, and legal and judicial writing. She is the author of numerous law review articles and is a frequent speaker at academic and law conferences. Professor Floyd has a particular interest in the ways in which higher education shapes students' ethical development and in the possibilities for cross-disciplinary collaboration within higher education. Professor Floyd was named a Carnegie Scholar by the Carnegie Foundation for the Advancement of Teaching and served as a member of the Carnegie Foundation's Life of the Mind for Practice Seminar. Her work and the findings of the seminar are discussed in *A New Agenda for Higher Education: Shaping a Life of the Mind for Practice* (Jossey-Bass 2008).

Timothy W. Floyd is Professor of Law and Director of the Law and Public Service Program at Mercer University Walter F. George School of Law. He has published two books and is the author of numerous articles in the areas of legal ethics, law and religion, and criminal law and the death penalty. His service activities emphasize access to justice issues and lawyer professionalism; he has been a member of the Supreme Court of Georgia Equal Justice Commission, chair of the State Bar of Georgia Access to Justice Committee, a member of the National Advisory Committee of Equal Justice Works, chair of the Advisory Board of the Georgia Council for Restorative Justice, and member of the Advisory Board of the Georgia Justice Project. In addition, he has represented several defendants in death-penalty cases.

Thomas J. Glennon is Reg Murphy Professor of Leadership in the College of Liberal Arts at Mercer University and serves as director of the Social Entrepreneurship Program. He has served on the boards of nineteen NGOs and has done program evaluation, program development, and non-profit consultant work throughout Georgia. He is director of the Georgia AmeriCorps Challenge Program and created the First Street Arts Pre-School

Contributors

Program and the Georgia Children's Museum. He is a past president of the Georgian Advocacy Office, the State of Georgia's program that advocates for better treatment, services, and programs for all individuals with disabilities in Georgia.

Harriet Anne Hathaway is Professor of Middle Grades and Mathematics Education in the Tift College of Education at Mercer University, where she was also the founding dean. She teaches courses at the undergraduate, master's, and doctoral levels. Prior to coming to Mercer, Dr. Hathaway taught seventh-grade mathematics and science; served as mathematics coordinator for the Guilford County, North Carolina, school system; served as mathematics consultant in the division of mathematics with the NC Department of Public Instruction; and was the founding dean at the Thayer School of Education at Wingate University. Primarily interested in the areas of curriculum design, mathematics education and problem-solving, and middle-grades education, she has made numerous presentations at state, regional, and national conferences, and has been principal or co-principal investigator for grants from the Knight Foundation and NASA. In addition, she has consulted on curriculum design for public and private P–12 schools and higher-education teacher education programs. She has also evaluated teacher education programs for a number of years. She has been active in the Mercer University cross-college symposia on professionalism, ethics, practical wisdom, and the Phronesis Project.

Mark Jones is a Professor of Law at the Walter F. George School of Law of Mercer University. For many years, his teaching, research, and service interests focused on the area of transnational law. In recent years, his interests have refocused and expanded to include legal history, legal philosophy, and issues of professionalism. Since 2005, he has coordinated Mercer University's "Professionalism and Vocation Across the Professions" Project and now co-directs the "Phronesis Project for the Exploration of Character, Practical Wisdom, and Professional Formation," into which the former project was incorporated in 2009. His long-term research agenda, which comprises several articles and at least one book, is concerned with exploring law in its broader historical, jurisprudential, and transnational context, and with tracing the influence of such a broader understanding of law upon evolving notions of legal professionalism and the historical development of legal education in the United States. He has been called to the bar of England and Wales, and is a member of the Honourable Society of the Middle Temple in London, England. He has also studied law in Germany and worked as a legal consultant in Brussels, Belgium.

Paul Lewis is Associate Professor of Christianity in the College of Liberal Arts at Mercer University, where he has taught since 2002. His area of specialization is theology and ethics, with special interest in moral development. He has presented papers in Hungary and Brazil as well as at schools in the United States. He has published several refereed articles and book chapters on a variety of topics. Common to them is engagement in a mutually critical dialogue between theology and other sources of insight and wisdom. His latest project is a treatment of "Christian Practical Wisdom as Faithful Innovation," one that grows out of his interests in Aristotle, Michael Polanyi, the psychology of moral development, and H. Richard Niebuhr. He also directs the Senior Capstone Program in the College of Liberal Arts and co-directs the Phronesis Project.

Thomas Lickona is a developmental psychologist and Professor of Education at the State University of New York at Cortland, where he founded and directs the Center for the 4th and 5th Rs (www.cortland.edu/character). His center's work was the subject of a *New York Times Magazine* cover story, "Teaching Johnny to Be Good." A past president of the Association for Moral Education and board member of the Character Education Partnership, he has written, co-authored, or edited eight books on moral and character development, including *Raising Good Children* and *Educating for Character*. The latter won a Christopher Award for "affirming the highest values of the human spirit." Dr. Lickona is the recipient of the "Sandy Award" for Lifetime Achievement in Character Education from the Character Education Partnership and the Award for Outstanding Achievement in Moral Education from the University of San Francisco.

Susan Malone is currently the Vice Provost for Institutional Effectiveness at Mercer University Press. Formerly, she was the associate dean for assessment, accreditation, and administration for the Tift College of Education at Mercer University. She also served for ten years as the director of English education at the University of Southern Mississippi. Her research interests include assessment and pre-service teacher preparation and induction.

Contributors

William F. May is Senior Fellow at the Institute for Practical Ethics and Public Life at the University of Virginia. Prior to his retirement as a university professor of ethics at Southern Methodist University (1985–2001), he was the Joseph P. Kennedy Professor of Christian Ethics at the Kennedy Institute of Ethics at Georgetown University (1980–1985). He served on the Clinton Task Force on Health Care Reform (1993) and on the President's Council on Bioethics (2002–2004). May is a former president of the American Academy of Religion, the Society of Christian Ethics, and a founding fellow of the Hastings Center, where he co-chaired its research group on death and dying. His books include *The Physician's Covenant* (rev. ed., 2000), *The Patient's Ordeal*, *The Ethics of Giving and Receiving: Am I My Foolish Brother's Keeper?*, and *Beleaguered Rulers: The Public Obligation of the Professional*. His latest book is *Testing the National Covenant: Containing Runaway Fear and Curbing Runaway Appetites*.

Darcia Narvaez is Professor of Psychology at the University of Notre Dame. She researches moral development through the lifespan with a particular focus on early-life effects on the neurobiology underpinning moral functioning (Triune Ethics Theory). She has worked on interventions for moral character development, including integrating moral character skill development into academic instruction. Her Integrative Ethical Education model was first described in the 2006 *Handbook of Moral Development*. She emphasizes "moral complexity" and the importance of both deliberative and intuitive processes in ethical expertise. She has co-authored or co-edited seven books, and in 2006, she co-authored the first chapter on character education for the *Handbook of Child Psychology* and has published articles in the *Journal of Educational Psychology* and *Developmental Psychology*. She is editor of the *Journal of Moral Education*.

Emile Paille is Associate Professor of Literacy Education in the Tift College of Education at Mercer University. She teaches courses in reading assessment, literacy, and children's literature. Her major research interests at present include improving literacy instruction in a developing country, including working through pre-service teacher candidates, and the long-term impact of learning to teach in a third-world country on American teachers.

Kelly Reffitt is an Assistant Professor of Education in the Tift College of Education of Mercer University. She specializes in literacy for students in preschool through grade five and primarily teaches language arts and assessment courses at the undergraduate and graduate levels. Her research interests include effective literacy instruction and issues in rural education. She is currently working on a long-term service-learning project with a local Head Start program to facilitate undergraduates' experiences in assessment and emergent literacy instruction, create a centralized media center for the county's numerous Head Start sites, and provide teacher and parent education workshops. She is also working on the establishment of a professional development school in conjunction with the Bibb County School district, the Macon Children's Promise Neighborhood Partners, and Mercer University. She is a co-director of the Phronesis Project.

David Ritchie is Associate Professor of Law at Mercer University School of Law, where he also teaches in the philosophy department in the College of Liberal Arts. He has published two books and more than a dozen articles and book chapters. His writings have appeared in the U.S. and abroad. Professor Ritchie has had fellowships at New York University, Temple University School of Law, and the University of Buenos Aires School of Law. He frequently teaches and lectures in Argentina and Brazil.

Jack Sammons is the Griffin B. Bell Professor of Law at the Walter F. George School of Law, Mercer University, where, in addition to teaching for thirty-three years, he also has served as Director of Clinical Education, Associate Dean, and Associate Vice President for Finance. Professor Sammons is the author of *Lawyer Professionalism* and over forty articles, chapters, poems, videos, and one commissioned play on the subjects of legal ethics, professional ethics, legal history, legal education, freedom of speech, and law and religion. He is a frequent speaker at law schools and at continuing legal education programs. Among his many service activities, Professor Sammons is a founding member of the Chief Justice Commission on Professionalism, the Georgia Judicial Campaign Ethics Task Force, the Georgia Center for Law in the Public Interest, Friends of the Ocmulgee Old Fields, and the Ocmulgee National Park and Preserve Initiative.

Barry Schwartz is the Dorwin Cartwright Professor of Social Theory and Social Action in the Psychology Department at Swarthmore College,

Contributors

where he has taught since 1971. Among his publications are *The Costs of Living* (1994) and *The Paradox of Choice* (2004). Schwartz has also published articles in the *New York Times, New York Times Magazine,* the *Chronicle of Higher Education, Slate, Scientific American,* the *New Republic,* and the *Harvard Business Review.* He has appeared on NPR's "Morning Edition" and "Talk of the Nation," and has been interviewed on "Anderson Cooper 360," "The News Hour" (PBS), and "CBS Sunday Morning." His latest book, *Practical Wisdom: The Right Way to Do the Right Thing* (2010), co-authored with colleague Ken Sharpe, is the basis for his contribution to this volume.

Kenneth E. Sharpe is the William R. Kenan, Jr. Professor of Political Science at Swarthmore College, where he teaches political philosophy, Latin-American politics, and foreign policy. Among his publications are *Drug War Politics: The Price of Denial* (1996), *The Transnational Corporations Versus the State: The Political Economy of the Mexican Auto Industry* (1985), and *The Real Cause of Irangate* (1987). Sharpe also has published articles in the *Washington Post, New York Times, Christian Science Monitor, Los Angeles Times, Boston Globe,* the *Nation,* and the *American Prospect.* His most recent work, co-authored with Professor Barry Schwartz at Swarthmore, is *Practical Wisdom: The Right Way to Do The Right Thing* (Riverhead, 2010).

Nancy Sherman is a University Professor of Philosophy at Georgetown. She served from 1997–1999 as a distinguished chair of ethics at the United States Naval Academy. She is also a fellow of the Kennedy Institute of Ethics and has received, for the academic year 2011–2011, a Public Policy Scholar appointment at the Woodrow Wilson International Center for Scholars (Washington, DC). She has appeared on numerous television and radio programs discussing military ethics, and ethics in general. She is the recipient of numerous scholarly awards, among which include NEH, Mellon, APA, and ACLS fellowships. She appears in the Who's Who of American Women. Professor Sherman's research interests include (1) moral philosophy, (2) the history of moral philosophy, (3) moral psychology and the emotions, (4) ancient philosophy, (5) ancient ethics, (6) psychoanalysis, and (7) military ethics. Her latest book, *The Untold War: Inside the Hearts, Minds, and Souls of Our Soldiers,* offers philosophical and psychological analysis of the moral weight of contemporary warfare.

William M. Sullivan is Director of Educating Tomorrow's Lawyers. He is currently Senior Scholar at the Center for Inquiry in the Liberal Arts at Wabash College. He was formerly Senior Scholar at the Carnegie Foundation for the Advancement of Teaching, where he co-directed the Preparation for the Professions Program, a comparative study of professional education encompassing the fields of engineering, the clergy, nursing, and medicine, as well as law. Sullivan is the first author of *Educating Lawyers: Preparation for the Profession of Law* (2007). He is also the author of *Work and Integrity: The Crisis and Promise of Professionalism in America* (2005). His most recent book is the co-authored study of preparation for business: *Rethinking Undergraduate Business Education: Liberal Learning for the Profession.*

Stephen Wills is Assistant Professor and Coordinator of Special-Education Programs at Georgia College and State University. Dr. Wills has spent the past several years researching, developing, and modeling cognitive-based interventions for students with learning disabilities. He currently serves as the vice president for the Georgia Federation Council for Exceptional Children. Dr. Wills also has twenty-one years' experience as a public school special educator, teaching elementary-school, middle-school, and high-school students with disabilities during his career.

Index

ABA Professionalism Committee Report (1996), 110
ABA Section on Legal Education and Admissions to the Bar, 111 (n 9)
"Abilities Are Forms of Developing Expertise" (1998) (R. Sternbern), 25 (n 8), 26 (n 13)
academy, academies, academic(s), 9, 19-20, 42, 49, 53, 63, 65, 81 (n 31), 82, 84 (n 36), 106-111, 117, 122, 126, 130, 133, 136, 145, 185, 199, 220, 227, 229, 230, 239, 247, 253-254
Academic Medicine (1993), 191 (n 33)
Academy of Management Review (2001): 172 (n 6)
accountants, accounting, 103, 105 (n 5), 107, 109, 113, 117, 124
additive (curriculum reform), 102, 110-111, 131
American Association of Colleges of Teacher Education, 92 (n 1)
"Answering the Call to Service: Vocation and Professional Identity" (Thomas Floyd), 9, 139
Answering the Virtuecrats: A Moral Conversation on Character Education (1997) (Robert J. Nash), 17 (n 2)
apprenticeship(s), 8-10, 32, 35, 38-40, 102-103, 105-113, 118 (n 6), 119 (n 6), 142, 149, 150-159, 161-63, 213, 224
Apprenticeship in Thinking: Cognitive Development in Social Context (1990) (Barbara Rogoff), 38 (n 45)
apprenticeships of professional education: academic, 9, 108-109; practical, 9, 108; socio-ethical, 9, 108. *See also* Sullivan, William
Aristotle, Aristotelian, 2, 17, 19, 21, 23, 26, 27 (n 16), 39, 53, 66, 78, 79, 130 (n 15), 150, 152, 153, 161, 173-175, 177, 187, 208, 209, 211, 215, 240
Aristotle's Ethics (1988) (J. O. Urmson), 39 (n 50)
Aristotle's Poetics (1986) (Stephen Halliwell), 79 (n 26)
"Assessing Dispositions: Five Principles to Guide Practice" (Mary E. Diez), 94 (n 6)
assessment(s), 6-7, 92-98, 106, 109, 169, 183, 214 (n 1)
Association of American Colleges and Universities (AAC&U), 144, 149
Association for Supervision and Curriculum Development, 47 (n 17)
Athens, 128
Authentic Happiness (2002) (Martin Seligman), 47 (n 15)
autism, autistic, 13, 237, 239, 243-245, 247, 250-251, 255, 267-269
autonomy, 6, 91, 171, 173, 175
"A Balance Theory of Wisdom" (1998) (Robert J. Sternberg), 20 (n 7)
balkanization, balkanized, balkanizing, 122
Baltes, Paul, 20, 24 (n 3), 25 (n 4), 26 (n 13)
banker(s), 183, 187n
Baptist(s), 115, 231-232
The Baptist Identity: Four Fragile Freedoms (1993) (Walter B. Shurden), 116 (n 3)
The Baptist Summit at Mercer University January 19-20, 2006: Three Addresses by R. Kirby Godsey, Walter B. Shurden, and William D. Underwood (2006), 115, 116 (n 4)
"Being Pragmatic about Practical Wisdom" (David Ritchie), 11, 199, 201, 203, 205
Beleaguered Rulers: The Public Obligation of the Professional (2001) (William May), 123
Benjamin Franklin's The Art of Virtue: His Formula for Successful Living (1996) (George L. Rogers), 56
Bennett, William, 19
Berkowitz, Marvin, 20, 22 (n 10), 42 (n 3), 59 (n 39), 60, 63 (n 46)
Big Questions, Worthy Dreams: Mentoring Young Adults in Their Search for Meaning, Purpose, and Faith (2000) (Sharon Daloz Parks), 40 (n 51)
Bloomberg Law Reports—Student Edition (2011), 219 (n 4)
brave, bravely, bravery, 146, 174, 176-177
Buechner, Frederick, 9, 134, 140
business, 46, 48, 61, 103, 117, 122-124, 127, 147, 187 (n 21), 218 (n 2). *See also* profession
The Call: Finding and Fulfilling the Central Purpose of Your Life (1998) (Os Guinness), 134 (n 1), 137
The Call to Service: A Witness to Idealism (1993) (Robert Coles), 137
Callahan, David, 60
Callahan, Sidney, 58
calling(s), 7, 9-11, 88, 104-105, 110, 114, 123-124, 134, 137, 139-142, 144-145, 147, 161-162, 193-194, 196-197, 218, 227, 234-235

Callings: Twenty Centuries of Christian Wisdom on Vocation (2005) (William C. Placher), 138
Calvin College, 120
capital: human, 103; intellectual, 103
career(s), careerism, 49, 104, 114, 118, 124, 135, 141
Caring, A Feminist Approach to Ethics and Moral Education (2003) (N. Noddings), 33 (n 34)
"Caring Moves: Seeing the Competence in Interpersonal Citizenship Behavior" (2010) (A. Wrzesniewski and J.E. Dutton), 172 (n 6)
Carnegie Foundation for the Advancement of Teaching, 102, 115, 199, 219, 225
case study, case-study, case studies, 1, 12 (n 4), 14, 154 (n 2), 202, 206, 207 (n 2), 214 (n 1), 217, 220, 221 (n 7), 226, 229, 231, 237-242, 243, 250
case-based learning, 191
Center for Ethics and Public Responsibility at Southern Methodist University, 130-131
"Changes in Dispositional Empathy in American College Students Over Time: A Meta-Analysis" (2010) (Sara Konrath, Edward H. O'Brien, and Courtney Hsing), 50 (n 25)
"The Changing Contours of Moral Education in American Colleges and Universities" (2010) (Julie A. Reuben), 18 (n 2)
character: development, 1-7, 10-11, 15, 17-18, 23, 43, 52-53, 226, 229; good, 2-4, 22, 51-53, 60, 175, 228-229; performance, 5, 43, 45-47, 53
Character Education in America's Blue Ribbon Schools (1998) (Madonna Murphy), 42 (n 2)
Character Education Partnership, 42, 42 (n 7)
Character Education: The Foundation for Teacher Education (1999) (Mary M. Williams and Eric Schaps), 42 (n 4)
Character Psychology and Character Education (2005) (Daniel K. Lapsley and F. Clark Power), 17 (n 2), 18, 38 (n 47)
"Character, Rules, and Relations" (2006) (Hugh Sockett), 93 (n 4)
Character Strengths and Virtues (2004) (Christopher Peterson and Martin Seligman), 45, 46 (n 12)
"'Cheater!': The Central Moral Admonition of Legal Ethics, Games, Lusory Attitudes, Internal Perspectives, and Justice" (2003) (Jack L. Sammons), 197 (n 3)
cheating, 49, 52, 57, 59-61, 182, 197 (n 3). *See also* dishonesty
The Cheating Culture: Why More Americans Are Doing Wrong to Get Ahead (2004) (David Callahan), 60

"Cheating: Why Students Do It and how We Can Help Them Stop" (2001) (Don McCabe), 60 (n 42)
citizen(s), citizenry, citizenship, 3-5, 19-20, 22, 23, 41, 45-47, 50, 59, 65, 104, 113-114, 117, 127-128, 143-144, 148, 151-152, 158-159, 162, 268
"Citizenship and Civility in a Divided Democracy: Political, Religious, and Legal Concerns", 231
citizenship education, 4, 19-20
civic: engagement, 22, 146; identity, 102; professionalism, 8-9, 105
"The Claim to Moral Adequacy of a Highest Stage of Moral Development" (1973) (Lawrence Kohlberg), 49 (n 22)
Clark University, 52
clinical training, 107
cognitive: development, developmentalism, 4, 18-19, 21-22, 108; knowledge, 108; skills, 108
Colby, Anne, 40 (n 51), 46, 50 (n 23), 112 (nn 10, 12), 188 (n 24)
Collaborative for Academic, Social, and Emotional Learning, 47 (n 17)
college(s), 1, 3, 18, 22, 40, 41-43, 48-50, 52-53, 60-61, 66, 96, 116-117, 119, 124-125, 143-144, 147-149, 185, 217-224, 228-230, 232, 238, 256
College of Liberal Arts, 145, 147, 149, 227-228, 230, 232
college undergraduates, 22
Colleges That Encourage Character Development (1999), 42 (n 5)
Colleges with a Conscience, 20
Columbia University Medical School, 188
common good, 21, 25, 114, 117, 124-125, 127, 148, 225
common ground (university), 116, 119, 121, 122
common marks of the professional (intellectual, moral, organizational), 125. See also May, William.
community of practice, community of practitioners, 107, 109, 113
competence, competencies, competency, competent, 5, 11, 19, 22, 44, 51, 54, 86, 105-106, 108-109, 113, 130, 199, 200, 205-206
The Complete Psychological Works of Sigmund Freud (1955) (Sigmund Freud), 74 (nn 11, 12)
complexity, 26, 155, 161, 186 (n 20)
conceptual framework, 8, 92-94, 96
conscience(s), 5, 37, 44, 51, 53-54, 56-58, 62, 70-73, 75, 77, 109, 146-149, 160-161, 180
"Contemporary Character Education in Context" (Paul Lewis), 4, 17, 19, 21, 23
context(s), 2-4, 6-13, 19, 21, 23, 25, 30, 34-36, 38-39, 74, 102, 105 (n 4), 109, 112 (n 12), 146,

Index

154-155, 165, 175-176, 185, 194-195, 199, 204-206, 208-209, 215, 217, 225, 226, 228, 232, 234-235, 239
"Correlates of Wisdom-Related Performance in Adolescence and Adulthood: Age-Graded Differences in 'Paths' Toward Desirable Development" (2003) (U. Staudinger and M. Pasupathi), 25 (n 7)
courage, 37, 52-56, 62-63, 162, 175-176, 196
Courage and Calling: Embracing Your God-Given Potential (1999) (Gordon T. Smith), 138
"Crafting a Job: Revisioning Employees as Active Crafters of Their Work" (2001) (A. Wrzesniewski and J. E. Dutton), 172 (n 6)
critical intelligence, 127, 148
"Cultivating Professionalism and Vocation Across the Professions: Challenges for Higher Education" (2006), 1, 8, 217
curricula, curricular, curriculum, 13, 42, 53, 63-64, 106, 109, 110, 131-132, 142, 143, 146, 181, 229-230, 232, 246
curricular development, 128, 131
curriculum reform, 214
daycare center (Israel), 182
The Death of Character: Moral Education in an Age Without Good or Evil (2000) (James Davison Hunter), 17 (n 2)
"Debating Moral Education: An Introduction" (2010) (Elizabeth Kiss and J. Peter Euben), 18 (n 3)
Debating Moral Education: Rethinking the Role of the Modern University (2010 (Elizabeth Kiss and J. Peter Euben), 18 (n 3), 23 (n 12)
de-moralize(s), demoralizing, 182, 186 (n 21), 189
decision-making, 2, 11, 21-22, 25, 36, 187, 193, 195, 198, 206
democracy, 19, 23, 50, 128, 200, 214
Descartes, Rene, 135, 200
desiring, 4, 21-22, 177
detachment, 176, 192, 209
"Developing the Ethical Thinker and Responsible Moral Agent" (Thomas Lickona), 5, 41, 43, 45, 47, 49, 51, 53, 55, 57, 59, 61, 63, 65, 67
"The Development of Purpose During Adolescence" (2003) (William Damon, Jennie Memon, and Kendall C. Bronk), 47 (n 20)
developmental psychology
Dewey, John, 11, 12, 173, 199-201, 203-204, 205 (n 19)
"A Deweyan Approach to the Development of Moral Dispositions in Professional Teacher Education Communities: Using a Conceptual Framework" (Erskine Dottin), 93 (n 5)
Diez, Mary, 94
Dijon Academy, 135
dilemma(s), dilemmatic, 22, 25, 59-60, 91 (n 44), 180, 194
disability, 245, 270
disability law, 13, 237, 239
disciplines, 107, 113, 132, 143, 145, 189, 213-214, 218, 228
discretion, 181, 191
dishonesty, 49, 61. *See also* cheating
dispositions, 2, 6, 19-20, 33, 92-94, 96-98, 112 (n 12), 174, 194, 213. *See also* professional dispositions
The Doctrine of Virtue (1797) (Immanuel Kant), 72 (n 8), 73 (n 10)
Doing the Truth in Love: Conversations about God, Relationships, and Service (19950 (Michael J. Himes), 137
due process hearing (special education), 248
Duke University's Center for Academic Integrity, 60
Dying Words: How Should Doctors Deliver Bad News? (2002) (Jerome Groopman), 168 (n 2), 190-91 (nn 29-32), 192 (n 36), 240
"The Economic Value of Liberal Education" (2010) (Debra Humphreys and Anthony Carnevale), 144 (n 2)
Educating Citizens: Preparing America's Undergraduates for Lives of Moral and Civic Responsibility (2003) (Anne Colby, E. Beaumont, and J. Stephens), 40 (n 51)
Educating Clergy: Teaching Practices and Pastoral Imagination (2006) (Charles R. Foster, Lisa E. Dahill, Lawrence A. Golemon, and Barbara Wang Tolentino), 112 (n 12)
Educating Intuition (2001) (R. M. Hogarth), 38 (n 46), 39 (n 49)
Educating Lawyers: Preparation for the Practice of Law (2007) (William M. Sullivan, Anne Colby, Judith Welch Wegner, Lloyd Bond, and Lee Shulman), 188 112 (n 10), (n 24)
Educating Nurses: A Call for Radical Transformation (2010) (Patricia Benner, Molly Sutphen, Victoria Leonard, and Lisa Day), 112 (n 11)
Educating Physicians: A Call for Reform of Medical School and Residency (2010) (Molly Cooke, David M. Irby, and Bridget C. O'Brien), 112 (n 11), 191 (n 34)
Educating the Reflective Practitioner (1987) (Donald Schön), 186 (n 18)
education: character, 1, 4, 18, 19-22, 41-43, 55, 226, 228, 231; citizenship, 4, 19-20; clergy,

283

112n; clinical legal, 110; continuing, 3; graduate, 14, 49, 117, 125, 142, 229, 238; higher, 9, 18 (n 2), 94, 102, 115, 119, 135, 137, 144; K-12, 3, 42; legal, 110-112, 157 (n 12), 219 (n 3); medical, 107, 117; moral, 2, 4, 17 (n 2), 18-20, 22, 39, 227; postgraduate, 3; professional, 3, 8-9, 11, 102, 105, 107-109, 111-114, 118 (n 6), 127, 148-149, 150, 152-153, 156, 157 (12), 167, 184, 187, 196, 205, 223-225, 227, 234-235; transformative, 13, 231-232; undergraduate, 3, 14, 18, 22, 49, 135, 143-144, 146, 149, 214, 225, 227, 230, 238

educational: continuum, 2, 7, 10, 226, 229; process, 3, 223; spectrum, 3

Educational Leadership, 47 (n 21), 64 (n 49)

emotion(s), emotional, emotionally: 5, 6, 21 (n 9), 22, 24, 28, 30-31, 33-35, 37, 44-47, 70, 71 (n 7), 73, 78, 84, 87-88, 95, 142, 175, 188, 209

Emotional Intelligence (1995) (Daniel Goleman), 47 (n 17)

emotional systems, 5, 28-29

empathic orientation, 62-63, 70, 77 (n 20), 78, 81

empathy, empathize, 11, 21 (n 9), 35-36, 50, 69, 73, 77-78, 86, 87, 146, 176, 177 (n 11), 189, 192, 209

Empathy and Moral Development: Implications for Caring and Justice (2000) (Martin L. Hoffman), 21 (n 9)

The Empathy Gap, 36 (n 43)

engaged campus (representative university as), 120

Engaging God's World: A Christian Vision of Faith, Learning, and Living (2002) (Cornelius Plantinga, Jr.), 138

engineering, 7, 81 (n 31), 111, 117, 124, 127-129, 131, 134, 143, 147, 218 (n 2)

epistemology, 11, 199-200, 204

Eros, 129 (n 12)

ethic of: action, 5, 11-12, 20, 22, 25, 30-39, 51, 55, 58, 62, 64, 70-73, 79, 90, 91 (n 44), 93-94, 98, 135, 145, 167, 194, 206, 209, 211; engagement, 5, 22, 29-32, 34, 95, 101, 129, 146; imagination, 5, 29-32, 34, 133, 155, 209; security, 5, 29-31; service, 103-104, 105 (n 5)

ethical: choices, 66, 173, 175, 177; expertise, 35, 186; intelligence, 11, 176-177; judgment, 5, 34, 36-37, 51, 194; leadership, 3, 41; learning community, 6, 67; motivation, 11, 177; orientations, 5, 29, 33, 40; sensitivity, 5, 21, 31, 34, 36-37; tests, 58-59; thinker(s), 3, 5, 41, 44, 46-48, 50-53, 55, 65

ethics: legal, 122, 171; medical, 122, 168; professional, 113, 122, 131, 195, 222 (n 8); special

Ethics in Practice (2000) (Deborah L. Rhode), 170 (n 4)

Essays in Experimental Logic (2010) (John Dewey), 200 (n 6)

Ethical Know-How: Action, Wisdom, and Cognition (1999) (F. Varela), 35 (n 40), 36 (n 42)

evolution, 12, 29, 42, 147, 225-226

Evolution, Early Experience, and Human Development (2012) (D. Narvaez, J. Panksepp, J. Shore, and T. Gleason), 28 (n 24)

Evolutionary Psychology as Maladapted Psychology (2007) (R. C. Richardson), 28 (n 23)

excellence(s), 5, 24, 42, 44, 46, 145, 196, 227 (n 1)

Excellence & Ethics, 43 (n 8)

exemplar(s), exemplary, 6, 30, 34, (n 35), 36-38, 40, 46, 53, 98, 189

experience(s), experienced, 31, 34, 38-40, 48, 65-66, 68, 76, 80-83, 85-91, 93, 96, 106-110, 116, 119, 128, 131-133, 135, 146, 157 (n 12) 170, 177, 187-192, 195, 200, 202-203, 206, 209-210, 217-218, 219 (n 4), 223, 225-226, 232, 238, 240, 242, 245, 250, 270-271

expert(s), expertise, 2, 4-6, 8, 12, 20-22, 24-26, 29, 31, 35, 37-38, 40, 113, 175, 177, 185-186, 188, 193 (n 1), 202-203, 205-206, 230

external goods, external rewards, 105 (n 5), 139, 160, 184, 197

failure, importance of, 181, 183, 209, 211

fair, fairness, 7, 24, 58-59, 72, 92, 96, 98, 136, 141, 171, 173, 175-176, 178, 192

Faithful Learning and the Christian Scholarly Vocation (2003) (Douglas V. Henry and Bob R. Agee), 137

"Faulty Towers: The Crisis in Higher Education" (2012) (William Deresiewicz), 143 (n 1)

fidelity, 9, 86, 125, 171

Finch, Atticus, 189

fine, 70, 76 (n 17), 171, 182

"A Fine is a Price" (2000) (Uri Gneezy and Aldo Rustichini), 38, 182 (n 15), 200

Flexner Report on medical education (1910), 107

flourish, flourishing, 2, 4, 5, 32, 39, 43, 46, 187 (n 21), 194-195, 215, 239

Forer, Lois (judge), 178-180

Forgetting Ourselves on Purpose: Vocation and the Ethics of Ambition (2002) (Brian J. Mahan), 136 (n 5), 137

formative dimension, 105

Index

"Forming Professionals and the Quest for Common Ground in the University" (2006) (William May), 8, 115, 177 (n11)
Four-Component Model, 35
Frankl, Viktor, 47
"Freud, Naturalism, and Modern Moral Philosophy" (2006) (John Deigh), 72 (n 7)
Freud, Sigmund, 71-74, 77-78
From Max Weber, Essays in Sociology (1958) (H. H. Gerth and C. Wright Mills), 118 (n 5)
Gilligan, Carol, 18 (n 3), 33 (n 34)
Gladly Learn, Gladly Teach: Living Out One's Calling in the 21st-Century Academy (2005) (John Marson Dunaway), 137
God, 69, 90, 124, 131, 134, 136, 139-142, 146, 151, 162-163, 197, 244, 268
"'God at Work': A Reflection on Vocation" (John Dunway), 9, 134-135, 137
good: life, 53, 174, work, 104
The Graduate, 119
Groopman, Jerome (physician), 168-169, 175, 188, 190-192, 240
"Guidelines for Observing Practical Wisdom at Work" (Jack Sammons), 12, 14, 237 (n 2), 207, 209, 211, 215, 237 (n 2)
guild, guild training, 106, 109, 113
guilt: accident, 6, 74, 85, 88; battlefield, 6, 81; collateral damage, 6, 88-89; luck, 6, 81, 84-86, 88; personal, 69, 74, 76, 78; rational, 84, 87; subjective, 77
habits, 2, 19, 33, 35, 40, 128, 130
Habits of the Mind: Intellectual Life as a Christian Calling (2000) (James W. Sire), 137 (n 7), 138
Handbook of Child Psychology, Vol. 3: Cognitive Development (1983) (J. Flavell Mussen and E. Markman), 35 (n 41)
Handbook of Moral Development (2006) (Melanie Killen and Judith G. Smetana), 20 (n 7), 32 (n 31)
happiness, 45, 56, 71, 185, 187 (n 21)
Harcourt Brace College Publishers, 52 (n 26)
Harvard: Law School, 124; Medical School, 191 (n 35); University, 63
health field, 112
Hogarth, R. M., 38, 39
holistic, holistically, holism, (education), 10, 30, 38, 56, 107, 111, 150, 153, 156, 236
honest, honestly, honesty, 31, 60-62, 141, 151-152, 156, 162, 169, 173-176, 196, 209-210,
"Honesty: Why It's Still the Best Policy" (2012) (Hal Urban), 61
hospital janitors, custodians, 171-173, 181,
"How Cognitive and Neurobiological Sciences Inform Values Education for Creatures Like us" (2008), 32 (n 32)

How People Learn: Brain, Mind, Experience, and School (1999) (J. D. Bransford, A. L. Brown, and R. R. Cocking), 37 (n 44)
"How 'Professional' are the Professions? A Review Article" (1995) (Sheldon Rothblatt), 103 (n 3)
Hutchins, Robert, 122
ideals, 103, 156, 159, 187, 200, 225
ideology, 186 (n 20)
IEP Team, 247, 250, 253, 255, 270
Implications for Caring and Justice (2000) (Martin L. Hoffman), 21 (n 9)
improvisation, improvisational, improvise, 11, 176-177, 181, 209
incentive(s), 11, 104, 177-178, 181-184, 186, 191, 234-235
"In Defence of Aristotle on Character: a Synthesis of Recent Psychology, Neuroscience, and the Thought of Michael Polanyi" (2012), 20 (n 7)
Indiana University, 120 (n 7), 126
Individualized Educational Plan (IEP), 247-248, 250, 252, 255
In Good Conscience: Reason and Emotion in Moral Decision-Making (1991) (Sidney Callahan), 58
injustice, unjust, 32, 48, 53, 63, 170, 173, 175
"Interpersonal Sensemaking and the Meaning of Work" (2003) (A. Wrzesniewski, J. E. Dutton, and G. Debebe), 172 (n 6)
institution(s), 37, 66, 92, 94, 98, 104, 113, 115, 119-121, 125-126, 132-133, 137, 184-185, 214, 222, 229, 231-232
Introduction to Service-Learning Toolkit (2003), 20 (n 6)
instrumentalism, 49
integrated competence, 108
integrated ethical thinking, 5, 51, 56, 62
integrative (curriculum reform), 4, 7, 10, 102, 110-111, 112 (n 12), 131, 150, 230, 236
"An Integrative Approach to Educating Virtue" (D. Narvaez), 230
integrative ethical education, 5, 32
"Integrative Ethical Education" (2006) (D. Narvaez), 32 (nn 31, 32), 36 (n 41), 38 (n 48)
intellectual training, 106, 108
intelligence, 11, 25-26, 36, 44, 81, 95 (n 8), 118, 127, 148, 176-177
interdisciplinary, 1, 13-14, 146, 206, 219, 221, 222 (n 7), 227 (n 1), 228, 230, 238
interdisciplinary pedagogy, 13-14, 238
interpersonal conformity, 49
Interstate Teacher Assessment and Support Consortium (InTASC), 94
intrinsic goods, intrinsic rewards, 104, 105 (n 5)

285

intuition(s), 25, 38, 207, 210, 218
"Invariant Sequence and Internal Consistency in Moral Judgment Stages" (1984) (Anne Colby and Lawrence Kohlberg), 50 (n 23)
Jabbari, Christine (kindergarten teacher), 180
John Hopkins University, 143
Journal of Happiness Studies (2006), 171 (n 5), 240
The Journal of Moral Education, 19 (n 4), 20 (n 7), 22 (n 10), 64 (n 47)
Journal of Research in Character Education, 32 (n 31), 42
journalism, journalists, 104, 122
journalism ethics, 122
judgment(s), 208, 210 (n 4), 237, 267, 270-271
just, justice, 17, 52, 55, 59, 62-64, 72, 88, 104, 113, 126, 127, 136, 148, 156, 158, 161 (n 14), 170-171, 215
"Justice by Numbers" (1992) (Lois Forer), 179 (n 13)
Kant, Immanuel, 27, 72-74, 174, 200
kind, kindness, 39, 173-176
Knowing and Being in the Intersection of Philosophical Traditions, Reconsidering Polanyi (2010) (Tihamer Margitay), 154 (n 2)
Knowing, Desiring, and Doing, 4, 21
knowledge: practical, 154, 210; theoretical, 11, 105-106, 112, 194-196
Kohlberg, Lawrence, 17 (n 2), 18-19, 26, 31 (n 27), 47 (n 16), 49, 50 (n 23), 59
law: clinics, 188; firm(s), 126, 170, 184; school(s), 2, 110-112, 156 (n 12), 188, 219-220, 228, 230
lawyers and clients, 170
lawyering, 112, 125, 224
"Lawyer Advice and Client Autonomy" (William Simon) (2000), 170 (n 4)
leadership, 3, 41, 45, 84 (n 36), 113, 117, 124, 147, 227
learning disability, learning disabilities, 269
leavening (curricular development), 131-132
"The Legacy of Transformative Education at Mercer" (Peter Brown), 232
legal knowledge, 111
legal skills, 111
Leibniz, Gottfried, 200
lesbian rule (Aristotle), 174
Let Your Life Speak: Listening for the Voice of Vocation (2000) (Parker Palmer), 141
liberal arts, 112-113, 127, 143-144, 147-149, 227
liberal arts college, 116-117, 119, 218, 230, 232. See also College of Liberal Arts
liberal education, 143-145, 147-149, 214-215, 225

Lickona, Tom, 1, 3-6, 12, 17 (n 2), 19, 21, 41, 42 (n 2), 43 (n 7), 47 (n 16), 56 (n 33), 59 (n 38), 65 (n 51), 193 (n 1), 213, 230
Life of the Mind for Practice Project, 225
life-span, 24,
Listening to Your Life: Daily Meditations with Frederick Buechner (1992) (Frederick Buechner), 140 (n 3)
Locke, John, 116
logic, 143, 184, 200-201, 204-205
Logic: The Theory of Inquiry (1938) (John Dewey), 199 (n 3), 200 (nn 4, 8), 201 (nn 11, 14), 203 (n 17), 205 (n 19)
"Love, Guilt, and the Sense of Justice" (1996) (John Deigh), 72 (n 7)
Love Your God with All Your Mind: The Role of Reason in the Life of the Soul (1997) (J. P. Moreland), 137
luck, 6, 77 (n 18), 79, 81, 84-86, 88, 215
Machiavelli, 133
Maguire Center for Ethics and Public Responsibility, 133
Maimonides, Moses, 121 (n 7)
"Making Citizens Out of Students" (2003) (Thomas Martin and Scott Richardson), 65, 66 (n 52)
Making a Necessity of Virtue (1997), 72 (n 8)
market, 103-104, 144, 148, 184-185, 234
marketplace, capitalist marketplace, 103, 124-125, 144
Marx, Karl, 187,
master virtue (practical wisdom), 2, 6, 11, 175, 194, 237-239, 241-242, 267
May, William F., 1, 8-9, 115, 123 (n 8), 144-145, 148, 177 (n 11), 193 (n 2), 213, 217
McIntyre, Alasdair, 162
mean, the (Aristotle), 11, 175-176
means and ends, 12, 208-209
medical school(s), 191, 218 (n 2)
medical students, 188, 191
medicine, 7, 104, 105 (n 5), 107, 113 (n 13), 117, 122, 124, 127-128, 143, 147-148, 218 (n 2), 224
mensch (being a) 176
mentor(s), 29, 38-39, 142, 160, 188, 191
Mercer: Commons, 115, 134, 219,-220, 227; on Mission, 146, 232; University; 1, 9, 13, 115, 122, 218 (n 2), 223, 229, 231-232, 240; University Academic Initiatives Monetary (AIM) Fund, 1, 220, 227; University College of Arts and Sciences, 147; University Phronesis Project, 1-4, 12-13, 199, 215, 217-218, 220-223, 226, 227-228, 231-32; University Professionalism and Vocation Across the Professions Project, 8, 12, 199, 217-218, 240 (n 3); University Quality Enhancement Plan Concerning the Engaged

Index

University Learning Together (QEP), 115, 219-220, 222 (n 8), 232, 237; University Tift College of Education, 4, 6, 7, 93, 147, 228
Mercer Law School, 219, 233
"Mercer Law School's Focus on Professionalism" (2011) (Patrick Longan and Timothy Floyd), 219 (n 4)
Merleau-Ponty, Maurice, 161
Michael Polanyi: The Art of Knowing (2006) (Mark Mitchell), 153 (n 2)
"Mike's Hard Lemonade" (NPR Morning Edition), 178
mindful morality, 5, 29, 33-35
mindfulness, 33-34
Mindfulness (1989) (Ellen Langer), 34 (n 36)
"Minnesota's Community Voices and Character Education Project" (2004) (D. Narvaez, T. S. Bock, L. Endicott, and J. Lies), 32 (n 31), 36 (n 41), 38 (n 48)
mistake(s), 11, 44, 80, 87, 89, 153, 159, 177, 181, 191-192
moral: abilities, 11, 12, 175-176; action, 5, 20, 22, 30, 32 (n 31), 35-36, 38, 51, 64; agency, agent, 5, 6, 18, 20, 41, 44, 46-48, 62-66, 86; anatomy, 20; autonomy, 6, 91; capacity, 2-4, 10, 226; character, 5, 19 (n 4), 20, 28-29, 32, 43, 45-46, 51, 53, 60; commitment(s), 44, 51, 109; competence, 5, 44, 51, 54; development, 1, 17, 19, 22, 31, 40, 49, 131, 213, 226, 227-228, 230; discernment, 5, 44, 51, 56, 60, 231; exemplar(s), 6, 34 (n 35), 40, 189; experts, 2; expertise, 5, 6, 12, 40, 177, 185, 193 (n 1); formation, 3-4, 6-7, 10-11, 15, 28, 38, 108, 119 (n 6), 128, 131, 226, 231; functioning, 5, 23, 25, 27, 29-33, 35, 37, 39-40, 212; identity, 5, 44, 51, 54; judgment(s), 26, 36, 47, 52, 110, 155; know-how, 44, 177 (n 11), 188; know-why, 177 (n 11); orientation(s), 29, 32, 33, 63, 186 (n 20); reasoning, 18, 19 (n 4), 22, 26-27, 44, 48, 50, 57, 59-60, 63; relativism, 52; rules, 174; skill(s), 11, 175, 177-178, 181, 186-187, 191; will, 11, 175, 177-178, 181, 185-187; wisdom, 5, 25, 32, 40, 53
Moral Behavior and Moral Development: An Introduction (1995) (W. Kurtines and J. Gewirtz), 35 (n 41)
"Moral Complexity: The Fatal Attraction of Truthiness and the Importance of Mature Moral Functioning" (2010), 29 (n 25), 32 (n 31)
"Moral Development Across Disciplines, Schools, and Life-Span: The Phronesis Project" 12, 227
Moral Development: Advances in Research and Theory (1986), 20 (7)
Moral Development and Behavior (1976) (Thomas Lickona), 47 (n 16)
Moral Development and Character Education (1989) (Larry P. Nucci), 17 (n 2)
Moral Development in the Professions (1994) (James R. Rest and Darcia Narvaez), 19 (n 4)
Moral Development, Self, and Identity (2004) (Daniel K. Lapsley and Darcia Narvaez), 47 (n 16)
"Moral Education and Character Education: Their Relationship and Roles in Citizenship Education" (2006) (Wolfgang Althof and Marvin W. Berkowitz), 22 (n 10)
Moral Education in America, 17 (n 2)
"Moral Functioning: Moral Understanding and Personality" (2004) (Augusto Blasi), 47 (n 16)
"Moral Judgment Competency Is Declining Over Time: Evidence from 20 Years of Defining Issues Test Data" (2008) (Stephen J. Thoma and Muriel J. Bebeau), 50 (n 24)
Moral Luck (1981) (Bernard Williams), 77 (n 20)
"Moral Luck and the Virtues of Impure Agency" (1991) (Margaret Urban Walker), 77 (n 18)
Moral Personality, Identity, and Character: An Interdisciplinary Future (2010) (D. Narvaez and D. K. Lapsley), 29 (n 25)
Moral Psychology: The Neuroscience of Morality: Emotion, Disease, and Development (2008) (W. Sinnot-Armstrong), 91 (n 44)
"Moral Virtue and Practical Wisdom: Theme Comprehension in Children, Youth, and Adults" (2010) (D. Narvaez, T. Gleason, and C. Mitchell), 26 (n 14), 27 (nn 18, 21)
morale, 101, 186 (n 21),
Morality, Moral Behavior, and Moral Development (1984) (William M. Kurtines and Jacob L. Gewirtz), 50 (n 23)
multiculturalism, 52
A Multidimensional Approach to Moral Identity: Early Life Experience, Prosocial Personality, and Moral Outcomes (2012) (D. Narvaez and J. Brooks), 31 (n 28)
Nagel, Thomas, 77 (n 18)
narrative(s), stories, 6-8, 12-13, 50, 53, 64, 188-189, 210-211, 213, 233, 245
Narvaez, Darcia, 1, 4-6, 12, 18 (n 3), 19 (n 4), 20, 23 (n 11), 24, 26-27, 28 (n 24), 29 (n 25), 31, 32 (n 31), 34 (n 35), 35 (n 41), 38 (n 47), 47 (n 16), 193 (n 1), 213, 230
"The Neo-Kohlbergian Tradition and Beyond: Schemas, Expertise, and Character" (2005), 32 (n 32)
neurobiology, neurobiological, 5, 24, 40

A New Agenda for Higher Education: Shaping a Life of the Mind for Practice (2008) (William M. Sullivan and Matthew S. Rosin), 225 (n 10)
New York: Library of Liberal Arts, 173 (n 7), 174 (n 8)
Nietzsche, Friedrich, 70, 72, 77-78
No Child Left Behind, 182
Noddings, Nel, 33 (n 34)
norm-centered motive, 62
Not in Our Genes: Biology, Ideology, and Human Nature (1984) (R. C. Lewonton, S. Rose, and L. J. Kamin), 28 (n 22)
Nucci, Larry P., 17 (n 2), 19, 59 (n 39)
nurse(s), nursing, 64, 102, 104, 113 (n 13), 124-125, 143, 153, 159, 163, 205, 218 (n 2), 219, 224, 225 (n 9),
Nussbaum, Martha C., 71 (n 7), 188
Oklahoma State University, 21
"The Ontogeny of Wisdom and Its Variations" (2003) (D. Kramer), 24 (n 2), 25 (n 6)
"An Overview of the Uses of Standardized Patients for Teaching and Evaluating Clinical Skills" (1993) (Howard Barrows), 191 (n 33)
palliative care, 127
Palmer, Parker, 47 (n 21), 141
Parks, Sharon Daloz, 40 (n 51)
Pascal, Blaise, 135
paternalism, 173
pedagogy, pedagogies, pedagogical, pedagogically, 2, 14, 19-20, 22-23, 106, 111, 112 (n 12), 114, 117, 142, 149, 151, 157, 213, 228-229, 238
perception(s), 10, 21, 30-31, 38, 151, 207, 209
performance character. *See* character, performance
Perry, William G., 18
personal identity, 141
perspective-taking, 59, 176
phronesis, 2, 26-27, 175, 239
phronimos, 11, 194-196
"Phronesis Project Conference on Character Across the Disciplines" (2010), 1, 4, 218, 221
Phronesis Project for the Exploration of Character, Practical Wisdom, Professional Formation, 1
physicians and patients, 168
Plato, 17, 26 (n 15), 66, 116
Platonists, 121
pluralism, pluralist, pluralistic, 18-19, 23, 120-121, 214-215
Poetic and Legal Fiction in the Aristotelian Tradition (1983) (Kathy Eden), 209 (n 3)
Poetic Justice (1005) (Martha Nussbaum), 188

Polanyi, Michael, 153-157, 158 (n 13), 160, 162, 227
positivism, positivist, 18, 107-108, 118-120, 144, 151, 153, 155, 159, 214
Postconventional Moral Thinking: A Neo-Kohlbergian Approach (1999) (James Rest, D. Narvaez, M. J. Bebeau, and S. J. Thoma), 26 (n 12)
practical reasoning, 11, 194-195
practical skill(s), practical know-how, 11, 105-106, 149, 157 (n 12), 194-196
"Practical Wisdom and Vocation in Professional Formation: A Schematic Account" (Mark Jones), 11, 193
"Practical Wisdom: Aristotle Meets Positive Psychology" (2006) (Barry Schwarz and Kenneth Sharpe), 171 (n 5), 240
"Practical Wisdom: The Character of the Professions" (2008), 240 (n 3)
Practical Wisdom: The Right Way to Do the Right Thing (2010) (Barry Schwarz and Kenneth Sharpe), 185 (n 17), 191 (n 35), 241 (n 4)
practice(s), 5, 9-11, 22, 32, 34-36, 38-40, 42-43, 47-48, 55, 60, 66, 94, 98, 104-110, 112-113, 122, 126, 128, 133, 145, 148, 150-62, 173, 175, 181, 184-187, 189, 193, 195-197, 214, 221 (n 7), 223-225, 228, 231, 234-236, 238, 239, 269
practice skills, 109
practitioner(s), 10-11, 105 (n 5), 106-109, 112-114, 153, 158, 162, 181, 186-187, 195-197, 221 (n 6), 223-224, 235-236, 239
pragmatic reasoning, 11, 200
pragmatism, 199, 206
Pragmatism, Postmodernism, and the Future of Philosophy (2002) (John Stuhr), 200 (n 7)
Preparation for the Professions Program (Carnegie Foundation), 102
preventive medicine, 127-128
Pride, Shame, and Guilty: Emotions of Self-Assessment (1985) (Gabriele Taylor), 72 (n 7)
principled thinking, 50
principles, 2, 13, 30, 55, 58, 62, 78, 94, 168, 171, 173-174, 176, 185, 187, 203, 209, 228-229, 239
problem-based learning, 112
procedure(s), 11, 39, 48, 176, 178, 181, 187, 190, 231, 240, 269
profession(s), 6-11, 13, 65, 84, 91, 95, 102-108, 112-117, 119, 122, 124, 127, 134, 136, 139, 142, 143-144, 148-149, 150-152, 158, 184-186, 189, 195-197, 199, 205-206, 218-219, 223, 225, 226, 233-236, 238-239
professional: attribute(s), 195, 197; calling, 7, 9-10, 123, 144; character, 2-3, 7, 19, 99, 148, 195-196, 225-226; commitment, 110; dispositions, 92-94, 97-98, 196. *See also* dispositions; educators, 9-10, 108 (n 7), 218;

Index

ethic(s), 103, 113, 122, 131, 195, 222 (n 8); formation, 1-3, 7, 9, 99, 144, 148, 193, 225-226, 228-229; identity, 103, 108-109, 142, 149, 151-153, 157 (n 12), 160, 225; judgment, 113, 148, 259; performance, 106, 127; practice(s), 9, 11, 106-107, 113, 184, 193, 195-197, 223-225; preparation, 106-109, 113-114; responsibility, 109; school(s), 14, 19, 106, 110, 113, 119, 122, 125, 130, 147-149, 185, 187-188, 213, 220, 223, 238; training, 106-108, 113, 149, 191

professionalism, 7-11, 13, 102-103, 105, 110, 114, 116, 122, 139, 143, 149, 160, 185, 205, 219, 221-224, 226, 233-234, 236

professionalism and vocation, 10, 13, 116, 122, 131 (n16), 139, 215, 219, 221 (n 7), 222 (n 8), 223-224, 233

"Professionalism and Vocation Across the Professions" (William M. Sullivan), 101, 103, 105, 107, 109, 111, 113, 115, 118, 150, 186 (n 19), 199, 207 (n 2), 217-219, 222, 225-226, 227-228, 233, 237, 240 (n 3)

Profiles in Courage (1955) (John F. Kennedy), 189

Proust, Marcel, 135

"Psychological Approaches to Wisdom and Its Development" (2003) (D. J. Shedlok and S. W. Cornelius), 24 (n 1)

"The Psychological Foundations of Everyday Morality and Moral Expertise" (2005) (D. K. Lapsley and D. Narvaez), 38 (n 47)

The Psychology of Moral Development: Essays on Moral Development (1984) (Lawrence Kohlberg), 26 (nn 10, 11), 31 (n 27)

"The Psychology of Wisdom and Its Ontogenesis" (1990) (P. B. Baltes and J. Smith), 25 (n 4)

public: benefit, 103; good(s), 104, 126, 144, 151; occupations, 104; purposes, 8, 105 (n 5); responsibility, responsibilities, 123; safety, 103; service, 8, 103, 105 (n 5), 110, 113, 124, 144; spirit, spiritedness, 9, 105 (n 5), 125-126; status, 102; trust, 103; undertaking, 102; value(s), 102-104; welfare, 104, 113, 148

Puritan Political Ideals (1965) (Edmund Burke), 124 (n 9)

purpose(s), 2-3, 5, 7-9, 13, 45-48, 62, 96, 101, 105 (n 5), 106, 108, 113-114, 122-125, 130, 134, 137, 140, 143, 148, 150, 154, 157 (n 12), 167 (n 1), 176, 177 (n 11), 184 (n 16), 187 (n 21), 201, 208-209, 222, 238, 240, 256

qualities of character, 2, 11, 194-197

racism, 170

"A Rational Superego" (1999) (David Velleman), 74 (n 14)

re-moralize, re-moralizing, 182, 186, 189

reason, 17, 59, 61, 63, 73, 88, 93, 111, 118, 156, 169, 176, 205, 210, 213, 225, 246, 254

reflection(s), 9-10, 23, 26, 53-55, 65, 75, 95, 102, 140, 142, 160, 171, 186, 189, 210 (n 4), 239

"Reform and Formation: Revisiting the Role of Liberal Education" (Peter Brown), 9, 143

regret, 58, 77 (n 20), 79-80

"Remarks on Some Difficulties in Freud's Theory of Moral Development" (2006) (John Deigh), 72 (n 7)

remorse, 77, 79, 80 (n 28), 87

"Remorse and Agent-Regret" (1988) (Marcia Baron), 80 (n 28)

representative university, 120-121

"Research on K-12 School-Based Service-Learning: The Evidence Builds" (2000) (Shelley H. Billig), 47 (n 19), 65 (n 50)

responsible, responsibility, responsibilities, responsibly, 3, 5-6, 37, 41, 44-48, 51, 59, 62-66, 70-71, 73, 75-77, 79, 80, 85-86, 90-91, 94-95, 104-105, 109, 113, 116-117, 123-126, 130, 133, 137, 144, 147-149, 151, 158, 187 (n 21), 188, 191, 193, 213, 227, 255, 268-271

Responsibility, Character, and the Emotions (1987) (F. Schoeman), 71 (n 7)

Rest, James, 19 (n 4), 20, 26 (nn 10, 12), 35

Reverence: Restoring a Forgotten Virtue (2002) (P. Woodruff), 30 (n 26)

Rogers, Will, 192

role models, 136, 192, 254

Rousseau, Jean Jacques, 135

rulers (professionals as), 123

rules, 10-11, 89-90, 148, 155, 157 (n 12), 173-178, 181-184, 186-187, 197, 209, 239

sacred canopy (university as), 116, 118-119, 121

Safe and Sound: An Educational Learner's Guide to Evidence-Based Social and Emotional Learning Programs (2003), 47 (n 17)

Savoring: A New Model of Positive Experience (2007) (Fred B. Bryant and Joseph Veroff), 34 (n 37)

Schwarz, Barry, 1, 11-12, 167, 171 (n 5), 184 (n 16), 185 (n 17), 191 (n 35), 193 (n 1), 214, 217, 231, 238, 240, 241 (n 4)

"Science as a Vocation" (1958) (Max Weber), 118 (n 5)

"The Secret Joke of Kant's Soul" (2008) (Joshua Greene), 91 (n 44)

self: deception, 58, 74; governance, 105 (n 5); identity, 21, 254; realization, 117; reflection, 140, 142, 160; regulation, 22

Seligman, Martin, 45, 46 (n 12), 47 (n 15)

service(s), 8, 13, 64-65, 82, 84 (n 36), 98, 103-104, 105 (n 5), 110, 112 (n 12), 113-114, 124-

289

125, 134-135, 138, 140-141, 144, 147, 158, 160, 185, 187, 197, 214, 230-231, 237, 239, 246, 268
service-learning, 20, 22, 47, 65, 146, 230-232
"Service-Learning Impacts on Youth, Schools, and Communities: Research on K-12 School-Based Service-Learning, 1990-1999" (2000) (Shelley Billig), 65 (n 50)
Shakespeare, William, 116
Sharpe, Kenneth, 238, 240, 241 (n 4)
Sherman, Nancy, 1, 4, 6, 7, 68, 79 (n 26), 83 (n 32), 213, 230
Simon, William (lawyer), 170-171, 173, 175
skill(s), skilled, 2, 4-5, 9, 11, 19-23, 24, 27, 29, 32-39, 43-47, 51, 58-59, 62, 65, 92, 103, 106, 107 (n 6), 108-109, 111-112, 117-119, 125, 128, 133, 142, 145, 148-149, 151-152, 155-157, 159, 175, 177-178, 181, 185-187, 191, 195, 209, 213-214, 230, 239, 247
skills training, 40, 110
Smart & Good High Schools: Integrating Excellence and Ethics for Success in School, Work, and Beyond, 43
social: contract(s), 102, 113, 151; justice, 104, 113, 148; responsibility, 65, 109, 113; science(s), 101; work, 104
"Sociomoral Development and Drug and Alcohol Abuse" (1991) (Marvin W. Berkowitz, Nancy G. Guerra, and Larry P. Nucci), 59 (n 39)
Soldier(s), 7, 68-71, 73, 75, 81, 85-89, 91
Some Do Care: Contemporary Lives of Moral Commitment (1992) (Anne Colby and William Damon), 46
"Some Further Reflection on Guilt and Punishment" (1999) (Herbert Morris), 72 (n 7)
"Some Reflection on the *Oresteia*" (1975) (Melanie Klein), 78 (n 21)
Sommers, Christina Hoff, 52-53
The Sources of Moral Agency (1996) (John Deigh), 72 (n 7)
Southern Baptist Educator (2005), 137
Sparta, 128
specialization, 107 (n 6), 214 (n 1), 228
Spinoza, Baruch, 77, 200
stages of moral reasoning, 26, 59
standards (professional), 44, 52, 56, 76, 93-94, 103-105, 146, 162, 182
Staudinger, Ursula, 20, 24 (n 3), 25 (n 7), 26 (n 13)
Sternberg, Robert, 20 (n 7), 21, 25, 26 (n 13), 46 (n 13)
Stewart, Jimmy, 187
Stockdale Center for Ethical Leadership, 81 (n 31)

Stoicism and Emotions (2007) (Margaret Graver), 72 (n 9)
student(s), 1, 3, 5-6, 10, 14, 19, 22, 32-33, 35, 38-40, 41, 48-55, 57-61, 63-66, 77, 92, 94-97, 106, 108-109, 111-114, 116-121, 125, 127-133, 135-137, 142, 145-149, 151, 154, 156-159, 162-163, 171, 173, 176, 180, 182-183, 186-189, 191-192, 202, 205, 213-214, 221, 225-226, 227-232, 238-240, 251-254, 256
Successful Intelligence (1997) (Robert Sternberg), 46 (n 13)
Sullivan, William (Bill), 1, 8, 101, 102 (n 2), 112 (nn 10, 12), 115, 118 (n 6), 131, 135, 139, 144-145, 148-149, 150-151, 156 (n 12), 157, 186, 188, 193, 199, 205 (n 20), 213, 217-220, 223-225
teacher(s): and students, 65, 171; preparation, 92, 94
Teacher Dispositions: Building a Teacher Education Framework of Moral Standard (2006) (Hugh Sockett), 93 (nn 4, 5), 94
teaching metaphors: engineering or manufacturing, 128-129, 131; inculcating or indoctrinating, 129; training, 130; parenting or dirt farming, 130; Holy Family (Joseph), 131
Teaching and Learning Professionalism, Report of the Professionalism Committee (1996), 110 (9)
"Teaching Note: 'Difference, Disability, and Professional Judgment" (Peter Brown), 14, 237, 242, 267
"Teaching to Form Character: A Polanyian Analysis of Practical Reasoning" (2010) (Paul Lewis), 154 (n 2)
"Teaching Professionalism" (2009) (Patrick E. Longan), 219 (n 4)
"Teaching the Virtues" (1991) (Christina Hoff Sommers), 53 (n 28)
technical: expertise, 8, 35, 185, 186 (n 21); intelligence, 118 (n 6), 127, 148; professionalism, 8; reason, 118
technicians, 118, 130, 148
technology, 127, 224, 251
theoretical knowledge, 11, 105-106, 112, 194-196
Tolstoy, Leo, 136
tradition(s), 25, 37, 109, 117, 120-121, 125, 129, 133, 139, 144, 151, 154-155, 157 (n 12), 160, 162, 200
Tradition and Discovery (2011), 23 (n 11)
training ground (university as), 116, 118-119, 121
"A Treatise of the Vocations or Callings of Men with Sorts and Kinds of Them and with the Right Use Thereof" (1965) (William Perkins), 124 (n 9)

Index

trial and error, 181, 190, 200
Triune Ethics Theory (TET), 29, 31-33
"Triune Ethics Theory and Moral Personality" (2010), 29 (n 25)
"Triune Ethics: The Neurobiological Roots of Our Multiple Moralities" (2008), 29 (n 25), 32 (n 32)
truth(s), 45, 58, 98, 129, 134, 136, 146, 156-157, 161, 168, 189, 200, 211, 222
tyranny, tyrant(s), 123
"The Ultimate Why: My Calling as a Christian Professor" (2005), 137
"Uncovering the Hidden Values about Values Assessment: Assessing Student Dispositions in Teacher Education" (2007) (Susan Malone, Emilie Paille, and Kelly Reffitt), 6, 92-93, 95, 97
United States Naval Academy, 81, 82, 84 (n 36)
university, universities, 3, 8, 41, 66, 101, 104-105, 107-108, 115-128, 132-133, 136, 143-144, 147-149, 150, 189, 217-220, 221 (n 7), 222-224, 227-229, 232, 238-239
University of Chicago Law School, 188
University of Michigan, 178
University of Virginia, 136
The Untold War: Inside the Hearts, Minds, and Souls of Our Soldiers (2010) (Nancy Sherman), 6
utilitarianism, 174
"The Value of a Developmental Approach to Evaluating Character Development Programs: An Outcome Study of Facing History and Ourselves" (2001) (Lynn H. Schultz, Dennis J. Barr, and Robert L. Selman), 64 (n 47)
values: clarification, 4, 19; statement exercise, 96-98
Values Education and Lifelong Learning: Philosophy, Policy, and Practices (2008) (D. Aspin and J. Chapman), 32 (n 32)
Varela, Francisco, 35 (n 40), 36 (n 42)
Vice & Virtue in Everyday Life: Introductory Readings in Ethics (1997) (Christina Sommers and Fred Sommers), 52
virtue(s), 2-3, 6, 9-11, 17, 22, 24, 26-27, 34, 39, 41, 45, 52-54, 56, 60, 72 (n 8), 73, 77 (n 20), 87, 97, 125-126, 129, 150, 152-153, 157 (n 12), 174-176, 177 (n 11), 185, 194, 196, 200, 206, 208-209, 214-215, 223, 225, 234, 239
"Virtue and *Hamartia*" (1992) (Nancy Sherman), 79 (n 26)
virtue ethics, 27, 174
"Virtue Ethics" (2003) (R. Hursthouse), 27 (n 20)
Virtue in Action, 55

vocation, vocational, 7-11, 13, 104-105, 116-117, 122, 134-137, 139-142, 144, 147, 187, 193, 196-198, 205-206, 215, 219, 221 (n 7), 222-226, 233-135
war: on wisdom, 177, 184; Vietnam, 48, 119,
"The War on Wisdom and how to Fight It" (2008) (Barry Schwarz and Kenneth Sharpe), 11, 167, 169, 171, 173, 175, 177, 179, 181, 183, 185, 187, 189, 191, 240 (n 3)
Weber, Max, 117, 118 (n 5), 144
Weberian, 120
What Works in Character Education (2005) (Marvin Berkowitz and Melinda Bier), 42 (n 3), 60, 63
Williams, Bernard, 71 (n 7), 77 (n 20), 79 (n 23)
wisdom, 1-6, 9-11, 12 (n 4), 13, 20-21, 24-27, 31-32, 40, 44, 51, 53, 86, 125, 130, 145, 150, 152-153, 154 (n 2), 165, 167, 169, 173, 175-178, 181, 184-192, 193-198, 199-200, 204, 206, 207-211, 213-215, 217, 221 (n 7), 225-226, 228-231, 237-239, 241-242, 267
"Wisdom" (2003) (P. B. Baltes and U. Kunzmann), 25 (n 5)
"Wisdom: A Metaheuristic (Pragmatic) to Orchestrate Mind and Virtue Toward Excellence" (2000) (Paul B. Baltes and Ursula M. Staudinger), 20 (n 7), 24 (n 3), 26 (n 13)
"Wisdom as Mature Moral Functioning: Insights for Developmental Psychology and Neurobiology"(Darcia Narvaez), 4-5, 24-25, 27, 29, 31, 33, 35, 37, 39, 40
wisdom-inducing experiences, 189, 190
Wisdom: Its Nature, Origins, and Development (1990), 25 (n 4)
wise, 7, 10-12, 46, 175-177, 181, 186 (n 20), 187, 194-195, 206
Wittgenstein, Ludwig, 161, 163
Wolterstorff, Nicholas, 120
Wordsworth, William, 116
work, 1, 3-5, 12, 17-18, 20-22, 23 (n 11), 25, 34, 40, 41-42, 44, 46-49, 51-52, 54, 59-60, 66, 72 (n 7), 73-75, 91 (n 44), 94-95, 98, 102-104, 107, 109-110, 118, 199 (n 6), 126-127, 131-132, 134, 139, 141-142, 145, 152, 154 (n 2), 157 (n 12), 158-160, 168, 171-173, 177, 179, 182, 186-187 (n 21), 189-191, 196, 199-202, 204, 206, 207-208, 213, 215, 219, 222, 225-226, 227-228, 231, 235, 239, 245-248, 252, 255-256, 268
Work and Integrity: The Crisis and Promise of Professionalism in America (2005) (William M. Sullivan), 8 (n 2), 102 (n 2), 115, 135, 151 (n 1), 186 (n 19), 218 (n 1)
Work in the Spirit: Toward a Theology of Work (2001) (Miroslav Volf), 138
Yale Law School, 136